TERRY FUNK

MORE THAN JUST HARDCORE

TERRY FUNK

WITH **SCOTT E. WILLIAMS**

FOREWORD BY **MICK FOLEY**

www.SportsPublishingLLC.com

ISBN: 1-58261-991-3

Publishers: Peter L. Bannon and Joseph J. Bannon Sr.
Senior managing editor: Susan M. Moyer
Acquisitions editors: Nick Obradovich and Noah Amstadter
Developmental editor: Dean Miller
Art director: K. Jeffrey Higgerson
Dust jacket/photo spread design, imaging: Dustin Hubbart
Project manager: Greg Hickman
Photo editor: Erin Linden-Levy
Vice president of sales and marketing: Kevin King
Media and promotions managers: Nick Obradovich (regional), Randy Fouts (national), Maurey Williamson (print)

Printed in the United States of America

Sports Publishing L.L.C.
804 North Neil Street
Champaign, IL 61820

Phone: 1-877-424-2665
Fax: 217-363-2073
Web site: www.SportsPublishingLLC.com

I dedicate this book to the wrestlers who have never worked a main event in Madison Square Garden, or anywhere, for that matter. I dedicate this book to the wrestlers who perform in Small Town, USA, the ones who know their night's pay won't even cover their transportation costs. I dedicate this book to the guys who have spent themselves totally, for what they consider noble causes—their fans and their families. I dedicate this book to the guys whose special brand of valor shows in their blood and their sweat. I dedicate this book to the wrestlers who have tried valiantly, even though they come up short, again and again.

In other words, I dedicate this book to the jobbers—the wrestlers who have put their shoulders to the mat, purposely and selflessly, to enhance other wrestlers in the fans' eyes. They do what they do in the unselfish hope of improving attendance in the weeks to come. They were, and are the unsung heroes of my profession.

This book is also written for my world. It's a small world, and I like it that way. It consists of the ones I love so dearly—my mom, Dorothy; my daughters, Stacy and Brandee; my daughters' families, Kelly, Jason, Daniel and Champe.

And this book is for the one, true love I have in this world – my wife, Vicki.

CONTENTS

FOREWORD

"What am I doing here?" I asked myself, a tone of dismay accenting my thoughts. It was the first week of January 1995, and "here" was an old, unheated gym in a small town in Japan, on the third day of a two-week wrestling tour. A genius in the IWA wrestling office had somehow managed to book our tour almost exclusively in unheated gyms throughout the southern part of the country, thinking, I suppose, that the gym's southern proximity would offset the brutally cold Japanese winter of 1995.

As a result, the small group of foreign wrestlers, or "gaijins," took to huddling around a portable kerosene heater, or, when lucky enough to find one, making a beeline for the "top-of-the-line" heated, Japanese toilets. Long after any "contributions" had been made, the gaijins could be found in these unique laps of luxury, savoring their last moments as warm men before the ringing of a bell, or the yelling of the boss, beckoned them back into the real world of pro wrestling. A world that, in the case of this particular promoter, often consisted of barbed wire, thumbtacks, fire, explosions and the occasional bed of nails.

Unfortunately, on this night, there were no kerosene heaters to comfort me. The heat-bearing bowls that babied my buttocks might as well have been a million miles away! They couldn't help me at that particular point in my life, as I lay underneath the ring, curled into the fetal position, trying to fight off the cold gym floor with the warmth of my own body.

At a designated point, I would emerge from beneath the ring, barbed wire in hand, ready to inflict damage on some more-than-willing foe. Upon my emergence, I would be the picture of pure terror, eyes wild with bloodlust, wielding my bat like a warrior's sword. But until that emergence, I would lay on that cold gym floor, continually thinking that same lonely thought—"What am I doing here?"

Actually, the reason was simple. There was one man to blame, and it sure wasn't me. The culprit … Terry Funk. Terry Funk was the reason I had traveled 10,000 miles from home. Terry Funk was the reason I was under that damn ring. Terry Funk was the reason I would return home from that tour (and 15 others like it) looking like some monster from Universal's glory days, swaddled in gauze, wrapped in athletic tape, bruised, battered and stitched, with the potpourri of analgesic balm and liquid antiseptic permeating the air around me. Yeah, Terry Funk was to blame. Why? Because Terry Funk was my hero, and I would have followed him anywhere.

I haven't seen them all, but I have seen quite a few. If a man of some distinction has graced a wrestling ring in the past 25 years, I've probably caught his act. I can't accurately state who the greatest of all time is, but I can say without any hesitation that Terry Funk is the greatest wrestler I have ever seen.

"What about Ric Flair?" I can hear the doubters cry. No doubt, Flair was great, and he and Terry Funk were the only workers I've ever seen who seemed to exude a love for the wrestling business in their every in-ring step. Funk was simply more believable. When watching Flair, no matter how great the match, with very rare exceptions, I was always aware that I was watching a performance. Terry Funk made me believe.

He made a lot of fans believe. I remember looking at the faces of the fans when the Funker was in action. Looking at the faces of his Japanese faithful in 1980, when he was at his most beloved. They believed. Looking at the faces of the Memphis fans, when he was at his most tyrannical. They believed. Looking at an Atlanta TV audience, when Terry returned from mainstream exile, middle-aged and crazy. They believed.

Maybe it would have been more accurate to say fans suspended their disbelief when Terry Funk took to the ring—or the microphone. But he sure made suspending disbelief a breeze. No one in the modern age of wrestling had the ability to make an impact so fully, or so quickly. The arrival of The Funker to a new territory or TV show would inevitably mean that a major change was taking place. Wrestling would almost instantly become a little scarier. A little funnier. A little more believable.

And that change could be infectious. He had that rare ability to bring out the best, not only in his opponents, but in onlookers, as well. Wrestlers raised their game, both physically and verbally, when the Funker came to town, lest they be swept away by the rising tide of increased expectations he left in his wake.

He was as kind as he was crazy. I first met this wrestling legend in November of 1989, a few weeks after his classic "I quit" match with Ric Flair—a match that remains my all-time favorite. You have to lean in kind of close to hear The Funker, for when a microphone isn't present, his voice is tough to hear. But the leaning close is worth it—a small price to pay for gaining access to his mind, a vast and fertile field of theories, anecdotes, parables and life lessons, which he is more than happy to pass on.

I met Terry for the second time at a WCW TV taping in Raleigh, N.C. A few novice wrestlers were in the ring, practicing the basics, working on the moves that they hoped would make them stars.

A few of the more seasoned wrestlers were laughing with each other, looking at the ring and then to the arena floor, where Terry Funk stood, observing all the ring holds and slams.

"I'll give him one more minute," Brian Pillman said.

Tom Zenk, known as the Z-Man (or as The Funker pronounced it, "Zea Man"), disagreed.

"No way," he said. "He can't take it. Look at him. He's not gonna last."

The countdown began. Well before the minute mark, Terry couldn't take it any longer. To the delight of Pillman and Z-Man, to the bemusement of myself and to the benefit of the novices, Terry Funk rolled into the ring. Within moments, he was rolling around with young wrestlers he had never met, dispensing wisdom and exchanging armbars. He couldn't help himself. He just loves this stuff too much.

In August of 1995, I became the "King of the Death Match" in Japan by virtue of my victory over Terry Funk.

"I wouldn't do this for too many people," he said, in that quiet Funker mumble.

I nodded my head. "I know," was all I said.

The victory was not without a price. I received 42 stitches from a variety of wounds, as well as second-degree burns that led to my arm turning a brittle brown by my return flight's end. My wife was a little concerned, and placed the blame exactly where it belonged—on The Funker.

"Mick," she asked. "Do you think you could find a different hero?"

Yeah, I suppose I could have. I would have had a whole lot fewer stitches. I would have never seen great flaps of charred skin fall from my arm. I might walk a little better.

But, man, I'd be a lesser man had I not known him.

There's a price to pay for everything in life. And in my humble, hardcore opinion, stitches, burns and the onset of arthritis are minor ones to pay for having known the world's greatest wrestler, and for having had the opportunity to be his opponent, partner, protégé and confidant—and a contributor to this great book.

—Mick Foley

PREFACE

Sometimes, when I was a child, my brother and I would wake up late at night to the sounds of my father coming home from a nearby town where he had wrestled. He would bring in his wrestler friends, and listening to their stories about wrestling, the Great Depression, or World War II was life at its best. These were great guys, with names like Benny Trudell, Herb Parks, Frankie Murdoch, Dizzy Davis, Ruffy Silverstein, Cowboy Carlson, Bob Geigel, Bob Cummings, Lou Thesz (with his manager, former world champion Ed "Strangler" Lewis), Dick Hutton, Joe Scarpella, and even Cal Farley, who founded the Boys' Ranch that would play a major role in our lives later in Amarillo.

A lot of these people are no longer alive, and you probably have either never heard of, or have forgotten some of these names. Where have all the flowers gone, my ass! Where have all the wrestlers gone? I'm not condemning the fans for not knowing—it's the wrestlers themselves, myself included, and the ones of the past who have failed to teach our profession's heritage. Someone needs to remember where we came from, and who the people were who sacrificed yesterday so we could have a business today.

I remember the boys' laughter and the stories that would fill our home with life until the wee hours. I remember how their eyes would sparkle with pride when they talked about the tough guys in the profession and the crazy ones, like Alex "One Punch" Perez, who ran himself into a corner post and split himself wide open one night. The next show, the crowd was up by a hundred people, which meant more money for all the wrestlers. He was half goofy for the next six months, but they loved him for it.

I listened to those stories for as long as I could, before my eyes got too heavy and I curled up in my mom's lap. When I grew up, I was fortunate enough to live the wrestler's life, a life that gave me stories to tell, just like the ones I had heard as a boy. Pirates, millionaires, kings and adventurers have nothing on me! I would trade my life with no one.

So, in that spirit, this is my story. And if you get sleepy, you can just stop reading, and you won't have to miss any stories!

ACKNOWLEDGMENTS

I would like to thank the fine folks at Sports Publishing for letting me tell my story to fans all over the world. I would also like to thank Scott E. Williams, my co-author, for helping me make sense, and for all his hard work in helping to put this together.

Thanks also to Mick Foley, one of the most genuine people in the world of wrestling, for writing a wonderful foreword, and for being such a wonderful friend.

A special thanks goes to the wrestling fans of the world, without whom I would never have been fortunate enough to live this amazing life.

Finally, I want to thank my wife, Vicki, for loving an old rascal like me for all these years. She kicks me in the butt when I need it, and she's there to listen to me gripe, when I need that. I love you, honey.

—Terry Funk

I would like to thank more people than I have room to mention here. Daniel Chernau and Richard Sullivan helped put together a lot of timeframes and were instrumental in helping me understand some of wrestling's regional history. Heath Grider, one of the funniest people I know, helped with a lot of history of the Amarillo circuit. Nick Kozak, one of the nicest pro wrestlers I've ever met (and the best 70-plus surfer in the state of Texas), was also very generous with his time, telling me his memories of Amarillo, where he was an integral component for years.

Jason Hess, Mike Mensik and John R. Williams gave me a lot of moral support and kept me honest by never being shy about telling me when I'd gotten something wrong.

Between scanning photographs and proofreading, Jim and Leann Sukman put in enough volunteer time on helping with this book to deserve a medal. Instead, they must settle for my genuine thanks.

I would never have had this opportunity without Dave Meltzer, editor of the *Wrestling Observer* Newsletter. It was Dave's recommendation of me that put Terry and me together in the first place. I will never be able to thank him enough. Dave was also kind enough to read over several chapters, giving me the benefit of perhaps the sharpest wrestling mind in the world. One man who could fairly challenge him for that title is Jim Cornette, who was also gracious enough to read the material and talk me through wrestling's rich history.

Thanks also to my editors at *The Galveston County Daily News* for giving me a chance as a reporter, and later, as a wrestling columnist. Every day on the odd island of Galveston is a revelation.

Several others helped me with a question about a date, name, or location, and whether they realized it or not, they helped keep us as accurate as possible. To whatever extent the book you hold is error-free, you can thank Jacob Christner, Max Levy, Jeff Luce, John McAdam, Barry Rose and Guerin Shea, among others (and I apologize to anyone I left out). Any remaining errors are solely the responsibility of Scott E. Williams.

It has been a rare privilege to work with Terry Funk. I always knew Terry was a great wrestler and promo man, but he's an equally great human being, and getting access to his incredible mind and seeing his generous heart have been among my personal highlights.

But when it comes to highlights, nothing can top the greatest blessings of my life—my wife, Brenda and our children, Brooke and Brody. Thanks for putting up with my burying myself in this work for all these months.

—Scott E. Williams

CHAPTER 1

Funk Family Tree

My generation is at least the third in a line of crazy people named "Funk."

My father was born in 1918. His given name was Dorrance Funk, which was the name his mother used to call him. However, his friends and schoolmates always referred to him as "Dory." He, his brother (Herman) and sister (Dorothy) were born and raised in Hammond, Indiana.

Their father, my grandfather, was Adam Funk, who was a Hammond police officer. He'd come from Krauthausen, Germany, where he had served as a member of the Kaiser's guard. After World War I, Adam moved to Hammond, where he started out walking the beat. He was a very good man, and he lived by a few rules—you follow the law, and right is right. He worked long and hard, rising through the ranks to become chief of police.

Hammond was just east of Chicago, stronghold of the criminal syndicate, run at this time by Al Capone during the prohibition era. Needless to say, there was never a shortage of action for Adam.

Adam was a no-nonsense kind of guy, and he was also willing to fight for what he believed in. Adam Funk shot and killed six people in the line of duty during his career. Marshal Dillon wasn't shit compared to Adam! Adam's no-nonsense attitude extended to his finances. He was very frugal, which I think was true of a lot of people who lived through the Great Depression.

Adam was no-nonsense at home, too. He expected his kids to toe the line, and when they didn't, he would not spare the rod.

I think a lot of that transferred to my father, who I saw get violent more than once, but he always got violent at the right time. He was a great man, although he was somewhat difficult to explain.

One summer, between my father's freshman and sophomore years in high school, Dory Funk had what he thought was a great idea—he would slug a few slots in syndicate-owned stores in Calumet City, on the Illinois-Indiana state line, between Hammond and Chicago.

Their plan was that my father's buddy would distract the store clerk, while my father would push slugs into the slot machines. He did well for about half an hour.

The only hitch to their scheme was a small window on the front of the slot machine that showed the last three coins played. When the clerk had finally taken more bullshit than he wanted to, he walked over to the machine. To try to keep him from seeing the slugs, Dory tried quickly to put in three nickels so they would be the only coins visible through the window, but he dropped his third nickel, and the clerk saw the slug in his machine.

Dory pushed him aside and ran out of the store, knowing the mob would be after him and knowing they wouldn't care that he was only a kid, or who his old man was.

Dory felt he had to get out of town, so he hopped on a train and rode the rails for much of the summer. He actually made it as far as Florida, but decided to head back before school started. He got to Chicago and walked the remaining six miles back home.

As he walked up the alley to the house, he wondered what he was going to say, when six-year-old Herman spotted him. Herman ran back in the house, screaming, "Pa! Pa! There's a bum in the alley … and I think it's Dory!"

My father was filthy, and he smelled awful. Adam made him take off his foul clothes, and my aunt "Dot" burned them in the trash can.

Adam asked his son why he had run away. When Dory told him about getting caught slugging the slot machines, Adam took off his belt and gave him the beating of a lifetime.

The next morning, Adam and Dory took a father-son trip to Calumet City. They went to the store, where Adam made Dory apologize for what had happened weeks earlier. Dory also promised to repay every penny he had bilked from the store.

Then Adam told everyone in the store, "If you harm my boy in any way you'll have hell to pay."

After Dory's brush with the mob, my father decided to buckle down at school. He became a good student, and an outstanding football player and wrestler. He won the state wrestling tournament three years in a row and became class president his senior year.

He took his wrestling to the next level after coach Billy Thom recruited Dory into the University of Indiana in Bloomington. Coach Thom, considered one of the best coaches in the country, was a strict disciplinarian and specialized in leg wrestling and hooks. His forte was the top body scissors and a variety of leglocks.

Coach Thom also taught how to cross a man's face while applying these holds, making them tortuous, but still legal under amateur wrestling rules. Used properly, these holds can knock a man out. In short, Coach Thom taught his wrestlers how to hurt their opponents.

My dad wanted a good education, but he got the best of all possible worlds. He got his education, learned how to break arms and legs and got to be close to home, close to his family and to his true love.

My aunt was not the only "Dorothy" in my life, or my father's. He ended up marrying his high school sweetheart, Dorothy Matlock, in 1940. They married secretly while my father was a freshman in college. She was a year older than him, and he often jokingly accused her of "robbing the cradle." She never did seem to think that was very funny.

Even though in 1940 they were now married, my mother stayed with her parents while my father was at school, because my parents didn't have much money. Bloomington was only about 200 miles from Hammond, so Dory would hitchhike home after his last class Friday, so they could spend weekends together.

The summer after my father's freshman year, he got a part-time job driving a truck for Inland Steel, and my mother worked in her father's drugstore. They had a few dollars in their pockets and were happy together, but that summer she found out she was pregnant, and they had a decision to make.

My father loved wrestling at the university, but he loved Mom even more. With a baby coming, he didn't want to go back. Dad went to work for Pullman Standard, which had started making tanks (as opposed to train cars, their usual fare) as the war heated up in Europe. Dory Funk's days as an amateur wrestler were over, but he played quarterback for Pullman Standard's semi-pro football team.

Dory Ernest Funk Jr. came into the world February 3, 1941. Less than a year later, the Japanese attacked Pearl Harbor, and the country was in a state of shock. My father thought seriously about enlisting, but held back because of his young family. Working for Pullman and making much-needed war materials kept him out of the draft.

All this time, my father missed wrestling. He liked the one-on-one competition. Beating someone on the mat gave him a rush that no other sport could supply. He went to local gyms and looked for opponents. He went through all of them, so he hit the bars and offered to take on all comers.

In the early 1940s, professional wrestling was very popular, and Chicago promoter Fred Kohler was one of the most influential in the country. Wrestling was treated as if it was pure competition, even though it was not competition, even at that time. Wrestling was even covered every week on the *Chicago Tribune* sports page.

My father wanted to get into this business, but didn't know how to go about it. Pro wrestling was a strange brotherhood, and wanting in and getting in were two different things.

If you wanted in, you had to have certain qualifications. Toughness and the ability to keep your mouth shut were two of them. Smartasses were not tolerated. Those who wanted in usually ended up with the shit beaten out of them. It was a closed business, and Kohler didn't want to let Dory into it initially.

Eventually, he proved himself in some shoots (legitimate contests), and they decided to take him under their wing and break him into the business.

Legitimate tough guys in wrestling were often called "shooters," or policemen. They relished getting a hold of a mark (a derogatory term for a fan who believes in wrestling) or a "wannabe." It was a feather in their caps if they made their victims scream with pain or piss their pants.

A.B. Scott, my father's former high school wrestling coach, decided to cash in on wrestling's popularity by opening a half-assed promotion in Hammond. He made a deal with Kohler to use two or three of Kohler's boys (wrestlers) on each show and fill out the rest of the card with locals.

The coach also wanted to use my father, and his big idea was for Dory to take on all comers. Every weekend Dory would have a shoot (legitimate match) against the best and toughest in the area. He even beat Walter Palmer, one of Kohler's top hands and a known shooter.

My father's pay was a grand sum of $10 per match. After several weeks, the mob caught wind of this and sent the toughest son of a bitch they could find to "beat this Funk kid." There was some betting involved, but these guys were mainly there to make the point that this mob muscle was tougher than any wrestler. I don't know if the guy was a collector, or what he did, but all he collected that night from Dory Funk Sr. was an ass-kicking!

Lou Thesz happened to be one of the main-eventers sent by Kohler into Hammond the night the mob's tough guy made his challenge. Years later he told me about it.

"One whole section was completely Mafia," he said. "Your father was on the first match against their tough guy. The bell rang, and in no time, your old man had him down. He top bodyscissored him and then ripped him across the face several times with his forearm. This broke the guy's nose. Blood was everywhere, and he quit. After the match, every one of those Mafia guys walked out, not saying a word. Their boy had lost. They could have cared less about the rest of the matches."

He laughed and added, "Including mine."

A reporter from the *Hammond Times* covered the match as if it were a major sporting event. The coverage made Dory something of a hometown celebrity. Fred Kohler, being the prototypical wrestling promoter, smelled a few bucks to be made. He brought my father into Chicago, where Dory worked occasionally in manipulated matches. The money wasn't great, but it was something my father loved to do. He still had to maintain his Pullman job, but he was hooked on the wrestling business. Soon enough he would be out of both.

In summer 1943, my father enlisted in the navy. He knew he'd be drafted sooner or later and always said, "I figured the food would be better on a ship than in some goddamned foxhole!"

I think he made the right choice.

He went to basic training in Chicago, on Lake Michigan, where he was allowed to see Mom on the weekends. Then he was assigned to a Land Shore Medium craft, more commonly known as an L.S.M. It was No. 182 and assigned to the Philippine Islands. The ship was only a few hundred feet long and about 34 feet wide, carrying 50 sailors and four officers, plus whatever troops the boat took to the beach for landings.

It was a small fish in a big pond compared to the destroyers, tankers and aircraft carriers in the fleet. My father used to say, "What goddamned Jap in his right mind would want to waste his life and plane on our little boat?"

Now, I want to make something clear—I don't condone the use of the term "Jap." I would grow to love the Japanese people, and so would my father, but he was at war with them at that point, and he had hard feelings toward them that took a long time to heal.

Even though my father's ship wasn't much of a target, whenever a squadron of Zeroes flew over, the ship's crew would man the 20-millimeter cannons along with the rest of the fleet, and they would claim any enemy aircraft that went down in the heat of battle. They didn't give a damn if 10 other ships were also firing on the plane when it went down—they would paint a small picture of a plane to represent each one they had "downed."

From the looks of their reconnaissance tower, you'd think that ship single-handedly wiped out the Japanese Air Force.

At the end of June 1944, my father's ship was hit by a typhoon, which tossed around that little boat like a matchbox in a washing machine. They ended up near the coast of China! But what he didn't know was that my mother was also in a dangerous situation at the same time. She was giving birth to a breach baby and started hemorrhaging. The only person in the area with the same blood type was her doctor, so he gave her his own blood.

And that was how I came into this world.

CHAPTER 2

The Little Funker

I was named after one of my mother's favorite characters from the funnies, Terry from Terry and the Pirates. Dory Junior, or "Dunk," as we used to call him (think about it), always said the first time he saw me, he thought I looked like a gangly little chicken. Later on, as we grew up, he would threaten to beat the hell out of me for one of the many reasons I gave him to do so. I ran like a chicken, but I never thought I looked like a chicken.

My mother spent the first three months of my life in the hospital, with peritonitis caused by a small piece of placenta remaining in the womb. My brother and I stayed with her family.

My father island-hopped until the war was over, and then came back to Chicago and to his family. He tried to get his job back with Pullman Standard, but they weren't hiring—there were no more tanks to be built.

He knew he needed money to feed his family, so he decided to try wrestling full time. By now a new local promoter was running Hammond for Kohler, a man named Balk Estes. Balk was also a wrestler. In fact, he and his brothers (Toots and Kick) were all in the business, and were all full-blooded Indians out of Elk City, Oklahoma. That little state put out some of the toughest amateurs in the country, and it still does!

Balk was one of those tough amateurs, and when he first met my father, he said, "So, you're the guy who's supposed to be so tough."

My father made no bones about it—he wasn't afraid of anyone, and certainly not Balk Estes, so Dory took Balk up on his offer to go to the gym the next day to see who was toughest.

That was the way things were done in the profession at that time. Two tough guys would go to the gym, more than likely alone, with no onlookers. Who won and what happened was the wrestlers' business, and sometimes never mentioned again.

Shortly before his death in July 2004, I tracked down Balk, by then 87, at his home in Oklahoma. I asked him what happened that day.

He said, "Dory took me down and hooked me in a top body scissors and facelock, but after several minutes, I got away. We wrestled about 10 more minutes with neither one getting the advantage, and then we both called it quits."

In my heart, I believed my father hooked Estes and crossed his face. I don't think Balk ever escaped, because with what I know about wrestling, I know that he would have had to have superhuman strength and the ability to withstand a hell of a lot of pain to get out of that hold.

Of course, I also thought if I were Balk Estes and Dory Funk were dead, I might tell a similar story, instead of one where I got my ass hooked.

As Ray Stevens, a legendary wrestler and a longtime friend, once told me, "If it's worth tellin', it's worth colorin' up a bit!"

And that, in a nutshell, is the wrestling business.

Whatever happened doesn't matter, because that day at the gym was the start of a lifelong friendship for Balk and Dory.

Balk decided it would be best for Dory to go to another wrestling area to get some ring experience. He talked to Toledo promoter Cliff Moppen and told him he had a green boy named Funk who needed some experience.

Moppen said, "*Funk?* Goddamn! That sounds downright nasty! How the hell can he draw a buck with a name like Funk?"

Balk said he didn't care what Moppen called him, and Moppen eventually agreed to use him and even let him use his name.

They borrowed a house trailer from my Aunt Dorothy and enough money for a used Oldsmobile. The Funk family was ready for the road.

I never really thought about us being nomads. It was just a way of life, traveling around and living in the trailer parks.

At the time, that old trailer didn't seem small to me. Heck, even the back window of our Oldsmobile seemed big. I remember crawling up in the space between the rear window and the back seat and riding for hours down the road. I always liked it best when we were traveling at night. Mom would make Dory Jr. a bed on the back seat with blankets and a pillow, and then fix me up a bed in that little rear-window nook.

We would listen to the radio for hours as we drove across the country. I loved "The Life of Riley," but "The Shadow" scared the devil out of me.

Wrestlers in the late 1940s were like a bunch of gypsies—roving vagabonds traveling throughout the country. We stayed at a trailer park in towns that were centrally located to the towns the promoter ran, as did a lot of other wrestlers' families, and we bonded with a lot of them. It was immediate acceptance with the other wrestlers' families. The kids stuck together, and the families did, too. It was much more of a circus atmosphere than what you might imagine—not as far as how they earned their money, but in the way of life. It was close to what the circus or carny's way of life was. You'd go into a territory, stay three or four months, or as long as you could, and then move on to your next territory.

In those trailer courts, we were all part of a big, extended family. I believe a lot of it was that we had common enemies. We might fight with each other, but we could come together against the people who called wrestling "fake" or "phony."

On weekends they would have get-togethers with plenty of beer and all the food everyone could eat. I never knew a wrestler or a wrestler's wife who couldn't make one hell of a meal!

Looking back, I guess that 30-foot trailer was a little small for a family of four, but it was home. My mother decorated the room Dory and I shared with paper stars that glowed in the dark. At night we said our prayers, and she kissed us good night. Then she turned off the lights, and the moment she did, the stars would glow. We were among the heavens, or at least we thought we were. You talk about neat!

For years, it seemed like the Trudells were always in the same territory as us. Benny and his wife, Lil, had four children, three beautiful girls and a boy. After seeing all of them packed into their trailer, I realized ours really wasn't so crowded.

They were from Montreal and originally spoke only French, but the kids picked up English fast. As for their parents, well, Benny did OK, but Lil brutalized the language and could not have cared less. All that mattered to Lil was that her husband was OK and her kids, too.

Benny was never really a great wrestler, but he was hard-nosed and pretty tough, pound for pound. He would fight for the wrestling business at the drop of a hat, but at five-foot-eight and with a pot belly, promoters would never let him be a main eventer. Like most of the wrestlers I've known through the years, Benny was hooked on the business. He doubled sometimes as a referee but just knew that if he had the right gimmick, he could make his fortune in wrestling.

Wrestling in the late 1940s and 1950s was a six-night-a-week occupation. No promoter would chance working on Sunday, or it would've been seven, but the guys wanted that day of rest to be with their families.

Driving to a different town every night could get monotonous, and good traveling companions were necessary. For my dad, Benny was the perfect companion, I believe, because he thought everything Dory did was grand, and thought everything Dory said was hilarious. Looking back, I guess he was living vicariously through my father.

My father worked in the Ohio, Florida, Oklahoma and Arizona territories before returning to Ohio for a second run under promoter Al Haft. Soon after we got there, promoter Moppen announced they were bringing in the heavyweights. Anything over 205 pounds was considered a heavyweight. At 190 pounds, soaking wet, Dad was a junior heavyweight, and he saw the writing on the wall—he was out, and the big guys were in. He gave his notice, and we were off to Texas.

By 1948, Mom and Dad were thinking about putting some roots down. Junior was in school now, but it was difficult for him. Moving from territory to territory, he had to change teachers and friends a couple of times a year, even though he usually did well and was an exceptional student. My parents wanted a home and some stability, like other families had.

I wasn't yet at school age, so it wasn't as hard for me as it was for my brother. He and I were like all brothers, I guess. We loved each other to death and hated each other, too, sometimes. We would get into terrible fights, and I usually got the worst end of it. My mom would stop it by hitting us over the head with a newspaper. For some reason, we were just like dogs. When the dog pisses in the house, you hit him with a newspaper, and that's what she did. Boy, we were scared to death of that newspaper! For some reason, hitting us with a newspaper was the worst thing she could do to us.

Our house had a kitchen with two doors leading to it on opposite ends and an island counter in the middle. Traffic would go in one door, around the island and out. It was almost like a circle. One time, when my brother and I got into a big argument, I said something that would turn it into a fight, as I often did. But it was only going to be a fight if he could catch me!

I took off with the idea I would try to get enough of a lead on him that I could make it to the bathroom and lock myself in before he could get to me. It was a great plan, except for one thing—I would also have to make it through the kitchen, where my mother was ready to spring into action with her newspaper, rolled and taped up.

I tell you, all she had to do after a while was take that newspaper out, and Junior and I would calm down as soon as we saw it. She had us trained, just like dogs!

It was always evident that my brother and I had different personalities. Junior would operate behind the scenes, while I was just goofy enough to try anything.

One time, he said, "Hey, Terry, I have an idea."

"What's that, Junior?"

"I think you'd be able to run really fast if we tied a piece of plywood to your back."

So that's what we did.

Well, the wind was blowing about 40 miles an hour that day. We found a large piece of plywood to put around my arms and tied me to it. I picked up a lot of speed, as I recall, but soon became the world's first manned tumble-board.

Junior was the quiet one, but he was the one with all the ideas. My dad was the same way. He always had stuff for me to do.

We had a skunk named Stinky. It'd had its scent glands removed, but at some point, Stinky ran away, so we went out looking. Soon enough, my dad spotted a skunk and said, "Terry, there's Stinky."

"Dad, I don't think that's Stinky."

"Goddammit, that's Stinky! Look how tame he is! Get out there and get him!"

So I went out there and got sprayed by the skunk. It sure was stinky, but it wasn't Stinky!

We lived for a while in the trailer court with the other wrestlers' families, but then my father got a job as superintendent at the Boys' Ranch under Cal Farley, who was also a professional wrestler. Dory Senior ran the entire thing for all 140-plus kids out there. He dealt with all their problems. Nowadays, you have to go through a tremendous amount of litigation to get a child to a place like that. Back then, they'd get a call from the sheriff, or sometimes even from out of state, with someone saying, "Hey, I have a boy for you here. He's a problem child, his parents aren't around, and he needs a place to live."

My dad would say, "All right. Bring him out."

The boys were anywhere from six to 18 years old.

Dad would work at the ranch all day and then occasionally wrestle at night.

As a child, I thought Dad was out there fighting for his life. Even though I knew that they knew each other, I never once questioned that their matches were real. I truly believed. I would go to the arena and bawl every Thursday night, terribly upset, the way my kids would years later, when they saw me getting beaten up. And I had fight after fight at school, defending it all my young life.

One time, a kid told me my dad was a phony, so I asked him what his dad did.

"He's a doctor."

"Well," I said, "what does he do? Give people sugar pills? I bet your daddy gives them sugar pills. He's not a real doctor."

Sometimes, that kind of response was sufficient. If it wasn't, we'd get down to business.

But I'm very glad it was presented to me that way. It made me respect my profession much more. It made me have a lot of admiration for the guys who were in it, and it impressed on me that it was not easy. It never has been easy, and I kept that with me. Over my career, there was just a handful who I smartened up to the business. Once you enter into the profession, you're in the fraternity.

When I was 14 or 15 years old, my father smartened me up. I don't think believing in it for so long did me any psychological damage. I think his waiting so long to smarten me up helped me to appreciate what a special thing it was to be smartened up in that day and age.

After he told me what the truth was, I continued to defend it as a shoot, because I understood it was necessary to present it as a shoot, especially in this area and at that time, because of the small populations of the areas and the number of performances they had to do. If it wasn't looked at as a shoot, they wouldn't be doing much business. Wrestling wasn't the circus coming to town—it was a weekly pastime.

I first saw how seriously my dad took protecting the business when I was five years old. We were on our way home from the matches and stopped off at Joe Bernarski's, a steakhouse in Amarillo belonging to and named after an old-time wrestler. I was sitting at one of the tables with my brother, who was nine. My parents were at another table, sitting and talking to some other people.

This man came over from another table and sat down next to me. "So," he said, "you're Dory Funk's son."

"Yes, sir."

Then he started asking me questions about wrestling—questions he really shouldn't have been asking me. He should've been asking my father.

Finally, he said, "Come on, you can tell me about this wrestling and how it all works. It must be all fake, right?"

My brother got up, got my father and told him what this guy was saying, and that was one of the first times I remember seeing someone truly get the shit beaten out of them.

A few years later, we owned a public swimming pool called Gem Lake Swimming Pool, and my father had mats on the roof so some of the guys could work out up there. One day, my father and Bob Geigel (a tough wrestler from Kansas City) were working out up there, and I mean truly working out, truly wrestling. While they were up there, this guy came onto the roof with them and said, "Hey, I think I can do that! Isn't all this wrestling phony?"

My dad said, "Is that right?"

My dad untangled himself from Geigel and beat the shit out of the guy. The guy took off running and jumped off the roof. He was trying to catch onto a tree that was about 20 feet from the building, but he missed. I think he ended up OK, but he spent a little time in the hospital.

When I got into wrestling years later, I took very seriously the idea of protecting the business, and I had a number of confrontations over that very thing. None of these confrontations ever started with me deciding I just wanted to punch someone out. Someone would tell me how phony my business was, and my answer was always, "Well, I'll show you it's not."

And I did just like my dad did. A lot of times, it was just easier to just shoot in on a guy, take him down and make him look like an ass.

One night, I was in a bar in Amarillo, talking with my wife, Vicki. A man came up to the table where we were sitting and asked her to dance.

I said, "Sir, would you mind waiting a little bit? I'm talking to her right now."

He said, "Terry Funk!"

I said I was, and he put out his hand. I put my hand out to shake, but he grabbed my hand and started squeezing as hard as he could.

He was about 300 pounds, not the most solid guy in the world, not a monster with muscles, but he was big.

I was trying not to register it, but his squeezing was hurting like hell. I rared back with my left hand and slapped the shit out of him.

A diamond ring I had just bought (and was really proud of) flew off my hand, and he went down to the floor. Now, this bar's tables were made of iron, including the one where we were sitting. They were very heavy, and after the big man fell to the floor, he grabbed one of the tables with both arms. I reached down to pick him up by his pants, and as I tried to lift him, his pants ripped right off of him and his underwear, too! I was looking down at his bare, fat ass!

I thought, "Shit, I might as well," and so I dove down and bit a chunk out of his ass, and that was the end of that.

Until the next day, when he sued me. I ended up settling out of court for $750. It was the most expensive piece of ass I ever had.

As I said, my father was violent at times, but other times, he was the softest person in the world. Laura Fishbacher was a girl from Umbarger, Texas, who had leukemia. She was 11 years old, and she was going to die. My father wasn't a rich man at this time, or ever, for that matter, but he took $1,000 of his own money and put it into a checking account in her name to let her buy anything she wanted to for herself. She wasn't related to us. That was just the kind of guy he was.

It was nice to stay put, not to have to go somewhere else and start anew. As I'd said, though, my brother Dory was the one who endured switching schools so many times. I started first grade at the Boys' Ranch where my father worked as superintendent. I would like to add that I received an award that year for being the best speller in the class. Of course, I was the only first-grader at Boys' Ranch, and they had a rule that each class got at least one award.

My dad didn't show any favoritism to me, even though I was his son. The first fight I ever got into there was when I was six, and I got into it with a kid named Dickie Harp, who was two or three years older than me. He was a tough kid, but when I got up from my seat at the mess hall during lunch one day, I came back, and he was in my seat, so I snuck up behind him and put the first illegal hold I guess I ever used on him—I grabbed him from behind, put both fingers in his mouth and pulled back as hard as I could. Come to think of it, I guess I invented the dastardly "fish hook."

Anyway, he was screaming and hollering, and my father came over, yelling, "All right, all right! What's going on over here?"

Dickie wasn't doing anything, so I was feeling pretty good, like a tough guy.

"Dickie," my father said, "what's the deal here?"

"Mr. Funk, Terry grabbed me from behind and pulled me down," Dickie said.

"Well, why didn't you fight him?"

"Well, I didn't want to, Mr. Funk. That's your son. I thought I'd get in trouble."

"That's OK, Dickie, you go on ahead."

In addition to being my first fight, that was also my first loss, because Dickie beat the shit out of me.

Every Thursday night, my dad would take the boys from the ranch to the matches. Each week, there'd be a bus out there to bring the kids to the arena, where we had our own roped-off area to sit in.

I went every week, but not everyone could. It wasn't an automatic deal—it was a treat. It was a good incentive for them, which they needed, because this wasn't exactly a bunch of good kids living out at the Boys' Ranch. There were some rough, troubled kids there.

One kid, Roger Landing, is probably worth a book all by himself. Roger was 10 years old and very street smart. Roger would sneak onto airplanes parked at the airport because they didn't have any of the security like they do now, and he'd get on the radio and start calling, "Mayday! Mayday!"

Roger didn't have any parents or anyone who gave a shit about him, so sometimes he'd just go to a motel at night, find an unlocked room, go in and crawl into bed right with the guy in the room. In the morning, the guy would wake up, look at Roger and say, "What the hell are you doing here?"

Roger would say, "Well, you brought me here."

One day at the ranch, after weeks of Roger on his best behavior (really, he was conning my father), my father made the big mistake of telling Roger, "Take my car keys down to my wife at the office."

"Yes, sir, Mr. Funk."

And that was the last my father's new Cutlass 88 was seen in one piece. Roger took off in that car, and Dad got a call from the neighbors a little while later.

"Dory," they said. "Your car just went by, and it was Roger behind the wheel, going about 80!"

About another mile up the road, he flipped it three times, and when my father got to him, he said, "Roger! What the hell are you doing?"

"I'm sorry, Mr. Funk, but I didn't want to run your battery down, so I shut the engine off."

The damned thing was totaled, but at least Roger saved the battery!

I was four years old out there, running around with kids who were in their teens. I thought they were my friends. Hell, I thought I was just one of the guys, so they'd have me stealing cigarettes. So there I was, four years old, smoking stolen cigarettes. I didn't know any better.

They didn't have any cigarettes on the ranch. Anyone my father caught smoking, he'd take to the gym. He'd make them drink a glass of warm milk, and then roll around on the gym floor until they puked.

I took a pack at a time of my father's, sliding the rest of the carton down, like they were all still there. Well, it only took my father a couple of times for him to figure out something funny was going on. He finally caught me stealing his cigarettes, so he took me outside where there was a big bell. He rang the bell, which meant everyone had to come running. All 140 kids came running.

He knew all the kids liked me, so he had everyone gather around, and he said, "I caught Terry stealing cigarettes. Now, Terry, climb up on this stepladder."

I climbed up on the stepladder he had set up out there.

"Now, pull down your pants."

I pulled down my pants, and he pulled off his belt and beat my ass in front of 140 kids.

Then he said, "If you want Terry to get his ass beat like that again, you just go on and have him steal cigarettes for you again!"

Well, nobody asked me to do that again. They liked me, and they loved him.

Dory Junior had a few scrapes at the ranch, too. My brother was on a wood-pile once, just playing, and there was also a beehive near the pile. I don't know if he touched the hive or what happened, but those bees went crazy after him. He had bees buzzing all around him, stinging him, and one even made it up his pants and stung him 13 times on the end of his pecker!

Well, naturally his pecker swelled up and looked like a gnarled tree limb. Now, my parents used to have the Boys' Ranch teachers up to the house in the morning for coffee. Dad's favorite deal became to show his boy's disfigured pecker to everyone who came by the house in the morning.

"Junior," he'd yell, "come here!"

My brother would come into the room, and my dad would say, "Show 'em where the bee bit you!"

"Dad, I don't want to show them!"

"Dammit, show them where the bee got you, boy!"

So Junior would unzip his pants and pull out this knotty, horrible-looking thing that used to be his little pecker, and those women would scream in horror!

I'm surprised Junior didn't end up with a lifelong complex about bees because of that.

My father also coached the Boys' Ranch football team. One time, not long after he got there, he brought his brother-in-law, Jack Thornton, to a game. Jack, who was married to my mother's sister, Eleanor, was only about five years younger than my dad, about 130 pounds and 25 years old. He was balding, though.

The Boys' Ranch hadn't won a game since two years before my father started there. They just didn't have many boys, and all the boys had to go out for wrestling, but they didn't have to go out for football. My dad's thinking was, if you're too small he could put you in another weight class to wrestle, but if you're too small for football, you couldn't participate.

On this day, the Boys' Ranch was ahead by 20 points—it was the first game they were going to win in years! But they had injury after injury, and pretty soon, they were down to 10 players.

My father had to weigh things now. On one hand, he didn't want to cheat. On the other, it was really important that these kids win for their self-esteem.

He got a football helmet and put it on my uncle's bald head and put bailing wire for a chin strap so it would stay on.

He told Jack not to run the score up, just to keep it close, and that's what he did. The Boys' Ranch finally got its win.

Don't ask me why, because my dad was really hard on those boys, but I swear, when he finally left that place in 1951, there wasn't a dry eye at the ranch.

Leaving was pretty hard for me, too, because I had made all kinds of friends at the ranch, from the other kids there to the adults working at the place.

At one point, after my dad left Boys Ranch, he got into a disagreement with Dory Detton, which resulted in us leaving the territory for a while. We headed north—far north. My father wrestled under a mask during one stretch in Vancouver, British Columbia, working for promoter Rod Fenton. That was actually where the "Double Cross Ranch" name came from. My father wrestled as The Outlaw and was billed as being from "The Double Cross Ranch." It was a great name because it had that double meaning, both as a brand (two "x"s side by side) and in the sense that The Outlaw would double-cross you.

It's a name that stuck with me. I've lived on the parcel of land known today as The Double Cross Ranch (yes, it's a real place) for 27 years. These days when I go to church, I tell people it represents two crosses.

The two Dorys eventually worked things out, but we ended up spending a lot of our summers in other areas. We went to North Bay, Ontario, Canada, where my dad wrestled the Vachons—"Mad Dog" Maurice and Paul "The Butcher." As ugly as those guys were, believe it or not, they were the babyfaces against the mean roughneck from Texas. And that feud drew well. The town had about 25,000 people living in it, and the matches drew 3,500!

Sometimes it drew too well. My father would get the fans so fired up that riots would break out in the arenas until they played "God Save the Queen" over the P.A. system. When the song started, the fans would stop throwing stuff and would stand at attention, which allowed my father a chance to make his escape out the back. This worked for three or four weeks, but those fans finally got tired of it, said, "Piss on the queen," and just kept rioting.

This was the first time I ever saw my father work as a heel, and it was before my father smartened me up to the business. But I never questioned why he was now being a "bad guy." We were from Texas, and we thought our home was better than Ontario, Canada. It made perfect sense to me!

Canada was a real experience, but I was glad when the two Dorys patched things up and we got to come back home. Not long after, my dad ended up as part-owner of the territory. Doc Sarpolis, a booker and promoter, had come in and bought the Amarillo territory in 1956 from Dory Detton for $75,000, which was a tremendous amount of money.

Sarpolis then offered my father a chance to buy in, and so Dory Funk Sr. became part-owner of the Amarillo wrestling promotion.

Nineteen fifty-six was also the year I met the love of my life. Vicki and I had gone to different elementary schools in Canyon, but were in the same middle school together. I always thought she was pretty great, but we were really just friends until high school, when we started dating.

On a couple of nights, this very rules-oriented father of mine would spend his nights wrestling under no rules in a Texas Death Match. I think my father invented the Death Match. I never heard of anyone doing them before he did. These were violent matches where there were no disqualifications and no countouts. In fact, even pinfalls didn't count. If one wrestler pinned the other, there was a 30-second rest period, followed by a referee's 10 count. The match only ended when one man could not answer that last count.

One of the most successful feuds in Amarillo in the early 1960s was when my father battled "Iron" Mike DiBiase for the right to be called "King of the Death Match." Their first death match went about 30 falls, well over the three-hour mark, without a winner. They called a curfew at 1 a.m., and they both went for hardways (where wrestlers are truly busted open, usually from punches to the head) in the match, so they both had to go the hospital to get stitched up afterward. That's just the way things were done for believability and to make things intense, which helped the business. You opened the sports page the day after a guy went hardway, and there was his picture, with a head looking like a melon. What would you think about the believability of what that guy was doing?

A lot of times they'd do a hardway if they had a bunch of smartasses in the front rows, yelling, "It's all bullshit!"

We'd go right out in front of them and let them see someone getting punched right in the face. It would keep them wondering if it was real or not. I've done hardways on other guys before, and I've had them done to me.

Both my dad and Mike had black eyes and busted mouths after the match, and naturally, after getting out of the hospital with his stitches, my dad was exhausted.

Over the next few months my father wrestled DiBiase just a few times, usually in tag matches, to build interest in the rematch.

The amazing thing was they came back a year after that first death match and did a rematch for the anniversary. The entire card was the Texas Death match and a standby match—only four people on the card. It sold out. I don't want to be one of these old-timers saying everything "in my day" was a sellout, but they really did have people lined up outside trying to get in to see this and getting turned away.

And the standby match didn't even go! They just had two guys dressed in their gear, just standing by like they were ready to go. Hell, they knew they weren't going on, so they weren't really even standing by, and they still got a payoff! Now, that's a hell of a deal!

My father won the Texas Death rematch with DiBiase, but that one also went long—more than 90 minutes.

My father also wrestled the original Gorgeous George. George Wagner was the original, bleached, flamboyant pretty-boy wrestler, and they wrestled in Dick Bivens Stadium in Amarillo. The match drew 7,000 people, which was more than 10 percent of the number of people living in the area at the time.

Even though we were based in Amarillo now, my father still wrestled outside the area occasionally. He was never the biggest wrestler, but he was a tough guy, and people knew it. In the late 1950s, there was a wrestling war between Houston promoter Morris Sigel and Ed McLemore, from the Dallas area. They would line their cards with shooters to protect themselves, because you never knew in that situation if someone from the opposition would come in and challenge your guys some night to make your wrestlers look like fools. Morris brought in my father, Rikki Starr and Ray Gunkel as his shooters, and those guys could damn well shoot. At that time, Dad was making $500 a week, which was huge money in those days.

Another one of my father's big feuds was with Frankie Hill Murdoch. They wrestled each other 32 times in 1948. The majority of them were singles matches, and every time Funk and Murdoch were matched up the building was full.

Later I got to be good friends with Frankie's stepson, Dick Murdoch. We played when we were kids. He always was a little asshole like I was, and we both ended up following in our fathers' footsteps as wrestlers.

We would sit around in the arena while our fathers waited to get paid. It took an hour or so, because they had to count the house and figure it all up. We'd go around the arena and collect cups. Once we got around 50 cups all stacked up, we'd set them down one at a time and stomp them on the floor to make them pop.

I learned a lot more about payoffs later. Here's what the honest cut of the gate was supposed to be—10 percent came off the top for booking fees, then the rest was to be split, 45 percent to the promoter, 45 percent to the boys. All the promotional expenses were supposed to come out of the promoter's half, and the boys would split the other 45 percent, based on the promoter's discretion in regard to where on the card each guy wrestled.

I started wrestling amateur-style at Boys' Ranch when I was five years old. My father brought a lot of the great pros to the Ranch to show the kids on the wrestling teams some techniques and pointers. Back then, almost all the pros could really wrestle.

CHAPTER 3

West Texas State: Running with the Outlaws

When I graduated high school, I was very small for my age—155 pounds. I got a tryout down at Cisco Junior College, and that summer I had a big growth spurt and shot up to 185 pounds. There were no steroids then, either.

I made the junior college team and just kept growing. I weighed 225 and played linebacker and guard down there. When I transferred to West Texas, I was at about 240 pounds. I was just late in maturing. West Texas was where I wanted to go because it was close to home. Junior, my brother, had just finished up there, and the football team had gone to the Sun Bowl where they beat the University of Ohio. I had been wrestling amateur but gave it up my sophomore year in high school. I still practiced my wrestling skills at home. I worked out in our garage, which had been transformed into a wrestling gym, with guys like my father, brother, Bob Geigel, Verne Gagne, Dick Hutton, Joe Scarpella and Lou Thesz, to name a few.

My relationship with Vicki also picked up a lot of steam during my college years. We had gone to the junior and senior proms together in high school, and I'd been in love with her right from the very first date with her.

I focused on football in college. Joe Kerbel was the coach, and he was a great coach, but he was also absolutely nuts. He'd come right out there and kick you right in the butt. He had been a sergeant in the Marines and was probably one of the toughest men in coaching. He had a hell of a program there—we were a bunch of outlaws.

And a bunch of those outlaws became big names in the wrestling business.

Frank Goodish, who later gained fame in wrestling as Bruiser Brody, had some go-rounds with Kerbel when he went to West Texas State. Brody was an asshole! He was on the third team—not because of ability, but because he had come to West Texas State after getting kicked out of Iowa State University. Another outlaw.

We used to go to the bar on 16th Street, where you had to parallel park. Brody used to be the champion of running cars. He would take off running at full speed.

Now he was a big-ass bastard, so when he got going, he'd jump and land one foot on the trunk, next foot on the roof, next foot on the trunk of the next parked car, and so on. That was the deal—you had to see how many cars you could do, and Brody was so damn big, he could do that for a whole block.

Brody was always tall, but he got huge after he discovered desiccated liver after college, and he lived on it. This was before steroids or anything else. When he left school, he weighed 240, and not long after, I saw this enormous guy walking down the street and damned if it wasn't Frank Goodish! That desiccated liver had made him huge, but it also gave him the worst-smelling farts of anyone I've ever known.

He was working as a sports writer for the *Odessa American* newspaper. When he did get into wrestling, I gave him his initial ring name: Frank "The Hammer" Goodish.

We had goal-line scrimmage the last five minutes of practice. Brody would play on third team, and everyone else was just practicing, but he'd go ahead and pump up the goddamned defense so much that we'd have be out there until the goddamned sun was going down.

Another West Texas player who became a great pro wrestler (and who became very close to Bruiser Brody) was Stan Hansen. He came to the school a couple of years after Brody. Stan is the greatest guy in the world and was a very talented wrestler. Like a select few others, Stan Hansen got his start in wrestling through the Funks.

Stan came to me one day in 1972 and asked, "Would you talk to your dad about me wrestling?"

I said I'd talk to my father. Stan, at six-foot-three and 280 pounds, was driving a Ford Pinto and was coaching high school football in New Mexico.

I told my father I thought Stan could be a good wrestler, and I set up a meeting between my father and Stan at my house. My father told Stan about all the training he'd have to do and how he'd have to learn some amateur wrestling. That was something that was important to my father, as he was breaking guys in. He also showed them that they could be beaten in an actual wrestling contest.

At the end of their meeting Stan asked my father, "So how much do you think I can make wrestling?"

My dad said, "Well, I think you can make $250 or $300. And that's just starting, Stan. I'll see that you make more than that before long."

Stan said, "Well, I don't think I can do that. I'm making $550 now, teaching."

My dad said, "A week?"

Stan's eyes got wide, and he said, "A week? GODDAMN! It's $550 a *month* I'm making now!"

Stan always talked loud because he was half-deaf. He'd use that as an excuse, too—"Oh, I'm sorry, I didn't hear you."

Four of Stan's favorite words were, "I didn't mean to," as in, "I didn't mean to take your head off clotheslining you."

Stan was smart, though, because he always saved every dollar he ever made from wrestling. Hansen wore tennis shoes all the time. For four years, he wore the ones they had issued him at West Texas State for nothing, until they had holes in them and were the most godawful-smelling things you ever smelled in your life!

Virgil Runnels was another West Texas boy who became a big name in wrestling as Dusty Rhodes. I met Virgil playing football. Virgil was a good linebacker, about 220 pounds at that time. He could move, too. That son of a bitch could play ball.

Truth is he was a better baseball player than anything else, but he was an all-around great athlete.

There was only one problem—he couldn't talk. I thwear, you jutht couldn't underthtand a wuhd he thed.

My future father-in-law had a filling station in town, and he had this idiot working for him—Virgil. One day, Dusty was working there, and I drove up in my 1965 Galaxy, the first new car I'd ever bought. I'd spent $3,200 on it.

As he filled up the tank, Virgil said, "Thay, Tewwy, I jutht dweem about a cah like thith thum day. If I could jutht get a cah like thith, it would be tho f-f-fine!"

As good an athlete as he was, he couldn't get into wrestling here. We wouldn't train him. We didn't have anything against him. It was just that guys would get interested in the business because of how it was portrayed here and its popularity. We had just started Bobby Duncum off when Dusty wanted in, and we didn't want it to seem like it was that easy for guys just to come in and start wrestling out of West Texas State.

But to Dusty's credit, he found his own way into the business.

Dusty went up to Pittsburgh, told the promoter he had worked for the Funks in Amarillo. They were having some kind of bullshit world title match, and the promoter put Dusty in as the challenger, even though Dusty had "left his gear." Of course, the truth was, he had no gear.

At the end of the night, the promoter gave Dusty his $10 payoff, and Dusty wanted to know where the rest of the money was, since he'd been in a world title match and all! It didn't matter to him that there were only 150 people there.

Then Dusty turned that into a chance to work in Detroit, for promoter Ed Farhat, who also wrestled as The Sheik.

He came back down here and said, "Tewwy, I been wukking fuh The Sheik!" He pointed to a bunch of scars on his forehead.

Well, I wasn't so sure he had been wrestling for the Sheik. He went into the dressing room, but nobody would talk to him.

I went in first and told the guys, "Hey, we're letting this guy into the dressing room, but we're not sure he's smart to the business, so watch what you say around him."

Dusty went in, pulled up a chair and sat down, and no one said a word to him.

But when we got word from The Sheik that Dusty had wrestled for him, it was like the arms opened up, and he was welcomed into that fraternity.

He was a living testament to the will of guys who truly wanted into the business. He made his own way in and became a tremendous box-office attraction.

The mystique of the business was that we hardly let anyone into it. If you got in, you were accepted in, but we let very few of them in. Some didn't really want in; they just wanted to prove a point. It never went well for those guys.

One time, while I was in college, there was a guy who said he wanted in the business. He said he'd been an amateur wrestler and was a tough guy. My father told him to come to the arena, and if he could beat me, then he could be a wrestler.

Sadly, he decided to bring his wife and daughter to his tryout. They sat in the front row and watched as I beat the living hell out of him and just made a fool out of him. He ended up busted open and blown up, and his wife and daughter were crying by the time it was over.

I really was dejected afterwards, because it had taken place in front of his wife and daughter. But my father told me, "Terry, don't feel bad. That guy brought his wife and daughter for only one reason—to show what fools we were."

I had never looked at it that way, but my father was right. That man had wanted to ridicule professional wrestling. Once that sank in, I didn't feel bad for the guy anymore.

Another guy we refused to break in was one of my football opponents in college. Bob Windham, who became known as Blackjack Mulligan, was a big kid from Odessa, Texas. He used to hang around the back row of ringside at the wrestling shows and say, "Man, I wish I could get into the wrestling business."

I would always tell him, "Well, kid, I don't know if you can or not," and walk off.

I had played against him when he was playing for the University of Texas-El Paso. We beat their asses that year, too.

We didn't end up breaking him into the business, but he did what Dusty had done. He went around until he found a small promoter to give him a shot, and he worked himself into the business. You might think we were too picky about who we let in, but that's one of the things that's wrong with the business today. If you have $500 and give it to someone with a "wrestling school," then BOOM! You're a wrestler! It used to be something of a process, not just in wrestling moves, but in some sense of respect for your business and the people in it.

Mulligan actually had some success, especially as part of the Blackjacks tag team with Blackjack Lanza in the AWA and Indianapolis areas. Lanza had a very distinctive look, which Mulligan came to emulate—slick black hair and a handlebar mustache, wearing a black cowboy hat and vest. Lanza drew a lot of money in the business, despite not having any kind of incredible physique.

And then there was Bobby Duncum, another West Texas player and future pro wrestler.

I knew Bobby because he and Dusty Rhodes would sit in the bleachers every Thursday night for the matches. Every week, they sat in the same seats—week after week, for years. We knew they wanted into the business, and we ended up breaking Bobby in. He certainly had that wandering spirit a wrestler has. When the school had the football players answer a questionnaire, Bobby answered the question about what he wanted to do when he graduated like this: "I want to be a truck driver, so I can see the world."

Well, he did end up getting to see the world, but not driving a truck.

When Bobby Duncum first got into the business, we stretched him. That's just the way it was done. We knew Bobby needed to be in the business when we put a hold on him, really sank it in and asked, "Now, Bobby, do you feel that pressure?"

He'd say, "Yes," as calmly as you please.

"Does that hurt, Bobby?"

"Yes," just as calmly.

That was all the emotion you were going to get out of that tough-ass bastard.

After Bobby had been in the business for about six months, we decided to try to give him a push in Albuquerque, so he could make a little money there.

One of Bobby's first opponents was "Spaceman" Frank Hickey, a bulbous wrestler who was out there, and who traveled around doing jobs. He was wrestling Bobby in Albuquerque, and we wanted to give Bobby a spectacular finishing move. We decided he would leap off the top rope as high as he could, and then land with one leg on the mat and the other foot on the guy's head. It was a great move for an agile 180-pounder. Of course, Bobby was 260.

Unfortunately we didn't have anyone courageous enough to try it out. We got a water bucket to serve as a guy's head for him to practice the move. He climbed up to the top and came off. He just crushed that water bucket.

We just told him, "Well Bobby, we'll work on this later, but we want to go ahead and get it going tonight."

That night, we went through the finish, complete with Duncum's new finish, and Hickey said, "Wait a minute—has he ever done this before?"

"Oh yeah, he's done it many, many times."

Their match that night went fine until Bobby climbed up to the top rope, and Frank looked up at him. I don't know what clued him in, but Frank Hickey made the right decision, because he got out of the goddamned way before Bobby could crash down onto his head. Frank Hickey had gone south on Bobby, and it was the smartest thing he ever did.

Frank had a hard time down here. One night he missed his match because he ran over a cow. He tried to drive up and over the cow and got the car stuck on top of the damn carcass with his back wheels in midair.

The West Texas State classes that came after us also contained some guys who would turn into big-name wrestlers.

Ted DiBiase was a good player. I knew he was going to high school and playing football in Arizona, and I wanted him up here. I love Teddy like he was my own boy. His parents were both wrestlers. His dad was Mike DiBiase, who worked in Amarillo while Ted was growing up, and his mother was Helen Hild, a woman wrestler.

He played football, but then he got under Dick Murdoch's wing and suddenly he didn't want to play football anymore. Murdoch always had to have somebody with him, and the great thing was, whoever it might be, Murdoch would make them the only two people with any brains. Everybody else was a dumbass.

"Ted, you and me are the only two smart sons of bitches here," he'd say. Then the next guy would come along, and Murdoch would tell him, "You know, you and me are the only ones who know what's going on around here."

Another one was Tully Blanchard, who was quarterback on the team with Merced Solis, an excellent tight end (who became Tito Santana in wrestling). Tully was a really talented quarterback, but he was in a bad auto accident. He had the window part of the way down, with his arm hanging out, and when his car and the other one collided, the glass broke and sliced through the muscle in his left arm, which was his throwing arm. I don't know if Tully was good enough to go pro, but I do know he would have won a lot of collegiate passing records had his career not been cut short. He would have had a chance at the pros at the very least.

Tully was a great athlete, and I think his success in the wrestling business was a testament to that, because he was a small guy by wrestling standards. Tully had a cockiness about him, and I guess I've never met a quarterback who didn't have that. Back then a quarterback had to have that confidence because the quarterback was often the one calling plays on the field. Tully was able to translate that natural confidence into a successful persona in wrestling.

A guy who didn't go into wrestling, but who became one of my dearest friends, also went to West Texas State a few years behind Stan. Ted DiBiase was the one who brought John Ayers out to the house.

My first thought about John was, "What a big goof," but I liked him from the first time we met.

He was just a big, South Texas boy, as country as he could be, and he didn't give a damn about much besides playing football. He didn't care much about getting grades, although he had a great mind. He'd been at the University of Texas and was doing great as a player there, but he finished up his freshman year with something like a minus-four grade-point average or something like that.

As I got to know him, I saw that this "goofy country boy" could run a bead a hell of a lot better than I could on a piece of metal when welding. That goofy country boy could figure out millimeters and make them match on the welding projects he did. He could build anything. That goofy country boy could start out with a pile of metal and have a horse trailer at the end of three weeks, which is more than I could do.

He could also shoot a gun a hell of a lot better than I could.

In the back of his mind, John knew what he wanted to do the whole time. He wanted to drink beer and play football. Later on, he loved working on his ranch and always loved his kids.

Finally, in regard to the great wrestlers who came out of West Texas State, I want to clear up a long-standing rumor. Dick Murdoch never went to West Texas State a day in his life.

He always played in the "Exes" (alumni) game, though. It was amazing! He just proclaimed himself an alumnus, and no one ever checked him on it! To make things even better, he was the defensive coordinator every year.

In the end I guess I just wasn't made for a classroom. One time I was late for an education class, and when I got there, they were taking a test. I looked over and didn't know what it was, so I just decided to copy the whole damn test off the girl sitting next to me. It was all multiple choice, and I didn't even bother reading the questions.

Come to find out, it was a personality test and for the next year the school officials thought I had female tendencies!

I left West Texas State lacking only four hours to get my degree. And today I still lack four hours.

I might have stayed, but I'd had a taste of the wrestling business from working in my father's territory for a few months, and in 1966 I had a chance to go wrestle for Eddie Graham in Florida. So I just said, "The hell with it," quit school and never looked back.

Sometimes I wish I'd stayed in school or spent more time studying things that I was interested in, but I didn't. And hell, Florida was a chance to be in the business I loved and still earn $25 to $30 a night! That was pretty big money to me back then.

CHAPTER 4

Breaking in

In 1965, as soon as football season ended in my senior year, I started wrestling in small towns on the Amarillo circuit. Growing up there was never any question that I wanted to follow in my dad's footsteps.

I had a couple of matches, one with Jack Cain, my uncle who had been the substitute football player for Boys' Ranch. These were supposed to be warmup matches, to help get me used to things, but these were little towns, and wrestling in front of 150 people didn't really get me used to the Amarillo audience.

My dad wanted me to use the spinning toehold as my finish hold, just as he had done. I don't know if Dory Senior invented that hold, but he certainly was the one who popularized it. The only other person I knew who used it as a finishing hold around the same time was a wrestler in Oklahoma named Wayne Martin.

The decision for my brother and me to use the hold was an easy one—it was over, and we weren't!

For something or someone to be "over," the people had to believe in it, or believe in that individual. Here's an example of how over a hold could get.

In the 1960s, not long after I started wrestling, we had a guy come in from Kansas City. He wrestled as the Viking, and used "The Hook" as his big finishing move. Now, The Hook was nothing but an imaginary nervehold, but his opponents sold it like it was torture!

Well, the Viking was driving home one night, but pulled over after he saw a guy fighting with a cop on the side of the road. It looked like a traffic stop gone bad, and this guy was pounding the hell out of the police officer. The Viking got out to help before the officer got hurt. He ran up and started to pull the guy off, but the guy turned around and recognized him and gave up, right there on the spot!

He was screaming, "Oh, God, no! Please Viking, don't put The Hook on me!"

It's amazing to me how people never get a hold over anymore. All you have to do is put a hold on, week after week, and if the guys scream, holler and give up, before you know it, people recognize it as the culmination of the match.

Baron Von Raschke used to get his clawhold over with the people in a spot where he didn't even put it on his opponent. He used to do a spot where he'd lunge with the claw, but his opponent would move, and Von Rashcke would have to pry his clawhold off of the turnbuckle! That was one of my favorite holds in the business. His clawhold grip was so strong that he couldn't make his own fingers let go of the turnbuckle!

And the people believed in that! They believed he was truly unable to release the turnbuckle. What was it he had, that he could get away with doing something so absurd?

In Japan they got the Japanese armbar over so well that the people screamed when someone did it. Well, the armbar's a whole lot harder to get onto a wrestler to cause real pain than what the Japanese viewers think from watching those matches.

My first match in Amarillo was against Sputnik Monroe. Sputnik was a great heel, but he didn't feel like giving too much to a kid having his first match. He led the match, and every time I started to look strong, he would say, "OK kid, that's good. Now let's get back down on the mat, and I'll get this hold back on you."

Also, I was gassed, just exhausted, early in the match from nerves. In fact, my nose started bleeding.

I was doing everything he said, and he was guzzling me until my dad ran down to ringside.

My father yelled, "Goddamn you, you dumb son of a bitch, you're letting him eat your ass up! Get up off of your goddamned ass and do something, or I'll beat your ass!"

When I heard that, I jumped up, hit some moves quickly and pinned Sputnik, but Dad had some more choice words for me when I got back to the locker room.

Sputnik was a great heel, but perhaps the top heel in Texas (and almost anywhere else he wrestled) for much of the 1950s and 1960s was Duke Keomuka. The irony was that Duke was a hell of a nice guy when he wasn't incurring the wrath of wrestling fans everywhere. I would run into him again in Florida.

I had a few matches under my belt when I had some talks with Bud Grant about playing pro ball in Winnipeg. They offered a contract paying $12,000 a year. I also went to work for Verne Gagne in the AWA up there.

I got on AWA television and, in my first match there, had Dennis Stamp as a partner against Larry Hennig and Harley Race. Well, they knew my father and liked us. We went out there, and those guys made me look like a million dollars, and I didn't know jack shit about the business. If anybody could wrestle a broomstick, they could, because they did it with me.

Then Verne sent me to Denver to wrestle Butch Levy. Butch was an old fart, tougher than nails. I thought I was going to do all this shit I did with Hennig and Race. They told me I was going 12 minutes, but that night I found out that 12 minutes with Butch Levy was like 12 days! I came out of that ring thinking, "Goddamn, there's something wrong with me. I ain't as hot as I thought I was."

I got so depressed about the match that I went right up to the hotel and went to bed after having a couple of beers with another wrestler, Silento Rodriguez.

When I left Amarillo my father told me, "Now Terry, I don't want you going and getting goofy-ass drunk up there. I want you to mind your Ps and Qs. You're working for Verne, and I want you to act like a businessman."

Well, this was the night he decided to check up on me, and he called my room. Unfortunately, Silento and I got our rooms mixed up I ended up sleeping in his room, and he ended up sleeping in my room.

Even more unfortunately, Silento Rodriguez couldn't talk. He was deaf. He could feel the phone vibrate, though. He reached for the phone and finally got it.

And he said, "Heh-ho! HEH-HO!"

My father said, "Terry!"

"RUH MUH BUH BUH!"

"Terry!"

Silento hung up, and my old man was hot at me. The next time he saw me, the first thing he said was, "Goddammit! I told you not to get drunk! You act like a nut, and then you hang up on me?"

I explained it, and he finally believed it wasn't me who hung up on him.

The football deal didn't work out, though, and I soon came back home.

It was a while before I understood what I needed to do to draw fans to the arenas. Dick Murdoch and I wrestled in a main event in Abilene when he was a rookie and my career was still very young. I'm sorry to say we did not continue the Funk-Murdoch tradition of sellouts our fathers had started.

We drew about 450 people and were going all out, to a one-hour, time-limit draw. We thought that would really bring the house up next time, because we had people standing the whole time we were out there.

Next time in Abilene, we drew the same 450. The reason was, we lacked maturity. We knew what to do, yet we looked like a couple of kids out there, instead of two seasoned pros. I still had a lot to learn.

In 1966, I left Amarillo for a place where I would do a lot of learning—Florida.

Sputnik was in Florida when I wrestled there in the second year of my career. Not long after I arrived, Florida promoter Eddie Graham was having some problems with a Puerto Rican wrestler named Don Serrano, because Eddie was running shows in Puerto Rico at the time, and Serrano was starting to run opposition there.

Eddie told us, "Sputnik, I want you to beat the shit out of him, and Terry, you just stay in the corner."

"OK, Mr. Graham."

Serrano was still working for Eddie at the time, because Eddie's was the only TV wrestling running in Puerto Rico then, and he didn't think Eddie knew about his plans to open up his own full-time office.

But Eddie did know, and since Serrano had given notice, his last chance to get him was in a tag match. The match was Serrano and me against Sputnik and Rocket Monroe. The idea was that if he got his ass beat on TV and looked bad, he wouldn't do any business down there, because people would see him as being unable to compete with top stars and be a champion.

"There's just one thing, Boss," Sputnik said. "I can't just go in there and do that to a guy without telling him it's a shoot beforehand."

"Well," Eddie said, "I don't give a damn how you do it. Just make sure you do it."

"OK, boss, I'm going to tell him first."

"OK, Sputnik, you just make sure you kick the shit out of him."

We had the match, and at one point, Sputnik had Serrano down on the mat. Sputnik got up, yelled, "IT'S A SHOOT!" and kicked him right in the head.

Sputnik stepped back to make sure Serrano wasn't going to get back up, and when he didn't, Sputnik guzzled his ass, but good!

Sputnik was a big white guy with a bleached streak in his hair and a tattoo of a cherry just above one of his nipples. Below the cherry were the words, "Here's mine. Where's yours?"

Sputnik always liked running with black people. A few years after my first Florida trip, Sputnik came back to work for us. One night, we were in Amarillo, and he wanted to go to a "black bar." He ended up getting so drunk that he told us he was going to sleep in the car.

We came out a little later, and there was no Sputnik. We figured he got a ride home, and so we took off.

What we didn't realize was that he had gotten mixed up and climbed into the wrong car to fall asleep. A black woman got into her car to get home, and she was driving down the road when he sat up.

She looked in the mirror, saw Sputnik sitting there and ran her car right off the road. The cops arrested Sputnik, so we had to go get him out of jail.

I also worked several matches with Ron Garvin, an excellent wrestler who was just starting out, and with Bill Dromo. Dromo was probably the most temperamental guy I ever met, but what a worker! Luckily he took a liking to me, and we had some unbelievable matches.

One thing I'll never forget during this time was a match in Lakeland, Florida. It was Bronco Kelly versus Bob Nandor. Those two had, quite possibly, the worst match I've ever seen. It was one of the first matches where I ever saw all the boys come out of the dressing room to watch.

That was the only thing that was going to get the boys out to watch. You really had to have a true stinkeroo going to get the boys out of the dressing room.

Eddie Graham had been a partner of Art Nielson under the name "Rip Rogers." That was what he was doing when Art and he came through Amarillo in the late 1950s.

He ended up buying into Florida the same way my father had in Amarillo, and he took the same approach that my father took in Amarillo in how he promoted and how he became a part of his community. I think he saw something that was successful for my father.

My father's mentor, Cal Farley, once told him, "Dory, to do great things in here, you have to do good stuff for the people who live here, and if you do, they can't knock you or hurt you."

My father lived by that rule. He did a lot of great things for people for no money. When he was out at the Boys' Ranch for years making $110 a month for running the thing, he loved what he was doing, but people also appreciated what he was doing. The community really accepted him for that. It was like arms were opened to him at every corner, businesswise and otherwise.

I think Eddie saw that, because when Eddie went to Florida, he also set up a boy's ranch, and it was successful for a while. He was also very active in the Florida Boys' Ranch and would visit burn patients in the hospital. He did a lot to build good will in that area.

Amarillo had been built on a great deal of wrestling, and Eddie also saw the success of that. He built Florida on great wrestling with guys like Don Curtis, Hiro Matsuda and so many others who were selling the product as real.

Eddie had a great mind for the business and a great feel for the fans. Eddie did not have a great deal of formal education, but he was a very self-educated person. He could fly airplanes, or captain a boat anywhere he wanted to. He was very much a self-made individual.

Eddie had a great mind for the manipulation and continuation of what you would call storylines today. Back then we just called it being a manipulator—not in the sense that he was crooked or anything, but in the sense that he would manipulate what was going to happen from week to week, month to month, year to year. Eddie had a great feel for what the people wanted and were interested in. He was also very progressive. He broke the territory in on wrestling, but he progressed with the times and was very ahead of his time in terms of how he promoted.

He was also fortunate in that he was in a growth area. Florida just grew and grew, and Eddie turned a lot of that growing population into wrestling fans.

He used very complex finishes, as my father did, but don't get the idea that means that the finish is the match. He also understood how to make the TV the lifeblood of that area, and he really educated Gordon Solie. Many times I heard Eddie lecture Gordon about what to say and how to get an idea across. Gordon, who passed away in 1999, would have been the first one to tell you that, too.

Eddie was also very influential in how I came to view the wrestling business. He was not only progressive in how he presented his angles and finishes, but he was also very heavy on the wrestling aspect of it. Eddie was very serious about maintaining kayfabe, the wrestling code of secrecy. Protecting the business was a big deal.

Announcing with Gordon was John Heath, who was wonderful for describing holds and getting into the wrestlers' athletic backgrounds. Gordon and John were able to announce with such sincerity because they'd been educated to it by Eddie.

Eddie was also able to get some great wrestlers into that territory just through the draw of the territory itself. It was the greatest place to live. It was a great life, the weather was beautiful, and everyone in the state knew you and treated you well.

The location was so attractive, compared to say, Minnesota, that Eddie didn't have to pay the boys what Verne Gagne had to pay them in Minnesota, to get them there. Amarillo was similar to Minnesota. Trying to get boys to come out to this little West Texas town, where there was nothing but sand (and not beach sand, like they had in Florida), it was pretty hard to compete with places like Florida. If you're running a place like Amarillo, you'd better have a lot more money for the boys, or they're not going to come.

His son Mike became a very good worker after breaking in in the 1970s, but Eddie looked at things a little bit differently than my father in that respect. Eddie would hold Mike back to a degree. He never tried to get Mike over as a superstar.

Eddie was also a great mentor to me. Eddie gave me so much advice about how to work, took me under his wing and taught me what to do. I can't say enough about how much I learned from Eddie Graham.

As I mentioned, another of my early mentors in the business, aside from my dad, was "Iron" Mike DiBiase, Ted's father. Mike was a star in multiple sports, including wrestling, at the University of Nebraska. He was a tough, wonderful guy who taught me so much about the wrestling business. He taught me to really understand the boys and the camaraderie there. He led me like I was a child in the ring, working 30 or 40 minutes, and working with him was the best education I could get as far as being solid and being believable. DiBiase was a master at getting heel heat, but he was really a highly moral man and highly intelligent. He was a great heel, which would be kind of surprising if you knew what a nice man he was. It takes a smart man to be a smart heel, because getting the kind of heat that makes people want to come in the ring after you is not easy, and he certainly could do that.

Throughout my own career I felt I made a better heel than a babyface. To be an effective heel, however, you have to have the ability to be a great babyface, because you have to understand the psychology of what the people want out of you. The first time I really got a crack at being a heel, in Florida in 1966, I had already been a babyface in Amarillo for years. I found it was a wonderful way to go. I found that I really loved to make people dislike me. I really enjoyed making people believe I was a thoroughly rotten person, which I must have succeeded at, or else they wouldn't have tried to kill me every night.

I also had some fun in Florida. We used to run Miami on Wednesday nights back then, in the same building Jackie Gleason used for his TV shows. They never locked Gleason's dressing room, so every Wednesday night, I'd go in there and piss on the toilet seat. And every week when I watched his show on TV, I would have a laugh to myself, because I knew that at some point that day, he had been sitting on my piss. Hell, that was my biggest claim to fame at that time!

I was still in Florida in 1966 when my father's partner, Doc Sarpolis, passed away. Dad called to tell me he had bought the remaining shares in the promotion from Sarpolis's widow.

"I want you to come back, Terry," he said.

"Dad," I told him, "I'm making a lot of money here."

"Well, figure out how much you're making a week, and I'll see if we can't come up with something better for you."

I called him back after my wife and I figured it out and said, "OK, Dad, I'm averaging $278 a week here."

"Aw, I can beat that," he said. "Come on back."

So I did, after I gave my notice. I wasn't leaving a huge hole for them to fill. I was a middle-of-the-road guy. I worked some with Wahoo McDaniel (a former NFL player and tough guy who had become a hell of a star) and those guys, but I was never a main eventer.

Now the Florida territory almost always made a lot of money, but the boys didn't see a great deal of it. One time, early in my career, my wife and I were on a 15-foot boat, enjoying a day on the water. We were near the base of the Causeway bridge that connected Tampa to Saint Petersburg. We were fishing when all of the sudden here came this gorgeous, 55-foot boat roaring by, horns blasting. Eddie Graham waved at us as his boat went by us and I thought, "Maybe I'm in the wrong end of this business."

I got to learn from some of the greatest promoters ever in the wrestling business, from exposure at an early age to not only my father, but also the likes of

Eddie Graham and Verne Gagne. I also got exposed to Jack Pfefer, who brought a new attraction into Amarillo in the 1960s. He had been a promoter in the Midwest using journeyman wrestlers and giving them names that were knock-offs of big attractions. When "Nature Boy" Buddy Rogers was the hottest wrestler in the country, he called a guy Bummy Rogers. He would use "Whipper" O'Connor since Pat O'Connor and "Whipper" Billy Watson were two of the biggest names of the 1950s. He had Hobo Brazil, instead of Bobo Brazil. I guess he thought people would come to his shows thinking they were going to see the real stars. I don't think that worked out too well for him.

By the 1960s he was bringing black women wrestlers from territory to territory. He had Babs Wingo and Princess Lamumba, "straight out of Africa." And Amarillo ended up being one of those territories.

Lamumba was actually this gal from Brooklyn, and he put a tin pot on her head and some chicken bones around her neck, and she became a princess. He'd bring her out on TV and explain that Princess Lamumba had a few words for the people. Our announcer would put the microphone in front of her, and she'd say, "MUMMA DA BABBA DOO DOO MA LOOBA BABBA LA POO POO!"

And it drew! People came to see the African princess!

That right there should show you how much times have changed. Let Vince try to pull some shit like that now! He'd have people picketing him at the arenas!

Pfefer had some strange habits. He believed in only using toilet water to comb down his hair. I don't know why, but it's the only thing he would use. He was always digging in his nose, too, and he'd wipe those boogers off into his hair! Why? Who knows? And he never spent a nickel on his clothes. He looked like the damned ragman of wrestling.

Amarillo had some really good wrestlers at that time. Bull Ramos was a hell of a performer. He was Apache Gringo's partner. When my father came up with that name, Bull wasn't sold.

Bull said, "What the hell does 'Apache Gringo' mean?"

My father said, "That's exactly what those fans are gonna say, and it'll create some mystery."

Well, Apache Gringo never did catch on, so I guess Bull was right about that one.

My father also gave Gary Hart a new nickname. Gary had been "Playboy" Gary Hart, wrestling around the country, but when he got here, my father decided to rename him "Gay" Gary Hart. I guess my father just thought Gary was a happy individual.

Gary and I were actually the ones in charge of driving Princess Lamumba and Pfefer around. For whatever reason, whistling drove Pfefer nuts. Once Gary found this out, he would spend the whole trip just whistling random notes until Pfefer couldn't take it.

He'd yell at Gary, in his heavy Polish accent, "Goddammit, Geddy, you qvit thet goddamned vistling! It hurts my ears, Geddy!"

Gary would stop for a while, but sooner or later, he'd "forget" and start whistling again. He drove poor Pfefer nuts!

My father was a great teacher to me, but I was also fortunate to be around some of the guys we had in Amarillo. One I learned a lot from was Ricky Romero. I made a lot of trips with him, and he was as good a Mexican wrestler as there was in the United States in the 1960s.

Cyclone Negro was another very talented individual and one of the nicest guys you'd ever want to meet. He always kept his body in great shape and had one of the greatest, most expressive faces I've ever seen. I mean, he had the greatest face in the business. It made him a perfect heel. He wasn't hideously ugly; he just looked like one mean son of a bitch!

And we brought Stan Hansen back in after he came back from a season with the Detroit Wheels, a Continental Football League team. He ended up hurting his knee and decided wrestling full time would be a safer way to go, so he came back down. We told him we were putting together a great highlight film to plug his return. We set it up on a monitor as if this was what was going out on TV, but it was only for his benefit as a rib.

It was a package of every moment where Stan had gotten the shit kicked out of him. He got punched. He got slammed. We had some goofy music set to it, and every few seconds this big, booming voice would come over the music and say ...

"Stan Hansen ... former Detroit Wheel!"

Then, it would have him just getting the hell pounded out of him some more.

"Stan Hansen ... former Detroit Wheel!"

Boy, was he pissed off.

"You're not going to show that, are you?"

He took a while to calm down, even after we assured him it was a rib.

Stan actually came pretty damn close to having his wrestling career ended not long after that. We were in El Paso, just goofing around at the hotel pool, and he was trying to throw me in. I got lucky and threw him in, which got him really pissed off.

He got out and came running after me with his clothes soaking wet. I was on the other side of the hotel door, and he was so ticked he kicked through the glass door. When he pulled out his foot, it caught the glass and cut his Achilles tendon right in half.

Stan was a tough guy, and he thought he could come right back in five weeks, after having it sewn back up. Well, all that did was tear it up again, and he ended up out for about three months.

He never did blame it on me, though, and I was always mighty glad about that.

One of the toughest guys was Amarillo's Mr. Wrestling. Tim Woods, an accomplished amateur wrestler, was Mr. Wrestling in much of the country, but in Amarillo the mask was worn by Gordon Nelson. Gordon was a hell of an amateur wrestler. He taught a lot of guys the sugar hold, a type of chokehold that could incapacitate a man. I knew the sugar hold before I knew Gordon, but I didn't want him putting it on me, that's for sure.

As Mr. Wrestling, Gordon would take on all comers with the deal being a cash prize for anyone who could last 10 minutes with him. I always admired anybody who did those open challenges, because you don't just get marks out of the crowd—you get some tough guys. You never know who you're in there with.

Another guy who did that was someone I got to know much better in San Antonio years later, named Keith Franke. Keith gained more fame using a name I gave him, Adrian Adonis. Adrian was not a classically trained amateur wrestler, but he was incredibly tough in his own way. His deal was a $10,000 challenge, and he handled it well. Adrian would con the challengers. He'd push them into the ropes and then let them push him into the ropes. He'd smile at them, and as soon as their guard went down a little, he'd deck them, and down they'd go.

Les Thornton was the guy who brought the European style to Amarillo, and he was a hell of a guy.

I know it might sound like I'm saying "hell of a guy" too much, but it's really the truth. These were good people. They were all friends. Hell, they were part of the family.

My dad also had an actual part of the family helping out behind the scenes. Jack Thornton (the uncle who had slipped into that football game for the Boys' Ranch, had originally come to Amarillo to help my dad out there. Soon after, he started refereeing and integrated himself into the wrestling business.

He and my Aunt Eleanor ended up splitting up, and Jack married a woman named Barbara, who had been married to a man named Braum. When they married, Jack adopted her son, Billy. Billy Braum changed his name to Billy Thornton.

Even after his divorce with Eleanor, he worked for Dory Senior and helped with booking, or paperwork, or whatever needed to be done. Later he went to work for The Sheik in Detroit as a booker. Believe it or not, Detroit was the premiere territory in the country at that time. Detroit was doing $100,000 houses before anyone else had heard of a $100,000 house. They were drawing even more money than New York for a while.

The Billy Thornton I knew was a strange kid. When he was 12 he stole a car! He was driving around town, and when he got caught, they thought the Boys' Ranch would be a good place for him. They took him out there, and that was where he stayed until he was 18.

After that he went to one of the Amarillo TV stations and became a cameraman. And he was still a goofy bastard! He would switch around the numbers on
the weather map so the weatherman would be there saying, "Well, in Amarillo
today it was 94 degrees," when it was actually 49 degrees.

I went years without hearing from him, until I went out to California in the
1980s looking for acting work. There was a big casting agent out there who
called me in to read for a part in some TV movie. After I read, she said, "By the
way, Billy Bob, the fellow who wrote this, says he's your nephew."

I said, "Billy Bob? I don't know any goddamned Billy Bob!"

She said, "Billy Bob Thornton."

I thought and thought and finally said, "Yes! Yes, I know who that goofball
is! He stole that car! Yes, I remember!"

Well, Billy Bob was apparently directing, too, so that was the last I heard of
that project.

Later I played a small role in another movie he was working on, *Friday Night
Lights,* and we were on the set together. He looked at me, and I looked at him,
and we both acted like we didn't know each other.

Amarillo was also where I encountered a really good tag team—Kurt and
Karl Von Brauner. Karl was a very smart guy and became a spray pilot after retiring. Kurt was a very dedicated professional. He was working for us when he got
word one night that his mother had passed away in Germany. He went ahead
and worked right on through it, fulfilling all his shots before going back there.
It wasn't easy on him.

Kurt Von Brauner was the man who taught my brother how to use the forearm. Kurt could throw a forearm check better than anyone back then.

The Von Brauners proved to be more than teachers, though. They were also
barbers, at least in one angle we did where they cut my hair off to build up a feud
with them against Junior and me.

Back then it took five weeks for the tapes of the shows to make it to all the
towns in the territory, in what we called "bicycling the tape" around. This meant
I had to cut all my hair off for five weeks, so the people who saw the tape of the
haircut show last would get to see a bald Terry the next time I wrestled there. Of
course, the people in the first towns where the show aired got to wondering,
"Damn, isn't his hair ever going to grow back?"

I also remember Ray Stevens and Pat Patterson coming in and just doing fantastic. Pat wrestled in Amarillo as "Lord" Patrick Patterson, and I had some great
matches with him. Ray Stevens was one of the greatest characters I ever met in
wrestling. Ray and I did rodeo together for a while in the early 1980s. One night
we were driving back from a rodeo show, and we would always shoot the shit.

This night I guess we ran out of bullshit, and we got quiet in the car. I
thought for a minute and then said, "Ray, what would you do if you had a million dollars?"

He said, as honest and truthful as he could be, "I'd play a whole lot harder." And he meant that.

I don't know how many times I was in a bar with Ray Stevens, and he'd ask me to borrow $50 or $100. Once I gave it to him, he'd set it on the table and buy drinks for everyone sitting at the table. He didn't care if it was his best friend or Joe Blow. He'd buy drinks until that $50 or $100 was gone, and he always paid me back.

Ray was an unbelievable worker. He could do anything.

One of our top heel teams was the combination of Black Gordman and Goliath. They came to us for a few periods after making their names on the West Coast. They were probably the ones who spearheaded the movement of Mexican wrestlers coming into the United States and being successful. When they were here, they were introduced as being from Mexico, but when they were in Los Angeles, they made the ring announcer say they were from "not Mexico, but New Mexico," and all those Hispanic fans would go nuts.

There's something I think a lot of guys don't realize about that generation of wrestlers—they could really wrestle. We have better athletes in wrestling than we've ever had, but we had more wrestlers back then. Heck, when I first got in the business, having amateur skills was almost a prerequisite. At least 50 percent of the guys then had some kind of background in amateur wrestling.

It was also an era when guys designed their own personas, and most of the time they could pull it off. I think that has its plusses. A guy knows who he wants to be and what he can play better than anybody else.

While I learned a lot about wrestling from the pros I worked with, I was also about to have a whole new learning experience on my hands. In 1967, Vicki gave birth to our daughter, Stacy. I took one look at this little thing and knew my life was never going to be the same again. Four years later, my life changed again, when my daughter Brandee was born.

One thing that didn't happen too often (except in Amarillo) but was always a thrill for me was when all three wrestling Funks—Senior, Junior and me—would wrestle together. Dad still wrestled periodically, and when he did, it was automatic box office. It was tough working with my father, because you always knew who was in charge. Still, it was a real pleasure, not just because he was my father, but because I got to be in there with someone who had such a great sense of the people in the audience. He had great ring psychology. I can't remember him ever having the same match twice, and my brother and I both learned from him. As many times as Junior and Jack Brisco wrestled for the world title, I don't think they ever had the same match twice, and I have never had the same match twice.

I think that's a creativity that's lost in the business. I can't ever recall sitting down and talking to Pak Song, Hiro Matsuda, or one of those guys about even one high spot before a match. You did it in the ring. You would have a finish, and that was it. The rest of it, you did by feel. You've got to dance, and today dancing is all but gone.

I was learning from my father and from people like Mike DiBiase to fully believe in what I was doing in a match, or while cutting a promo (an interview of a wrestler, aimed at hyping an upcoming match). When I was a babyface, I truly loved the fans and would go to the extent with fans that you'd see few people go to, because I realized what they did for me. Yet—and this is where the foggy part comes in—when I am a heel I truly hate the people. My brother would continually get mad at me. He'd say, "Hell, you don't come back down for 10 minutes."

And I didn't. As a heel, I didn't just walk into the arena. I was the heel before I even got there, and don't even ask me when that transformation took place, because I don't know, but I think that is the lure for me of the business—that I can immerse myself in what I'm doing.

When I get hit, I am hit. When I show being hurt, I am hurt, and when I am beating somebody up, I am beating him up—and I don't mean that I am out there throwing potatoes (legitimate, full-force punches or kicks).

Junior and I worked together in a lot of tag-team matches over the years, though. He also learned some, I think, from Mike DiBiase, but he also picked up things from a lot of people, incorporating a lot of styles into his own work. I think he learned a lot about psychology from Johnny Valentine.

I thought that being a second-generation wrestler helped give me a good foundation for what to expect in the business. It didn't seem to work that way at first for Johnny's son, who wrestled for us as Johnny Fargo in the early 1970s before becoming Greg "The Hammer" Valentine.

Greg was 18 or 19 years old when he started for us and was never happy with his money. One day they were passing out the checks. His was about $500, and he wasn't happy with that. Well, this was a surprise to us, because $500 for a week's pay in the early 1970s was pretty damn good, especially for a young guy! He opened up his check and started cussing up a storm, and I looked over and watched him tearing his check up! He threw the pieces on the floor and stomped off.

I didn't do anything. Neither did my father, my brother, or Uncle Herman, another old police officer from Indiana like his father. Herman retired from police work and worked in the office at that time. We just sat there. About five minutes later, he walked back into the room, picked up the pieces, put them in his pocket and never said another word about it.

But Greg was a good man deep down and a tough guy just like his dad. He had that way about him where I knew that he was always going to do all right for himself. He wasn't what you might call a loner, but you weren't going to get a phone call a day from Greg Valentine, to see how you're doing.

A lot of the guys were obviously tough, but some of the really tough ones might surprise you. What a lot of people don't realize is that my brother is a tough man. I think that's because he is a fairly quiet man. He certainly knew how to hook somebody. He was also a good football player and a much better athlete than I ever was. He could always run faster than me.

We paid the TV station in Amarillo $500 to use their studio and shoot our show. Then we'd bicycle the tape around to the different towns. Our announcer was Steve Stack, who learned everything he knew about wrestling in Amarillo. He had been running a gas station. His co-announcer was Nick Roberts, the old Lubbock promoter. Nick was a former wrestler and the father of Nickla Roberts, who worked as a manager named "Baby Doll" in the 1980s.

Some of the most outrageous characters we had in the Amarillo territory weren't wrestlers at all; they were the promoters of the towns.

Chief Little Eagle ran Hobbs, New Mexico, on an old air force base. God, what a rat-trap that place was! The closest thing to a shower in the building was a hose connected to a horse tank. Unfortunately, he never changed out the water in the tank, so the "shower" water got filthier every time it was used, because it just kept recycling through there.

Little Eagle walked around with a .45 pistol sticking out of his waistband, and he'd wave it at anyone he got mad at.

Our Albuquerque promoter was Mike London, and he had TV there Sunday mornings at 11 a.m. We'd have to leave Amarillo at 6 a.m. to get there. He had a one-day promotion. We'd go on TV that morning and beat the NFL and everyone else for viewers. Seriously, wrestling was the top-rated show there for years. Then, at 5 p.m. on Sunday he'd open up the box office and by God, they'd better be out of there by 9 p.m. or 9:30 p.m.

Mike did his own ring announcing, introducing all the wrestlers, but he had some problems on the microphone. Sometimes Mike would forget who was in the ring, or who they were supposed to be. One time we had Nick Roberts out there under a mask as Mr. X, to fill in for a no-show, and London introduced him, saying, "Ladies and gentlemen, in this corner, from parts unknown ... uh ... NICK ROBERTS!"

About every two years, Mike would have a robbery at the box office. He'd come into the locker room with his shirt torn up and a story about how he'd been beaten up and the money stolen. He always seemed to have some extra money after those weeks, and then he got an insurance payment to cover the "robbery!" It was like Albuquerque had a big holiday once every two years— Mike London Day!

Actor Ernest Borgnine came to one of the shows in the late 1960s. Junior and I were talking to him backstage. Borgnine was amazed at the size of the crowd and couldn't believe we ran the town every week.

"This is really great," he said. He started to say something else, but Mike walked up to him and asked him, "Do you have a ticket?"

Borgnine didn't.

Mike asked, "Well, who are you?"

"I'm Ernest Borgnine. I'm an actor."

"But you don't have a ticket?"

"No, I don't have a ticket."

"Then get your ass out of here."

The other Texas promotions were undergoing some upheaval during my first years in wrestling. In 1967, Houston promoter Morris Sigel died, and his assistant, Paul Boesch, took over the city.

In Dallas, a mid-1960s promotional problem broke out between longtime promoter Ed McLemore and Fritz Von Erich, who was trying to take over.

Even though McLemore was the established promoter, my father backed Fritz because he and Fritz had always done good business together. Fritz talked to Dory Senior about taking Dallas over before he even tried it. My father was really a great deal of help to him. He had a great deal of respect for Fritz, and he liked him. They were friends.

Professionally, Fritz Von Erich was an immediate box office draw wherever he went. It was heartbreaking to see what happened to his kids later on. Fritz outlived five of his six sons, and four of them had some kind of chemical problem. A lot of people tried to talk to Fritz about them, but I don't think he was capable of listening because of who he was. He was their father, and he believed in those kids no matter what.

I know Jack Brisco wrote a book stating that when he first came to Amarillo, Dory and I both beat him in a bunch of one-sided, two-minute squash matches after playing up his amateur credentials on TV. I can't remember ever having a match with Jack that only went two minutes. I also don't think pumping up his credentials so heavily is something we would have done in Amarillo—our audience was made up of people with names like Gomez, Martinez and Hernandez, and those folks didn't give a shit about Oklahoma athletics.

Jack Brisco was a great wrestler, though. His brother Gerald was also a hell of a wrestler and was a good babyface, even though he had that big potato nose (just kidding—Jerry actually has a lovely nose, really).

We actually had the Briscos in as a heel tag team for a while, and they were great heels! It was a unique feud in the 1970s—they would come to Amarillo and we would go to Florida as heels to face them. The funny thing was, we could use the tapes from one place in the other place. So the Amarillo fans got to see us as heels in Florida, and the Florida fans got to see the Briscos as heels in Amarillo. It was kind of groundbreaking in a way, because it became more of an atmosphere like the Texas-Miami game in college football. Everyone had their local favorites.

Junior and I also went into Georgia in the late 1960s, to battle the masked Assassins—Tom Renesto and Jody Hamilton. We had lines of people wrapped around Atlanta's City Auditorium with people who couldn't get in. We did a hot angle with them on TV, with the Funks as the babyfaces. The Assassins were a great team. Everywhere they went they did big business.

The Georgia crowd was actually very similar to the Amarillo fans. And the product was very wrestling-oriented. Vince McMahon's World Wide Wrestling Federation in the Northeast was seen as the place where there was more showmanship than wrestling at that time.

One thing about Amarillo—it was the Funks' territory, and that fact alone taught me a lot about wrestling. The best thing about being a performer in your own territory is that nobody can steal you—no one can take you out of there.

But it has its drawbacks, too. From Verne Gagne in the AWA to the McMahons of WWE today, it can get easy to rely too much on yourself as a pushed character. The booker, or creator, needs to be someone who can live vicariously through others, so he can remove himself if need be.

The excuse for a booker pushing himself too much is usually, "I know I can count on myself not to leave the promotion without notice, or hold us up for more money. I'm not going to leave myself."

It's the greatest excuse in the world, and it lets you push yourself forever.

The demise of a great many areas over the years was that the wrestlers who owned them inserted themselves into too many top slots, and when you do that you're taking away an opportunity for your talent to prove itself, and it ultimately lessens the quality of what you're putting out.

Still, knowing the other NWA promoters made a big difference in my professional life. No matter where I ever went it was never, "Hi, how are you? What's your name?"

I already had a relationship with every one of them, and that helped me tremendously.

CHAPTER 5

Road Stories

Travel in the old territories was just something you lived with. I would drive 250 miles to Abilene and back for a $25 payoff, thinking this was the greatest way of making a living in the world. It never even occurred to me there were people in the world making more than I was. We laughed a lot and shot a few rabbits along the way. We'd shoot rabbits, birds, anything that moved along the side of the road, and even the occasional cat in town.

There were some real characters in Amarillo when I wrestled there in the early part of my career.

I could tell Dick Murdoch stories all day. What was great about Murdoch was he was just completely goofy.

When I first broke into the business, Dick was still in high school. Since he was about two years younger than me, he'd referee the matches. We went to Abilene one night, and the wrestlers didn't even want the fans to know the referees traveled with them—that's how serious they were about keeping appearances to protect the business.

That night in Abilene, we did a deal where Dick, as the referee, got involved in the match, and he and I went at it in the ring.

So later, we were getting ready to leave, and I said, "Dick, we can't go out together. People will see us! You get in the trunk, and I'll let you out as soon as we're out of sight."

I shut the trunk and let him stay inside for the entire 165 miles to Odessa, and was he ever pissing and moaning!

"Goddamn you, Funk! Let me outta here!"

Finally, he just gave up and went to sleep.

And he never changed. In 1989, he, Mike Shaw (who wrestled as Norman the Lunatic), referee Tommy Young and I were on the road, and anytime Tammy Wynette came on the radio, Murdoch would give the high sign with his fingers crossed and bump me, as if to tell me he and she were real close. He never knew the broad! He didn't know her from Adam, but he'd act like they were sleeping together for years!

I used to like to change his country station while he was driving. I'd find some rock station, and he was like lightning, changing it right back.

"Hey! Goddammit, you leave that goddamn thing alone," he'd say.

Murdoch was always afraid to go into a restaurant with me. He had his favorite places in every town, and I'd always screw things up by acting like an idiot. I'd ask where the restroom was and then walk into the kitchen, shit like that.

One time we were in Saint Louis, and we were coming out of this bar next to a grocery store when I said, "Dick! You know what would be the funniest thing in the world? If you got into one of those grocery carts and let me push you in the cart. That would be really funny!"

"All right, Terry!"

So he got into a cart, and I started him off. Pretty soon he was going about 30 miles an hour when I slammed on the brakes and let him go. He went about a block and a half down the road, cussing me the whole way.

"Goddammit, Funk, you son of a bitch!"

I loved that goofy bastard. I really did.

Dick Murdoch was really one of the greatest workers in the entire business, but he was temperamental. If Dick, for whatever reason, decided he was going to go out there and have a stinkeroo of a match, he'd have one. It would be stinkier than what anyone else in the world could do. But when he wanted to work, by God, he could work.

I am serious about Murdoch being an incredible worker. His name actually came up once in the early 1970s as a possible NWA world's champion, but he just didn't have the political allies even to be strongly considered for it. The world title was a very political deal, as I would find out first-hand.

What kind of champion would Murdoch have made? There's no telling. He'd have drank a lot of beer every night. Hell, he probably would have traded the world belt for a case of beer on the right night.

Murdoch had a son running around at six years old wearing a hat that held a beer and had a plastic straw going from the beer to his mouth. That kid would run around sucking on that beer, and Dick was so proud of him.

"That's my boy," Dick would say.

Murdoch also had a dog—a bull mastiff. One day, he said he was going to the lake and asked me to come around and check his place while he was gone. It was only about four miles from The Double Cross Ranch, so I said I would.

He had been gone for about four days when I went down there to check the place out. I went to the pen where he kept that bull mastiff. Dick had put a big bowl of water and 50 pounds of dog food in there. I guess the dog was supposed to regulate how much he ate every day. Dick must have thought the dog would sit there and say, "OK, Dick's going to be gone for six days, so I need to eat two pounds today and two pounds tomorrow."

Dick had the dog tied with a thick rope around his neck, and when I went out there, the 50 pounds of dog food was gone. That had made him thirsty, so he drank all the water. I guess he got hungry and thirsty because he had gotten so wound up that he'd pretty well hogtied himself with that rope. The dog's tongue was hanging out of his mouth.

It was really sad how Murdoch died in 1996. The Thursday before he died, he ran a show in Amarillo and did about 800 people, which was a big plus for him. Now, Dick Murdoch was one of the tougher guys that I knew in my life, but Murdoch's idea about working out was, "Hey, I don't need to do shit."

He'd do a set of bench press, get in two hours of bullshitting, and then he'd go home. He had a big gut on him, but that son of a bitch could go. I saw Murdoch run cross-field with John Ayers, and Dick ran about a 4.8-second 40-yard dash, big gut and all. Ayers only beat him by about three and a half yards.

What I think Murdoch didn't realize was that he had been keeping in shape by wrestling. Well, when he promoted his show in Amarillo he had done a match here and there, but hadn't worked regularly in about a year. He was so enthusiastic about having such a good crowd that he went about 30 minutes that night.

And to this day, I think that was the night it happened. Something happened internally to him. I think guys have to watch that. When you haven't gone for that long, don't put yourself out there for 30 minutes.

The next night, Friday, he was pushing cattle at a rodeo. He and his wife owned a bar called Dick's Dive, and he told his wife, "Dadgummit, honey, I'm not feeling good. I'm going to go on home. You go close up the bar."

She did, and then when she got home, he was lying on the couch. He had a bloody nose and he was dead. The bloody nose makes me think he had a stroke or something like that.

Dick lived well when he was making money wrestling, but he had no money when he died. But this is an example of how Dick inspired loyalty among the people close to him. Janet, Dick's ex-wife, paid all the funeral expenses, and she works hard for her money.

Murdoch should be remembered, but there are things like the Wrestling Observer Hall of Fame, where Murdoch's not in, and I don't think he'll ever make it in. I'd like to tell Dave Meltzer, the editor, to put him in, but he can't just do that. He has to go by the balloters. I do think if you had the boys in the business vote, they'd vote him in. But you don't have a true, balanced hall of fame if it's just the boys voting.

Murdoch and I certainly didn't invent ribs (practical jokes) and ways to keep ourselves entertained on the road. In particular, jokes involving hitchhikers were always popular. Once when my father and Benny Trudell were traveling together, my father was driving when Benny spotted a hitchhiker in the distance.

"Do-ree! Do-ree!," he shouted, in his heavy, French accent. "There ees one! Let's reeb (rib) the cock-suck-ier!"

My father pulled onto the shoulder about 50 yards ahead of the hitchhiker, who came running. When he got about 20 feet from the car, my father took off, leaving the man in a cloud of dust.

"Do-ree! Do-ree!," Benny shouted, laughing. "That ees so funny! Do eet again!"

My father stopped again, and knowing the hitchhiker wouldn't believe him, stuck his head out the window and said, "Come on, I was just kidding."

The hitchhiker stood there and shook his head.

"I promise we'll wait for you this time," my father said.

Finally the hitchhiker came to the car. He got within inches of the back door when my father took off again. The hitchhiker was enraged, screaming every expletive known to man as he tried to run beside the car. Finally my father stopped again ahead of him, while Benny laughed hysterically.

My father said, "Benny, you know what would be funny? Stick your ass out the window at the guy!"

"Ha ha ha, Do-ree! I weel do eet," Benny said, and he pulled down his pants and mooned the hitchhiker, who was screaming like a banshee in a rage.

He raced up to the car, and as he got close, Benny said, "That ees so funnee, Do-ree! Here he comes! Let's go!"

Instead, my father turned and braced Benny's shoulders with both hands, holding his ass in place outside the open window.

The hitchhiker ran up and began pummeling Benny's bare ass!

Benny started screaming, "My God, Do-ree! My ass! He's heeting me in the ass! Do-Ree!"

My father finally let him go, and they raced away from the furious hitchhiker.

Benny had his ass bruised, as well as his pride, because he knew the story would follow him the rest of his wrestling days.

My father also rode a lot with Tokyo Joe, a wrestler who was actually from Hawaii. They were going to Borger, a town 50 miles away that they ran every Friday. The referee who was working the town that night was known as the office snitch, so Joe and my dad decided to have a little fun at his expense.

The referee always left at 6 p.m., so my father and Joe left at 5:30 and drove slowly, knowing that the referee, with his girlfriend in tow (she went to a lot of the matches with him) would pass them. Sure enough, the referee passed them soon enough.

Then, my father pulled off the road and had Tokyo Joe get in the trunk of the car. The idea was, Joe would be inside the trunk, which was shut, but not locked. When they caught up to the referee/snitch and passed him, Dad was going to honk twice, which was Joe's signal. Joe would then pop open the trunk and horrify the guy and his girlfriend with Joe's ugly ass.

Well, Dad got in such a hurry to pass the guy that he sped right by a highway patrolman. The patrolman came up behind Dad to pull him over, and Dad suddenly thought of something that would be even funnier than embarrassing the snitch and his girlfriend.

He honked twice, and Tokyo Joe popped up from the trunk, only to find himself exposing his hairy ass at an officer of the law. I think he figured he was in hot water pretty quick, because that patrolman hit that siren immediately. Joe just reached up, grabbed the latch and pulled the trunk closed again.

Of course, the patrolman let them go, but not until my father had gone to great pains to explain the joke that was being played.

But when it came to ribbing, the greatest of all was "Killer" Karl Kox, especially on hitchhikers. Kox would make kung-fu artists out of every one of them.

He'd pull up to the hitchhiker and roll down the window. Kox was a big, mean-looking guy, and he carried a glass eye that he put in when the occasion arose, so he looked pretty scary. He'd say, "You dumb son of a bitch! I'm gonna open up the goddamned door and come out there and kick your ass, you bastard!"

He'd get about six feet from the guy and then he'd say, "Hey—you don't know karate, do you?"

The hitchhiker would just look at him.

Kox would back up a couple of steps and say, "You do! You know karate, don't you?"

Pretty soon, he'd have the guy in a karate stance, like Bruce Lee, or something. Kox would say, with a terrified look on his face, "I don't wanna mess with you if you know karate!"

He'd run back to the car, and we'd take off. The guy would be back there doing goddamned kung-fu thrusts and everything, chopping and kicking at thin air!

Sometimes we weren't even trying to cause trouble, but trying to stop it. One time I was out with Chris Taylor, the 400-pounder who had wrestled in the Olympics. We were coming out of the Claridge Hotel in Saint Louis, and we saw a man and woman having a huge fight right there on the street.

Being the gentleman I am, I went to break it up and got between them.

"All right," I said. "That's enough of that shit. Dadgummit, you guys break it up!"

The guy went into his car and pulled out a .45-caliber revolver. I jumped right behind the biggest thing I could find, which was Chris. God bless him, he was about to shit his pants. The guy couldn't even see me back there!

He finally calmed down, but Chris and I were both scared shitless.

Murdoch and I knew that when Art Nielsen and Eddie Graham were a tag team, they'd literally drink a case of beer every day. We idolized them when we were young, so we figured we'd be just like them. Well, many nights, Murdoch and I, and sometimes Dusty Rhodes, pulled up to my house at 2:30 in the morning, but we still had two six-packs left. We'd drink that up so we could say we finished our case of beer.

One time, Dusty and I were coming back from Albuquerque, and we were getting drunk. We had Cowboy Lang, the midget wrestler, in the car with us. We drank and drank the beer, and pretty soon we couldn't drive anymore, either one of us.

Lang was the only sober one in the car, so Dusty took off his boot, and I stuffed two beer cans down in it, and we put that big boot on Cowboy Lang's little leg, because that was the only way he could reach the gas pedal. That son of a bitch drove 120 miles and got us home!

Nick Bockwinkel and I were in Abilene once. I was driving my 1965 Galaxy, and the air-conditioner wasn't working. Well, this was the middle of summer, so it was hot as hell! We got all our beer ahead of time.

I had my match, took my shower, put on my underwear, threw the rest of my clothes in my bag and tossed them into the trunk of the car. Nick and I had our beer, and the car was gassed up and ready to go. I was driving 90, 95 miles an hour, and here came the cops.

He pulled us over, and I went back to talk to him, still in my underwear. I said, "Goddamn, tonight just isn't my night. Somebody stole my bag with all my clothes in it, and now I'm getting a goddamned ticket!"

The cop said, "Dadgum, Terry, that's OK. I didn't know that. You guys just go on."

Good thing he never looked in the trunk.

I remember when Bobby Jaggers got a new convertible Corvette. God only knows who he talked into loaning him the money for it, because I know he didn't pay for it! We were going through Tulia, Texas, and it had been raining, so the underpass was just full of water. Ray Stevens and I were in his pickup truck, and we made it through the underpass, but just barely. It was a raised pickup, four-wheel drive, and the damned water was still getting up to the floorboards.

Jaggers got on his C.B. in his Corvette and said, "How is that underpass?"

Ray got on his radio and said, "Just fine, Bobby. Come on through."

He did, and that convertible was just sunk. That poor son of a bitch.

Even the referees weren't safe from being the targets of ribs. Amarillo had a referee named Ken Farber, and at the time there was this synthetic drug called Dilaudid, only prescribed to cancer patients, that was about halfway between heroin and morphine and was popular in drug circles. I read about it in a newspaper, and so the next week, when Ken and I were riding to a show together, I said, "Ken, would you mind going into the pharmacy for me and picking up something for me?"

He said, "Sure."

"Thanks," I said. "Just go in there and tell the pharmacist you need to pick up an order of Dilaudid. They should have it ready by now."

A few minutes later, he came running out of the store. They had pitched a goddamn fit on him, and he was mad.

"Damn, Terry! You trying to get me thrown in jail?"

Farber used to take his pet pitbull, Buffy, to the matches. He and that dog would make the loop to El Paso, Odessa and Lubbock. Usually, one of the locker rooms would have a four-legged table, and Ken would leash his dog to one of the table legs. Every match he went out, that dog would go crazy with barking until Ken got back.

This used to drive Al Hays (one of our top heels) nuts, and he'd ask, in his dainty English accent, "Farber, please, please don't leave that dog here. Please do something else with him. Leave him in the car, or something. The dog drives us nuts when you're not back here."

But each week Farber would bring that dog back. And every week that dog would be leashed to a table and bark its head off. And every week, Hays would ask Farber not to bring the dog anymore. Maybe he didn't believe Al. After all, the dog stopped all its barking and crying whenever Farber came back to the room, so Farber just didn't realize how obnoxious that dog got when it was crying for him.

One night, Farber leashed the dog to the table in the room and went out to referee. When he came back, Al Hays was waiting for him.

"Well, Farber, look what your dog has done," he said, pointing to a big turd on the floor near the dog.

Farber fussed at the dog and rubbed its nose in the crap. Then, as he looked at the pile of shit, he noticed a kernel of corn and a peanut, and he realized his dog didn't eat corn or peanuts.

Al Hays did, though.

Farber never brought that dog to the matches again.

Yes, Al Hays was a wonderful worker and every bit as good a ribber. He was also a great talker and even did some commentary for us in Amarillo. People who only heard him in the WWF would probably never believe how sharp and smart he was.

Sometimes an idea for a rib would just pop into my head.

For example, at one point, Gary Hart was managing a guy called the "Moon Man." I think he also wrestled as Masabu. He had no front teeth and crazy, spiked hair going in all directions. He was working for Fritz, and was drawing pretty well, so Junior and I brought him in to work a shot in San Angelo, Texas, as an attraction. He was Mexican and couldn't speak a word of English.

I picked him up at the little airport in San Angelo and told him, "I TAKE YOU TO HOTEL."

He looked at me for a second and said, "HO-KAY!"

No English whatsoever. We were going down the road when we came upon an old folks' home.

I thought to myself, "Wouldn't it be funny to set him loose in an old folks' home?"

We pulled into the driveway and stopped. I pointed to the building and said, "HERE HOTEL."

He said a bunch of shit in Spanish I didn't understand and then, "HO-KAY!"

He got out of the car and I motioned between myself and his bag, letting him know I'd get it.

"You go in door," I said, pointing at the door. "Ask for room. ROOM!"

So this crazy-looking Mexican walked into the old folks' home shouting, "Room! ROOM!"

A bunch of those old sons of bitches were looking around like their world was about to end, and then he realized where he was and ran out of there, back to the car. I was laughing. He wasn't.

One of the best ones I ever did was with Rick Martel when he was a rookie and coming down to Florida. He was riding with Dick Slater and me one day, and I said, "Hey, Rick! You know what would be really funny?"

He answered in his thick French-Canadian accent, "What, Ter-ree?"

"At the next stoplight we come to," I said, "It would be a funny son of a bitch if you took off all of your clothes when we stopped, got out, ran around the car naked and jumped back in the back door!"

He laughed and said, "Yes!"

Now, you have to understand—in Florida, they have these gullies that are full of water, to keep the roads from flooding and help with drainage.

He got out of the car, naked, and started running. When he got behind the door, Slater locked the door, and I took off. He was running down the road, totally naked, shouting, "Wait! WAIT!"

He didn't know what to do, so he jumped into the damn gully! When we went back around to get him, he looked like a damn turtle, with just his head sticking out of the water!

Nowadays, they travel by plane, and I think one of the problems with the wrestling business today is that they don't have the bonding to the same extent that we did. Of course, as I was living proof, it was entirely possible to have as crazy an experience in an airplane as you could in a car.

Junior and I used to love playing tricks on the other passengers on planes. One of our favorites was the "empty luggage trick."

Junior, who's been bald-headed for most of his adult life, had this awful-looking toupee, which he put on the top of his head before getting on a plane. He would always get on board before me. When I got on, I would have an empty bag with me, and I'd be struggling with the thing as if it weighed a thousand pounds. I'd carry it for about 10 feet, then set it down and make like I had to catch my breath. Junior would be in his seat while this was going on. I'd finally lift the thing up as I got to the overhead compartment over Junior, who would be acting like he didn't know me. Everyone around would be watching as I staggered back and forth before finally getting it into the overhead rack. When I did, I would bring my hand down and knock his toupee to one side—not all the way off, but enough to be seriously lopsided. Then, I'd go to my seat, a couple of rows behind him.

The funniest thing, to us, was that no one would ever tell him about it! He'd be sitting there with the wig on the side of his head for the whole flight!

Boy, the things we did to occupy our time.

CHAPTER 6

The Doctor is Out (of His Mind!)

And there's one crazy bastard, in particular, who deserves his own chapter, if anyone does.

One of the craziest weeks in my entire career happened a little while after Virgil Runnels came back to Amarillo, now calling himself "Dusty Rhodes" and wrestling as a heel. We decided to give Dusty a manager, Dr. Jerry Graham.

Jerry Graham's mother had recently passed away in a Phoenix hospital while Jerry was there. Jerry was so upset that he picked up his mother's body, slung her over his shoulder and ran out of the hospital room. The interns tried to stop him, but he pushed through them and got onto an elevator. He took that elevator down to the first floor, where he pushed his way through another batch of interns. He made it out of the hospital and down the street to his car. When he got to the car, he was so tired and blown up, he just bodyslammed her onto the car. The police showed up and he started fighting them, until one of them cracked him on the head with a billy club, giving him 110 stitches in his head. I tell you, he looked like the goddamned Frankenstein monster!

He made his bond to get out of jail, and somehow Dusty and I heard that he was available, so we suggested him to my father. My father said, "Well, if we bring him in, you guys are gonna have to handle him."

We thought that was a great idea. Jerry Graham was one of the all-time great characters in wrestling, and we were going to make a load of money by making him Dusty's manager.

His first night, we were in Albuquerque. He managed Dusty against me, in a best-of-three-falls match Dusty won the first fall, and I won the second. Between the second and third fall, I was sitting in one corner, and Dusty was in the other. Jerry was in his corner, and told him, "Open your mouth!"

Dusty opened his mouth, and Jerry threw two pills inside.

Dusty swallowed and said, "Damn, Jewwy, what wuth that?"

Jerry shrugged and yelled, "Nobody knows! Nobody knows!"

That night, we drove from Albuquerque to El Paso. Back then, we went to extremes for opponents not to be seen together, so I met Dusty in the alley behind the arena, and we got going. Along the way, we stopped to get some beer.

At this time, you had to go into the bar and buy the beer in New Mexico, so Jerry said, "I'll go!"

We gave him the money, and he went in, with our beer money, plus his $85 payoff for that night. About 10 minutes later, he came out and explained, "Sorry, I couldn't get no beer."

We stopped at the next bar we came to, and the same thing happened. The third bar, we waited almost 10 minutes again, before we got to wondering just what the hell he was doing. We went into the bar, and there he was, shooting damn shots down, one after another.

He was still drunk as a skunk when we got to El Paso. The next morning, Jerry decided it would be a good idea to dye his gray suit black. It was his only suit, but he thought it was time for a new look, so he bought a box of Ritz dye. He filled up the motel room bathtub with water, poured the Ritz dye into the tub, and then got into the tub with his suit on.

We came in there later, and he must have been doing somersaults around the damn room, or something, because there was dye on the curtains, dye on the walls, dye on the sheets—there was dye everywhere in the damn room!

So now he had taken his suit off to let it dry, and this pale, 400-pound nutcase was walking to the restaurant wearing nothing but his bikini briefs and a Hamburg hat, shooting at airplanes flying overhead with his umbrella.

Dusty and I finally talked him back into his room, and I called my dad.

"Dad, Jerry Graham's terribly drunk. We can't handle him."

My father yelled, "You guys! You got him that way! You damn well better get him to the next town!"

Well, Harley Race was in the territory at the time, and he happened to be staying at the same hotel. We didn't know what to do, but we knew Harley could handle anyone, or anything, so I asked for his help.

"Harley, please help us. Take Jerry Graham to the next town for us!"

Harley took one look at the huge drunk now back in his dyed suit, and Harley growled, "He's not getting in my car! You guys are gonna have to figure out some other way than that."

So we rented a U-Haul trailer, hitched it to Harley's car and coaxed Jerry up into the trailer. Once he was in, we locked the door shut, and Harley drove him the rest of the way to Odessa, where he managed that night.

A few days later, we were driving to a show in Littlefield. One of our favorite things to do on the road was to shoot at ducks, rabbits, or whatever creature happened to be roaming about. Well, Dusty figured out pretty quickly that we didn't need Jerry Graham around a loaded firearm, so Dusty put his shotgun in the trunk. Unfortunately, that's where Jerry found it when he went to put his bags in.

"Guys!" he said. "Let's shoot some ducks! Let's shoot some ducks!"

Dusty didn't want to break his heart, so Dusty said, "OK, Jewwy, let'th thoot thum duckth, but I don't want you methin' with the gun."

Along the way, we came to a pond. We saw some ducks sitting on the pond, and Dusty rolled down the window, grabbed his gun and shot at them. One of the ducks fell. Jerry Graham jumped out and dove into the water on our side of the fencing! He wasn't a very graceful diver, either.

He submerged at the fence, and came up on the other side. God only knows how he maneuvered his bulbous body through the fence, but he did. He swam all the way to the duck, about another 30 feet. And then, instead of picking the duck up, he stuck the damn thing's neck in his mouth, like he was a 400-pound bird-dog!

He swam back, went under the fence again, and came out of the water back by us. He put the duck down and then proceeded to shake himself like a dog drying itself off.

Dusty told him, "Jewwy, look at yourthelf, now! You're gonna have to run until you're dry."

And that's exactly what he did. He ran alongside the car.

The following night, back in Amarillo, Jerry got thrown in jail because he had been in a go-go bar and had grabbed one of the dancers between her legs. Not only that, but he wouldn't let go! The police had to come and force his hand off the poor girl.

With Jerry Graham back in jail, my father decided it was time to send Jerry out. Usually promoters would give guys at least a two-week notice, but I think my father was scared Jerry Graham would have burned Amarillo to the ground by then.

So instead of giving him a two-week notice, my father told him, "Jerry, I have a deal for you. I'm gonna give you $50 and a one-way ticket to anywhere in the United States you want to go."

Jerry was heartbroken, but he said, "OK."

Uncle Herman drove him to the airport, got him on the plane and waited until it took off. He was under strict orders from my father not to leave until he saw Jerry Graham fly out of Amarillo.

Later that day, we got a call from Dallas. Jerry had disrupted the damn plane so much that they threw him in jail! Of course, he was now in Fritz's territory, which officially made him Fritz's problem. Fritz got him out, put him on a plane for New York City, and that was the last we saw of him.

CHAPTER 7

My Brother, the World Champ

The year was 1968, and my father had some big news.

I didn't know about it until my father came to Junior and me and said, "Gene is ready to give it up."

"Gene" was Gene Kiniski, the National Wrestling Alliance world's heavyweight champion, and what he was ready to give up was the championship. Champions tended to run that route. The world champion went from territory to territory, wrestling the top stars in each, often in long, grueling matches. The grind would run through a guy physically and mentally, and they'd be ready to give it up. Some lasted longer than others. If one worked, the promoters wanted to keep him, because he was a proven draw. It was almost always the champion himself who wanted to end his reign.

Now Kiniski wanted out, and he had told my father immediately before making it known to the NWA board because they were good friends. Gene also told Fritz he was done as champion.

After he told the board, and it became official that Gene would be stepping down as champion, my father told us, "I'm going to push for Junior to be champion."

This meant he was going to talk about Junior becoming champion to the different NWA promoters who made up the NWA board. The board voted on who would become champion.

My father was very smart about the business, he could count alliance members and knew who was going to vote which way. He knew how many he had to carry. With Junior, there was pretty widespread support, although it wasn't unanimous.

My father's push worked, and on February 11, 1969, Junior won the world title from Kiniski in Florida.

This isn't a knock against Gene, who worked hard every night to make the local territories' stars look good and did big business everywhere he went, but I don't think a step was lost when Junior got the slot. It just got stronger.

I've been asked more than once my opinion as to who was the greatest NWA world champion. You really have to put them into eras to be able to make an apples-to-apples comparison. Having said that I can't even give you one name, but I'll give two.

First is Dory Funk Jr. Sure, I'm biased, but Junior was as versatile as anyone who ever held the title. For that point in history, and for what was needed to produce revenue at the box office and to "make" people in a territory, Junior was a great one.

Also first is Harley Race, partially because he was another great, versatile champ who could make anyone look like a million bucks, and partially because if I don't say Harley, I will be in an absolute fight the next time I see him.

Junior winning was also the best thing that could have happened to us. Amarillo was a small but influential territory. You might think having one of our top stars out of the area defending the title might hurt business, but it helped business. When Junior came in periodically, we had someone built up for him, and it was automatic business. There was also the prestige of having the world's champion be someone from this area.

Sometimes my father or I would go into a territory as heels and challenge whoever was the top contender for Dory's title, prior to the guy getting his shot at the world title. A father and brother trying to take out challengers to keep the world title in the family was a great scenario that had never been done before. My father could go anywhere and get instant heat with his promos.

Out of my entire career, my favorite time might have been when Junior was champion and we were all traveling through the territories, here and there. I was treated very well by the different promoters, although I wasn't getting rich. It taught me a lot, because I had to be able to help a challenger by making the fans convinced that because he beat me, he could beat the world champion. I had to be creative constantly, within the ring, to make that opponent and still keep myself strong enough to come back again. It was a bit of a tightrope walk but I loved the challenge.

Johnny Valentine was one of the later challengers who battled me on his way to Junior. We had a short feud in February 1973 in St. Louis, over the Missouri title. We wrestled 30 minutes for TV. It was so damn good—because of Johnny, not because of me.

At the end of the match, we had a deal where I clipped his leg with a chair. Johnny sold it so well that the people were coming unglued. I mean, the whole arena was ready to jump in the ring, and believe me, I've had them do it, so I was watching. It was chaotic.

Later on, Sam Muchnick, the Saint Louis promoter, came and told us he wasn't running it on the TV show because "it was too hot."

That's one thing people fail to realize, when they talk about a fluke finish, where there is no finality. It's what you do going into those finishes that's so important. A screwy finish can be just me hitting you and you being laid out, if the match is popping and the people are being set for it.

That St. Louis crowd was hot, because of the way we set it up in that long match, and because of the way Johnny Valentine sold the pain of his leg.

I'm not trying to put myself on a level with Johnny Valentine, but I truly think he and I took the same approach. When he was selling that chair, he was really hurting. To be able to totally do that is rare, but he had that power, not to just portray it, but to deliver the truth of what he was doing to the people in those stands and have them feel that.

Sam was a smart man, though. To this day, I think part of the heat for my issue with Valentine was Sam showing part of the angle, but not all of it. But at the same time, cutting that angle short was caused by Sam not wanting to put so much power in our hands. If he'd shown that whole thing, Johnny and I would have been locked in for a long run there, and Sam had other plans. Those plans included not letting anyone get so hot that St. Louis was too reliant on one piece of talent. Sam always kept control of his town, and wisely so.

Johnny was never world's champion, but he didn't need to be world's champion. He went to Dallas and popped it for years. He went to Charlotte, St. Louis, cities all over, and he popped every place he went. And he didn't do it by doing goddamned moonsaults, he did it by making people believe in him.

Hell, if he were here today, Johnny Valentine at age 35 or 40, he could walk into Vince McMahon's company and pop the WWE. You might think he wouldn't, but I have a feeling he'd give it hell. He understood the psychology of what he was doing, and you know, if he were there now, understanding the business and the fans like he always did, hell, he might climb up there and do a moonsault.

Speaking of McMahon, let's go ahead and clear something up. I am well aware that the old WWWF promoter was Vincent J. McMahon, while his son, the owner of today's WWE and the guy who led the nationwide push starting Christmas 1983 is Vincent K. McMahon, but everyone in the business who dealt with both called them Vince Sr. and Vince Jr., so for the sake of clarity, that's how I'll usually refer to them throughout this book.

Anyway, in late 1972, my brother Junior told me that, like Gene Kiniski before him, he was ready to drop the belt. He'd had enough of the grind. It was hard on him, but it was easy on me. I could go into a territory ahead of him here or there, and I'd rant and rave about whomever I was wrestling. It was really one of the best times of my career, in terms of creativity. Just laying out a five-minute promo and starting and finishing right on cue was something I loved doing.

Junior ended up losing the title to Harley Race in Kansas City on May 24, 1973. Kansas City was Race's hometown, but that didn't really have much to do with that being where the match was held. It was more a matter of Bob Geigel having control of that area, and Kansas City had never had a title change to that point. A world title change was a great thing for a city, and any promoter would have loved to have had that match.

Junior was going to lose the title to Jack Brisco but ended up having a pick-up truck accident on the ranch and hurting his shoulder. Here, I have to stop again, because Jack Brisco's book claims that he thinks there was no wreck, that the Funks were only trying to maneuver him away from the title.

First, there was a wreck. I saw the truck. The hood ornament was slightly twisted, and there was a little dent in the right front bumper. Junior even had to comb his hair, because it had gotten mussed!

No, I'm just being silly, but that's what the Briscos seemed to assume. The truth is, the truck was totally torn up, and Junior was hurt. He and our father were at a creek on the ranch. The creek had a good, steep bank, and he went off the bank and into the creek.

That same shoulder had been bad for a long time. He'd even had surgery on it previously after hurting it in college playing football.

Second, has anybody thought that the Briscos might have been trying to maneuver the Funks out of the picture through Eddie Graham? We had guys biting at our asses—they wanted us out. There's no one-way street in the business, and there never was. But that's the business. Someone didn't just decide one day to make Dory Funk or Jack Brisco world champion, and it suddenly happened. Someone had to push for them—it was a promotional thing, and there was a lot of politicking, on all sides, before votes were cast.

If Jack had gotten it six months earlier he might have made less money, because the money for the champion only increased as the years went by, so the Funks possibly made him some money by putting him off! He would have only lasted the same amount of time, so what's the difference when he took it? But there's no doubt, Jack Brisco later became a great world's champion.

While Jack was a great worker, it was Eddie Graham who made him what he was. Eddie, Jack's biggest supporter, was the great manipulator, and he groomed Jack to where Jack had to be a star. Eddie was the right mind to get behind Jack's push. Eddie was capable of seeing Jack's potential and knowing how to get the most out of him.

So yes, there were some political struggles between Eddie and Jack and the Funks, but I don't have a single complaint about it. Geez, that's the stuff that makes the past worth talking about.

CHAPTER 8

My Japanese Debut

The first Funk team to visit Japan on a wrestling tour was Dorys Senior and Junior, in 1969. My dad still had an aversion to the Japanese because of the war. They had an aversion to him, because they could tell how he felt about them. They pelted him with fruit, which was very unusual for the time. They hated my father, and my father certainly hated them.

There were a lot of hard feelings left over from the war, as I would find out. A few years later, when Junior and I visited Hiroshima for the first time, we walked into a bar, only to be told, "No Americans! Get out!"

About three years after Dory and Dory's tour of Japan, we had two Japanese guys, Okuma and Masao Koma, come to work as a tag team in Amarillo. Koma in particular was a great guy, very tough and very sharp. He was also one of Shohei Baba's young boys (protégés), so he had some say with Baba, who was one of Japan's top stars. Koma also had a tremendous knowledge of the business.

Baba made a trip to the States while they were here, and he stopped in only two places—Dallas and Amarillo. He was talking to Fritz and to us, to line up an American promotion to work with for talent. After hearing from both promotions and talking to Koma, he decided our promotion would be the better one to work with. Fritz made Baba an offer that included money that Fritz would be paid as promoter. Our offer had no upfront money paid for the promoter or booking fees. Still, we didn't think we would be the ones picked, but we were, because Koma thought a lot of us and told Baba that he did. It also helped that Junior had done such a good job and gotten over so well over there when he had toured before.

Japan was in turmoil the first time I was there, which was my only trip for the Japan Pro Wrestling Association.

Junior and I worked several dates on that December 1971 tour. The biggest match we had was a tag-team win over the two biggest stars in Japan—Shohei

"Giant" Baba and Antonio Inoki. Inoki didn't want to do the job in that match but he did it anyway. I think he did it for the company, which was on its last legs. He certainly didn't do it for Baba.

There was tension between Inoki and Baba, and a lot of tension in the company overall. Both men ended up forming their own groups, which became huge, and becoming lifelong rivals. Their rivalry was rooted in business, but it was always personal. There was true animosity between those two, which probably made for one of the truly greatest wrestling eras in the world. There was great wrestling on both sides. It produced the talent mixtures and the variety of styles that enabled people to see so many different types of wrestling.

My brother had a match with Inoki on this tour. A lot of the guys were worried that Inoki was going to go south on Junior, but Junior was tough and could take care of himself, so he wasn't afraid of being crossed up. Just to make sure, I was standing at ringside, ready to punt Inoki's head like a football if there was trouble.

This was the beginning of our long relationship with Baba, as we joined the All Japan Wrestling group that he started. He never did anything except impress me as a very smart businessman. He was a very wise man who would only say what was necessary and nothing more. I never have met many people who would contemplate an answer and give as much thought to the consequences of that answer to the degree Baba did.

My first tour for All Japan was the inaugural tour for All Japan as a company. It was also the only time I ever wrestled with Bruno Sammartino. He was a perennial champion for Vince McMahon Sr.'s WWWF, while I was always an NWA man in the 1970s, so our paths rarely crossed. Bruno, a burly power lifter and an incredibly strong man, was a great guy and a really underrated worker, because he knew how to get a response out of a crowd. Bruno also had a great heart and a lot of love for Baba.

Bruno's loyalty to Baba ended up putting him at odds with Vince Sr., who was aligned with Inoki's New Japan Pro Wrestling. Even though he was Vince McMahon's champion and doing so meant heat with McMahon, Bruno refused to go to Japan for Inoki. He was just loyal to his friends to the end, putting his own livelihood in jeopardy over his loyalty to his friend Baba. I really admire that.

Bruno Sammartino was one of a rare breed in the wrestling business—a guy who was always as good as his word, with a lot of integrity. With Bruno, what you saw was what you got. And if he told you something, you could bank on it. Even on the tour I met him on, he was one of the top stars in the world and could have been making a lot more money than he was by appearing for his friend Baba, who wasn't able to pay very well at that time. The highest compliment I can pay to a guy in the wrestling business is that he stands up for what he believes in, stands up for his friends, and is true to his word.

One of the real characters on that tour was "Bulldog" Dick Brower. He said repeatedly, "I got to get my little girl something from Japan before I go."

This burly, mean-looking wrestler always talked about his little girl and what a sweet girl she was. One day he finally went to a store and got a kimono, but it was a size 24! I guess his "little girl" must have weighed 300 pounds! Or maybe he was a cross dresser. Who knows?

One of the most memorable series of matches I ever saw in Japan was during one of my first tours there, when Don Leo Jonathan went up against Anton Geesink. Don Leo, at six foot eight, was one of the most amazing athletes I've ever seen, and Geesink was a famous Olympic judo champion before getting into pro wrestling. But physically, he was no match for Don Leo, and Don Leo goosed him pretty good every night. I mean, he just ate Anton's lunch. Of course, their matches all had preplanned finishes, and they were both professional enough to stick to those plans, but Don Leo had a little fun with him every night along the way. But on the last night, they had a judo jacket match, and that match was a different story. Anton was in his element, and on that night, Don Leo met his match. That was the one night he got a little revenge on Don Leo.

There were differences in how Baba and Inoki promoted their products to the fans. Baba was into gradually changing the business. He would stick with his formula and only develop and tweak it slightly. Inoki, on the other hand, was always trying to put out something different. He wanted to innovate in the world of wrestling. Inoki was more experimental. For example, he was the first one to really make good use of the European wrestlers and their unique, mat-based style.

That was out of necessity, because as the NWA-backed promotion, we pretty much blocked him from using any talent from the United States, except for talent from New York.

We were also involved in training Tomomi "Jumbo" Tsuruta, who would be one of Baba's biggest stars for about 20 years. To be honest, Junior had a lot more to do with training him than I did.

The first time I met Tsuruta, he was wearing a pair of size-14 sneakers, a shirt and a pair of pants that had been worn too much. It was the best stuff that he had. He was just an overgrown kid. Baba told us he had been in the Olympics and now wanted to be a pro wrestler.

Tsuruta took to pro wrestling like a duck to water, and it was immediately obvious he was destined for big things. He picked up a lot of Junior's style, including the European forearm smash that my brother had seen Billy Robinson, the shooter from Great Britain, use. Tsuruta also had a lot of financial sense, too, which was very important. He kept his mouth shut and learned by listening. He ended up spending his entire career with Baba, and made good money under him.

Unfortunately, Tsuruta died of liver failure while undergoing a transplant in 1999. I was out of the loop with Baba at that point, so the only way I found out Tsuruta was even having health problems was through a couple of the boys who called to let me know.

My relationship with Baba wasn't always harmonious. When I called in 1977 to cancel a tour because I was filming *Paradise Alley,* Baba just said, "OK," although he was very, very unhappy about it. And I knew how he was going to answer that before I even called. It probably came back to haunt me, though. Later they had a date for a big show, and didn't have me on it. Well, I was over with the fans in Japan at that time. I also know Baba was presented with some ideas for me to do some commercials in Japan, but they were never followed through on, strangely enough.

Anything I did on the side, the All Japan office wanted more than its fair share of, but that's just the way it was. Baba was not happy with some of the licensing deals I made over there. He wanted the company to have a piece of things, like the record I made in 1983 (which contains some of the most godawful singing you've ever heard). Jimmy Hart wrote the songs for me because I was too cheap to pay for the rights to songs that people had already heard. All the songs on that album had one thing in common—they all sucked. One of them was called, "I Hate School"! Can you imagine? Who in the hell would think it would be a good idea to have a 35-year-old man singing "I Hate School"?

After we finished recording, I flew back home, and that was when I found out this country isn't as free as we might want it to be.

I had been working with studio musicians, and when we finished they presented me with an electric guitar that I couldn't play, but I wanted to bring it back because my kids might have wanted to bang on it someday.

I was only in Japan for a day before flying right back to the States. As I came through customs, with my long hair and guitar, the customs man said, "Come with me."

He took me into a room and asked, "Where are you coming from?"

"Well," I said, "I was coming over from Japan, you know, just cutting an album."

"You got a guitar in there, sonny?"

I said I did, and they searched me like I was Public Enemy No. 1.

I had some Motrin, an anti-inflammatory, and they broke up my pills, pulled down my pants, made me spread my cheeks, and stuck a finger up my ass! I think it was his finger. Hell, I hope it was his finger!

I swear to God, they tore everything apart in every bag I had. They thought they had a goddamned hippie, punk-rock singer, or something. Hell, who knows? Maybe the guy knew who I was. He had an Indian look to him. Maybe he was a Brisco fan. Maybe that was a tomahawk he'd stuck up my ass.

Baba inspired a great deal of loyalty on the part of guys who wrestled for him in All Japan, the group he formed after Japan Pro Wrestling collapsed. I would like to say it was only because of money, but that wasn't all of it. I often like to think of myself as a good soldier, and I think a lot of Baba's success came from his ability to select good soldiers. Those soldiers transformed into money guys over a long period of time.

When Inoki formed New Japan, he didn't try to get the Funks on board. He didn't reach out for very many established stars. Inoki went at it as very much a loner. When he started up I knew there was no way he'd be anything but successful. He landed the TV slot he needed, and with his talent and ability, there was no question he was going to make it over there. Inoki had talent, and he had a mind for the business. He still continues to be creative in 2005. But it wasn't a matter of making it at that time. It was a matter of one side preventing the other from finishing the war, because in Japan, with those two organizations it was a 15-year battle that we thought would only end with one of them swallowing the other. Many times they had us in the casket, but didn't get that last nail in, and vice versa.

The war between Inoki and Baba had effects in the States, as the NWA promoters argued over which side to give NWA backing to. Inoki had the support of Los Angeles promoter Mike LaBell, WWWF promoter Vince Sr. and San Francisco promoter Roy Shire. My father backed Baba, as did NWA president and St. Louis promoter Sam Muchnick, Carolinas promoter Jim Crockett, Portland promoter Don Owen, Oklahoma promoter Leroy McGuirk, Houston promoter Paul Boesch and Georgia's Jim Barnett. It was almost like the major population centers on the two coasts against the Midwest, but we ended up having the votes, and the NWA went with Baba.

Florida promoter Eddie Graham was almost in the middle, but he was leaning toward Inoki. He and my father had a friendship, and I think if my father wasn't there, he'd have gone with Inoki totally, because of ties between Hiro Matsuda (one of Florida's top wrestlers) and Inoki.

Six years later, we watched as our rival tried to bury us by making himself a superstar on a completely different level. Inoki put on a show where he had a boxer-versus-wrestler match with Muhammad Ali. It was a big undertaking, with the match going out over closed-circuit television into arenas nationwide. Local wrestling promoters would show their own cards, then switch to the feed of Ali-Inoki.

I knew that show would have been the coup de grace for us if it had been successful, so I was very happy to see that it wasn't. It was a true stinkeroo.

We were almost always over as babyfaces in Japan, but the match that really pushed us over the top was a 1977 tag match against The Sheik and Abdullah the Butcher. That match was really hot, and both the Sheik and Abdullah were excellent.

The Sheik truly could convince you he was the meanest bastard in the world. Hell, when he'd come to Amarillo to wrestle and I was a teenager, I'd run like hell from him! He scared me to death. The Sheik was one of the reasons Lubbock became the best-drawing city in Texas for a short period of time.

Years later, when I wrestled The Sheik in Amarillo, those were the only matches where my wife and kids didn't want to be anywhere near ringside. If he made a move in their direction, they were gone!

The funny thing is, when I'd sit and talk to him in the locker room, he was really a sweet guy, but you'd still be thinking of the insane Sheik, and you'd be scared to death of him, even as he spoke.

The American wrestlers in Japan had always been the big heels, playing off of the very real animosity left over from World War II. When I went over there, the fans would bring up things for wrestlers to sign. The American wrestlers would write insults like, "You look like you could eat salad out of a fruit jar," or something stupid like that.

I realized these Japanese fans weren't dumb—they could read the English we were writing. It was really something for them to associate with an American wrestler, and so I signed all the autographs, without the stupid insults. I showed those fans I really cared about them, and they appreciated it.

The fans in Japan always reacted to wrestling differently than the fans here. A lot of it was the way it was presented to them, in the ring and from the commentators. The sense of realism stretched from their training to their booking. It created a domino effect—from the promotion, to the reporters and then onto the people. We all lived, and were all a part of, the suspension of disbelief. If you don't believe in what you're doing, the fans won't.

One time, Bruiser Brody and I were to appear on a Japanese television talk show. When we got there, they were making fun of the business, with one of Baba's boys sitting right there, laughing right along. We looked at each other and both said pretty much the same thing: "Fuck this shit. We're getting the hell out of here."

We weren't just going to sit there while these guys sat there and made fun of what we did to make our livings, messing with the suspension of disbelief that was such a key to our business. They were going to present us as a couple of phony-baloney wrestlers. We got up and left.

You might think storming off a TV set like that would have hurt us in the public eye, but it did nothing but help.

To this day I think that suspension of disbelief is important. Yes, I know Vince McMahon sat in a courtroom in 1989 and said it was all predetermined, so he wouldn't have to pay taxes to the athletic commission. I know the wrestlers do interviews on talk shows and in magazines every week, talking about it as entertainment. And I know that if you were to ask the guy next to you if wrestling was fake, he'd say, "Oh, sure, of course."

But if I were sitting next to the same guy, we'd get to talking and we'd be talking with that suspension of disbelief.

That's what we wanted to keep with our fans. They knew, in their heart of hearts, that what they were watching was not purely competitive sport. But we maintained that suspension, whether it was in the ring or walking around on the street.

Today someone asks me about wrestling, and I'll say, "It's entertainment," but that's about it. I'll take the conversation somewhere else, because the more I talk, the more I'm afraid I'll be destroying their fun and emotional investment in watching it.

Whether I like to admit it or not, I am something of a cartoon character from years of appearing on television as a wrestler. I'm not talking about the guy I go and buy feed from, or the waitress who brings me my eggs benedict. I'm talking about the fan. To that fan, I am not a guy who buys feed, or orders eggs benedict. I am the person that fan sees on TV, and I have to remember that. It's pretty hard for some people to understand, even in this day and age, that maintaining even a fraction of that sense of mystery is the key to our business. The wrestlers have to have a mystique about them. The fan has to wonder, "Is this guy really the guy I see on TV?"

Now I'm not saying that the heel, even back then, needed to be the world's shittiest person to everyone he met, all day long. But he didn't need to expose himself completely and destroy his façade, either.

CHAPTER 9

Losing Dory Funk

Just a few weeks after Junior lost the world's championship to Harley Race, he and I lost something much more precious.

My father had a cookout and a get-together with a bunch of the guys at his ranch.

During the evening, my father began to talk about shooting and its virtues with Les Thornton and a few others. This was nothing new—I had seen these discussions between my dad and Larry Hennig, Harley Race and too many others to count. These guys would always get into some kind of debate. It was just something they did when they got together.

Eventually, someone said, "OK, move the furniture, and let's wrestle."

The deal this night was Les challenging my dad, saying, "Bet you can't hold me in a front facelock."

My dad put the hold on, and Les struggled to free himself, but ended up passing out after a few minutes.

My dad let go and sat on a bench in the kitchen next to me. He looked at me and said, "Not bad for an old man, huh?"

A few moments later, it was very late, and everyone had gone, when my father walked out onto the patio and found my wife, Vicki.

"Get Dunk and Terry," he said. "I think I'm having a heart attack."

We took him to the Canyon Clinic, a small hospital that was the closest one to the ranch, but all they had was this old EKG machine that would take 30 minutes even to get going. At the time, Canyon only had two doctors. They had to call the doctors at home to get them to come in. They told my dad, "You've had a massive heart attack. Just roll with it, and we're going to get you to Amarillo in an ambulance."

The ambulance took another 20 minutes.

The whole thing took us about an hour and a half from the time he told us he was having a heart attack to the time we pulled into the bigger hospital in Amarillo.

But by the time we pulled in, he was already gone.

We were on our way to the hospital, and my father asked how long until we got there.

I asked the ambulance driver, who said, "Five minutes."

Dad looked at us and said, "I'm going. I'm not going to make it," just as calm as could be.

The thing that haunts me is wondering, if we'd just gone to Amarillo first, would we have been all right? Would my dad have lived through it?

My dad was only 54 when he passed on. Hell, I'm past 60, and I've done a lot of living between 54 and 60.

After my dad died, I had anxiety attacks, thinking I was having heart problems. Six months after his death, I was coming back from a show in New Mexico when I started feeling flush. I went to the next hospital I got to, and my blood pressure was sky-high. I had just scared myself into it because of what happened to my father.

A little later we were in El Paso, and Junior and I had just finished a tag match. We got to the locker room and I sat down and said, "Junior, I'm having a heart attack. I don't want to move real fast, but get me to a hospital."

Junior said, "My God. OK," and he got me in the car.

We buzzed down to the hospital and I sat down in the emergency room. There must have been 20 people in there, and I sat down while Junior went to talk to a nurse about me.

He came back over and said they would be over in a minute, but someone in the waiting room screamed.

"Terry!"

Junior kept trying to tell me what was going on, but...

"TERRY FUNK!"

I looked over, and coming my way was a guy who must have been waiting to see a doctor. Obviously, he was a wrestling fan.

"I can't believe it! Terry Funk! How the hell are you doing? I want to shake your hand! How's it going, Terry? HONEY! Come over here! It's Terry Funk! You got some paper, honey?"

"Just a Kleenex," she said.

"Terry, would you sign this for me?"

I just tried to stay calm as I signed the autograph.

"Well, how are you? Here you go. Hope you enjoy it. Thanks for stopping by."

All the while, I was thinking, "Please, pal, have a little courtesy. Please, God, I don't want to die like this."

I should have blown my nose on the damn thing!

The doctors told me I had been causing myself anxiety and had been pumping up my own heartbeat. It's pretty amazing what the mind can do.

Eddie Graham and my father had one of the strangest relationships. They loved each other, but it was strange. Every once in a while they'd just get into a damn fistfight.

I'll never forget, one time we were in Florida, at my grandfather's house, and Eddie pulled up in his big, beautiful boat. He climbed out, and he and my father were walking together. All of the sudden, out of nowhere, Eddie hauled off and hit my father, and they went after it.

But as many times as they kicked the shit out of each other, and there were many times—a little later—they'd be on the phone talking with each other.

I think it went all the way back to Eddie's days in Amarillo, when he teamed with Art Nelson. I loved Art, Eddie's partner, but Art was sure capable of needling and instigating.

Art would tell him, "You shouldn't take that," after Eddie'd had a disagreement with my father, and the next thing you know, there was a fight in the locker room. They'd wind up underneath the dressing room table, just beating the shit out of each other.

But when my father passed away, the first guys who called, the first guys who came around and offered their support, were Bob Geigel and Eddie. We were having to deal with Japan, and titles, and who was going to get what in the territory, but they were there to talk us through.

Twelve years later, when I got a call that Eddie had killed himself, I was stunned. Since then I heard a lot of stories about what happened, and I just don't know what to believe. I know what I'd like to believe, that he was having financial problems and had an insurance policy on himself that would pay off for his family.

I don't know if that's true. I might be so far wrong that it's not even funny. I never asked his son, Mike, about it, although I've had the desire to, and I believe Mike would probably tell me if I asked. I just never have felt like it was enough of my business to ask. That's a pretty damn personal thing, so I'll just take the one that I think is true, because it's a nice one.

One time my brother and I were in an airplane being flown by Eddie, when business was just sky high, and when business is sky high, expenses get sky high. Junior said, "Eddie, what are you gonna do when the business goes down?"

That's just something that we all have to face in this business, because it does run in cycles, but when things are good, it's easy to get full of yourself.

Eddie looked at us and said, "It's not going to go down."

Being a realist is hard, at times.

Junior and I grieved a lot after our father died, but we were also filled with an obsession to show we could carry on the business and do well. It was an obsession to the point that I eliminated my family time and became entirely business-oriented, day in and day out. We did it and were very successful.

But there was a cost. I got so obsessed with keeping the family business from going down the tubes, and so obsessed with making it better than ever, that I was neglecting my family at home, and Vicki eventually filed for divorce just a few months after my dad died.

I was devastated. That reality was the hardest thing I've ever had to swallow. I didn't want her leaving, but she was going, by God. She'd had enough of that isolation. I don't think I could have salvaged things at that point if I'd offered to give up the business entirely. And as soon as it hit me, I knew what a terrible mistake I'd made by isolating myself like I had.

Junior and I, along with Uncle Herman, had expanded into Colorado Springs, Pueblo and a few other towns. It seemed like it kept on getting larger, and we would have continued to do so if the national situation had not changed the way it did.

I also got more experience dealing with wrestlers as an owner, and I found I wasn't exactly one of the boys anymore. I was now on the other side.

One time I went over a finish with Bob Roop, and he wasn't thrilled with it. "They said this is what you need to do," I told him.

He said, "Terry, will you do me one favor? Tell me who 'they' are."

I said, "Well, uh … uh … that's me, Bob."

But it wasn't long before I couldn't handle being in Amarillo, with Vicki and me apart, so I went to Florida in 1974.

Dick Slater did me a great favor when I moved down to Florida to get away from all of it. I couldn't sleep at night. I was a complete mental and physical wreck, and weighed 195 pounds.

I called Bill Watts, the booker in Florida at the time, and told him I wanted to come in and work. He said, "Hell, yeah! Come on down!" He was expecting Terry Funk to walk through the door. Instead, here came this skinny, 195-pounder, looking like death warmed over.

I lived with Slater while I was there, for several months of insanity. One time, we decided to try to help the promotion by getting some front-page publicity. Our plan was to drive to the middle of the Sunshine Skyway Bridge, leave a note in the rental car and then leave the car there, as if I had jumped off the bridge. Then we went home and I stayed in the bathtub for about four hours. Once I was good and wrinkled, we drove out to the beach and I laid down at the edge of the coast, as if I'd washed up onto shore.

Hell, nobody came to my rescue! I laid there for three or four hours and just got up, went back home and forgot about it.

CHAPTER 10

Terry Funk, World Champ

The vote over who would succeed Jack Brisco as world champion, held in Summer 1975, was a tough one for NWA promoters. It came down to Harley Race and me. My brother fought hard for me, and it got him a lot of heat.

Sam Muchnick had been president of the NWA for years but retired from it in 1975, I think because he saw some possible legal trouble coming, in terms of us being an alliance of promoters. They had withstood an antitrust investigation years before, but Sam was very smart about watching out for problems, and he took himself out of that position.

I think another major part of it was that he saw the alliance falling apart, which it sure did after he stepped down.

Fritz Von Erich, in one of his first major acts as NWA president, had to break the tie from the vote of members, because half wanted me, and half wanted Harley.

Fritz said, "By God, I didn't want it to come down to this, but I'm gonna vote for Terry."

And that decision really caused that guy a lot of heat, too, because Fritz was the only one whose vote was public. All the rest voted their own way with secret ballots. I was grateful to Fritz, because I knew this was a great opportunity.

I also knew it was now my job to make stars in each territory I visited. For anyone, including myself, who would seriously say to another boy in this business, "I am the world champion," I would think, "Are you out of your goddamned mind? They *made* you the world champion!"

The guys, the other wrestlers, make someone the world champion, and the world champion exists to make the guys seem like world-beaters. Gene Kiniski was good about that, but Lou Thesz wasn't.

I have great admiration for Lou, who held the title through most of the 1950s, and for a few years before and after that decade. But he was a very self-centered champion, one who didn't take into consideration the time and effort that some of his challengers and the other guys on those cards had put into making certain guys the top stars of the areas. If he didn't like someone, or didn't think they should be in there, he'd chill them in the ring, which he was certainly capable of doing, because he had legitimate skills.

He wrestled Baron Michele Leone in California in 1952. Now Leone wasn't a legitimate wrestler, but by God he could draw some unbelievable houses. Lou ate him alive, and Leone never was the same again as an attraction.

He did the same thing to Bull Curry in Houston, and to my friend Ricky Romero in El Paso. That was one thing I never have understood. He wasn't helping the territories he visited, and that was the champion's main job. To me, that meant that as great a wrestler he was, Lou was not a great champion.

One of my biggest gripes about the wrestling business has always been when a guy would stiff another guy in the ring, not giving them anything and making them look bad, and the other guy didn't even realize it until it was too late. What does that prove? It just sours the other guy, and it's a horrible way to treat a guy. Promoters would sometimes tell a guy to stiff his opponent, telling them something like, "Don't give that guy much in the ring."

Well, what the hell kind of fair deal is that? Why not just tell me if we have a problem? Even if the other guy said beforehand, "I'm going to try to kick your ass," that was fine with me. But don't stiff me in a work. That is bullshit.

Baba did that to me once, in October 1986, when Riki Choshu came to All Japan. I felt that Choshu was just off. I was trying to perform and do my best for the match, but I was being shortchanged and didn't even know it. You do the best you can, but if you're in a situation like that, nothing you do looks good.

When I was champion, I usually got to come up with my own scenarios, and it was always important to me to leave a place at least as strong as it was when I got there. My question to the promoters was always, "OK, what do we need to do to draw a buck?"

My first big chance at making a challenger actually began about a month before I won the title.

Jim Crockett's Mid-Atlantic Wrestling had a tournament for the United States championship on November 11, 1975. The title had been vacated after former champion Johnny Valentine was crippled in a plane crash that also broke Ric Flair's back. Flair, at the time, was an up-and-coming wrestler with a lot of promise. I won the tournament, beating Paul Jones, one of the area's most popular wrestlers, in the finals. It was an incredible night. We sold out Greensboro, and the newspaper there even covered it, saying it was the first sellout in the building's history of wrestling. It was also the biggest crowd Crockett ever had up to that point.

The whole thing was set up for a rematch a couple of weeks later, and I lost that title to Paul Jones. The idea was that he beat me, so when I came back through with the world title, he was a natural contender.

In the rematch, I also got busted open doing a hardway for Paul. I ended up getting 18 stitches, but I thought it would help make the return even stronger.

A couple of weeks after that, on December 10, it was my night. The match was in Miami. The scheduled match was Jack Brisco defending the NWA world title against Dory Funk Jr. That night, it was announced that Dory couldn't make it, and I was his replacement.

It was great booking, because when I won, it created a situation where fans felt like, "Dadgummit, Jack didn't know it was going to be Terry! He thought it was going to be Dory the whole time! The Funks screwed him again!"

It made for a nice program, because it set him up as the challenger looking for revenge. It also made Jerry Brisco an automatic contender, since he'd be looking to avenge his brother's loss.

I was a heel during the match, but as soon as the referee counted three and the title change was official, I became the *de facto* babyface for a few seconds. The crowd just exploded, because it was so rare to actually see a world title change that it was like they were there for history. Even though they were Brisco's fans during the match, the week before and the week after, when that moment took place right in front of them, they couldn't believe it, and they were elated.

I always enjoyed coming back to Florida to defend the belt. It was always a hot territory, because there was always an issue with Dusty Rhodes or Jack Brisco that would pop the territory. Another favorite of mine was Houston, because promoter Paul Boesch always treated me great, and the money there was always top-notch. Same thing with Sam Muchnick in Saint Louis.

Actually, as I went through all the territories, the promoters all treated me great, as they had when I toured areas in advance of Junior defending his title. The money was a little better this time around, though!

My becoming world champion was also a big boost to the Amarillo territory, as it had been when Junior won the belt. Even though it meant Amarillo was without one of its biggest names, winning the title told fans we were as good as anyone in the world, and placed a spotlight on the territory.

During my whole time as world champion, there was never any question that I would make every guy I was in there with look more like a champion than he did before he got in there with me. I was there not to promote the world title, but to promote that top guy in each area.

I knew those people wouldn't be happy leaving the building, since their hero hadn't won the world title, so I had to make them believe he was a better athlete and a better wrestler than the world's champion, and it was only a fluke that he didn't win. If it was done right, the world champion's business would go on, and the territory's business would flourish.

As champion, I worked a totally different style from the way my brother worked as champion. Since I was most interested in making as much money as possible with the title, my title programs tended to be shorter than Junior's. I was in town to produce the most revenue in the shortest period of time.

I wasn't there to debase the championship or to tear apart the NWA, but I was there to make as much money as I could, as fast as I could. If that meant going out and blowing the lid off the house by doing something insane or absurd, that was what I did.

In Tulsa, Oklahoma, wrestling the top guy meant I was defending the title against my old friend Dick Murdoch. Working with Dick was always a pleasure. Murdoch would jack around with people on occasion if he got a hair up his ass not to have a match, but for a high-profile, world title match, Murdoch was there!

In Florida I once defended the title against Andre the Giant. Andre was a hell of a guy, but I'll tell you, I was afraid of him. People don't think of him this way, but he was a great performer in the ring, a great worker. One time, I was in a tag match with someone against him and Dusty Rhodes. I walked right up to Andre and said, "You big son of a bitch, you ain't gonna touch me."

He had that real low voice and he just laughed. "Hurh hurh hurh."

The bell rang and here he came. I jumped out and turned the corner of the ring as fast as I could, and here he came behind me.

I cut the next corner by rolling into and back out of the ring, because it was quicker, and I didn't figure Andre would be able to get under those ropes. He went right under the ropes and on through, though! He kept chasing, and we got to the next corner. I rolled in and was about to roll out, when I felt something grabbing my leg.

He had me by one hand, holding my leg just above the ankle, and his fingers were touching his thumb, encircling my boot!

One time, a couple of years after I was NWA champion, Junior and I were finishing up a Japanese tour and were having dinner in a nice restaurant, when we saw Andre.

I said, "Junior, let's get Andre over here. We can buy him dinner."

"I don't know, Terry."

"Aw, come on! The bill can't be that bad."

And so we had Andre come over.

About seven bottles of wine later, they brought our $600 bill for supper.

During a swing through the Pacific Northwest, I defended the world title against a young wrestler who had taken to calling himself Jesse Ventura. Jesse was green, but was Jesse ever not green?

Jesse knew that he wasn't the greatest technical wrestler, but Jesse had a ton of charisma. He was a heck of a talker, so he didn't really have to do a lot. He got his shit over before he ever even set foot in the ring.

Another Pacific Northwest challenger was Jimmy Snuka. He was more famous later on in the WWF, where he was awfully hot with his top-rope splash. Jimmy Snuka was a great in-ring performer, and the greatest tag team Junior and I ever worked against was Snuka and Bruiser Brody in Japan in 1981. The Andersons were great, the Briscos were great, and the Assassins were great. But Brody and Snuka were phenomenal, and that was as well a put-together team as there ever could have been.

Brody had become a tall powerhouse with wild hair and a sense of menace, and Snuka was a muscular, agile Polynesian who could work like a maniac. They complemented each other. I think Junior and I did that, too, but Brody and Snuka just melded together, and they were both so solid.

I've heard stories about Snuka being screwed up, but I'm here to tell you— every time I was ready to work with him, that son of a bitch was there. He was a class act and could do stuff in the ring that was just phenomenal.

A territory that doesn't make many people's lists of the best is Los Angeles, but I always looked forward to going there to wrestle against Chavo Guerrero. I had first met Chavo when he was about four years old. His father, Mexican wrestling legend Gori Guerrero, promoted El Paso for us in his later years. Gori used to take four-year-old Chavo and balance him in a handstand in the palm of Gori's hand. Gori had four sons, and those kids had a whole acrobatic routine worked out with Gori.

Gori Guerrero had been a very popular wrestler both in West Texas and in Mexico. I remember Eddy Guerrero running around backstage in diapers, but he grew up to be a man I have a lot of respect for, as far as his work is concerned. I think it's a real plus to WWE (formerly WWWF and WWF) to have guys like him, Kurt Angle, Triple H and Chris Benoit on top.

And Eddy's brother Chavo was also a great wrestler. In the ring Chavo was a great seller. I think, in the early 1970s, Chavo, Jose Lothario and Ricky Romero were the top three Hispanic wrestlers in the United States in terms of ability. What set them apart was they knew how to sell, and they understood their people. Anytime I was in the ring with Chavo Guerrero, I knew there was going to be a riot. Time after time, I had to fight my way through the chaos to get back to the dressing room after a match with Chavo, and it was all because of the way he could sell his injury to the people.

The other two Guerrero brothers, Hector and Mando, were also very talented, and I see great things for Chavo's son, Chavo Jr., who works for WWE today. The Guerreros were just a strong, solid family, and I can't say enough good things about them.

Looking at their careers, it doesn't seem like Hector achieved quite the same amount of fame his brothers did. I tend to think it was because he was a light guy who looked even lighter, because he was taller than his brothers. But Hector was another really fiery performer who could have been a bigger star. I just tend to think Hector had more outside interests, another job and a family, and he wasn't as consumed by the wrestling business as the rest of the family. Hector found himself a wife, and I bet he's as happy as he could be. He was a smart kid who went to college (and even graduated, which is more than I can say for myself!). Whatever Hector's doing these days, I bet he's damn good at it.

Wrestling Jose Lothario was the same deal, in the Corpus Christi-San Antonio territory. The Mexican fans would be hanging from the rafters, almost—I mean, they were packed in there like sardines! Sometimes the match would never even get started. I'd fight my way to the ring, then worry about keeping those people out of the ring, do whatever it was I could manage to do and then get out of there, all in a couple of minutes, because that's all the time I had before they just wouldn't be held back anymore.

Jose was such a great worker because he was believable. There was nothing funny about Jose. Everything he said on his promos, everything he did in the ring, it was all dead serious. He was completely professional as well. He never felt like losing a match would hurt him, if it was done properly, and it never did hurt him. And at the time in this part of the country, with such a strong Hispanic fan-base, that would have been a perfect excuse for getting out of doing a job.

"Oh, my people won't understand me losing."

But Jose never tried to play that card.

I always regretted not getting to work against Ricky Romero more. We wrestled a few times in Amarillo, in babyface matches, but I never got to have a long program with him.

I know it sounds strange, but I loved the Mexican fans, because I loved the heat. And boy, they were hot people. They were great to work in front of.

Another group of guys who were great workers but are guys you don't hear a lot about were the Fullers in the Southeastern U.S. I know I'm sounding like a broken record, but the Fullers could *work*. As goofy as they were, they were good, and they were over (accepted as a star by the fans). Every time I went down there to wrestle one of them, it was an automatic riot. I sent a tape to Harlan, Kentucky, one time, and had a unique promo on TV to promote my match with Ron Fuller.

I said, "Look at these hands. Look at these nails. There's dirt under these nails. You people in Harlan, all you do is sit there and take welfare, except for the ones who go down to those stinking coal mines. All you coal miners do is sit at card tables and play all day long. You don't do anything, you idiots. You have no brains, and most of you are married to your sisters or brothers."

At the arena that night, security took away something like 17 guns. I know it sounds like bullshit, but they did. We finished the match, and I had to fight my way to the back, because the fans were rioting.

Vicki and I had reconciled by this time, but this was a trip she probably wished she had stayed home for. We were leaving the arena that night and were driving down the road, coming down the mountain out of Harlan, when a pick-up truck came up behind us and started ramming us.

I started to pull over, but my wife said, "Don't stop! Don't stop!"

We kept going and finally they stopped following us, but it was pretty damn scary.

I also faced hostile Southern crowds when I faced Bob Armstrong, who would be an opponent for me off and on for years.

I knew him when he was a fireman, just starting out in Atlanta in the early 1970s. He was just a natural, and his four sons who went into wrestling were the same way. Working in the ring and understanding how to be a great babyface just came naturally to Armstrong. He was a real pleasure to be in the ring with. He would sell and sell and sell, but he knew when it was time for his comeback.

I also made several trips to Japan as champion. After a match one night I went to a hot bath house. As I was under the faucet, a blast of hot water shot down and burned a hole in my back, three inches wide and about 18 inches long. I put some salve on it and wrestled the next night.

As champion, you had to go, and you had to be in top form when you got to each town. Whether it was Japan or Harlan, Kentucky, those fans were expecting a championship match, and you'd better be there!

One time, I left the arena after a match in St. Louis and went to the Whiskey A-Go-Go, a bar in the Gaslight Square district. I ended up getting pretty drunk, and I had to make it to one of those red-eye flights bound for Atlanta. I boarded the plane after midnight, and there weren't even 20 people on the plane. There was no one in the seats next to me, and I was still drunk, so I laid down to go to sleep. OK, OK, I didn't go to sleep—I passed out.

I ended up rolling off the seat and halfway underneath it. When I woke up, I crawled out from under the seat, and the only other person on the damn thing was the guy sweeping out the plane.

I asked him, "Are we in Atlanta?"

He looked at me like I was crazy and said, "Atlanta? That was two stops ago! You're in Memphis!"

Did I mention that the travel schedule was godawful? I criss-crossed the country constantly. Any of the NWA world champions would tell you the same thing. It's not as glamorous as it might seem, when you're wrestling in the last match in Jacksonville, Florida. I was always in the last match of the night, and when I was done, I was the last one in the dressing room. I left a lot of arenas alone, walked across a lot of streets and tried to hail a lot of taxicabs. That was how glamorous it was.

I gripe about the travel, but don't misunderstand me, there were a lot of glorious things to being champion. Still, pretty soon, it can burn you up.

The world champion traveled alone, not as part of a group of wrestlers. There was a real loneliness to it, because nobody made the champion's reservations. I handled everything myself.

Sometimes you couldn't even get a flight into the next city at a decent hour. The Dallas airport had a tram that went around it, and I picked up a trick from Junior. Whenever I picked up a redeye into Dallas, I'd land a few hours before sunup, so I'd get on the tram and just go to sleep, while it went around and around. I would wake up after a couple of hours, sit up and ask some befuddled stranger what time it was.

One of my most memorable trips as champion was one I made to western Canada, for Stu Hart's Stampede promotion. Stu was the father of Bret and Owen Hart, both of whom became stars for the World Wrestling Federation years later. He was also one of my favorite characters in the wrestling business. When I went as world champion into his territory in 1976, he was taking part in the city of Calgary's annual Stampede Week parade.

Every year they had a parade to promote their rodeo, and Stu made his wrestling promotion part of the event. Stu had a wrestling ring hooked to a trailer, pulling it through the streets as part of the parade. In the ring Stu had a menagerie of human oddities. There was a hunchback, and I don't know if he was working around the house for Stu or what, but there he was. That ring contained several other people, including midgets, and many of the people were not wrestlers. Hell, I think there were even a couple of goats in there!

The gigantic, obese Maguire twins, Benny and Billy, were also in the parade, riding alongside the ring. They were on mini-bikes, but their cheeks hung down so far they looked like a couple of two-wheeled asses. And I don't mean donkeys.

The trailer had small airplane tires, and after a few blocks of traveling on bumpy streets beneath that ring, the tires started popping out. One tire went, then the next and the next. When the last tire went, the decision was made just to shove the ring out of the path of the rest of the parade. I guess the human menagerie stayed behind, too.

I was riding in the back seat of a Cadillac convertible behind this collection of humanity. Andre the Giant was supposed to be in the back seat next to me, but he wisely decided he wasn't going to be a part of this, and he stayed in the hotel room.

On one side of the Cadillac, the words "World champion Terry Funk" had been written. On the other side, it read, "Andre the Giant," and they never bothered to take Andre's name off of there. The parade was being televised live, and as the car went by, the side reading "Andre the Giant" was facing the cameras.

The host said, "Well, here comes Andre the Giant. And, well, he certainly is a good-sized fellow, but he doesn't look like a giant to me."

Riding with me in the car was Babette Bardot, a big-name stripper up there who spoke in a thick, French accent. Owen, the youngest Hart boy, was sitting in the front. At one point, Babette's zipper broke, and the crack of her ass was hanging out of her dress.

After the ring collapsed, Owen decided he'd just about had it. Ten-year-old Owen was so embarrassed that he hopped into the back seat and crawled down onto the floorboard. He just lay there, refusing to get up until the parade was over! He was hiding.

As we drove slowly along the parade route, a cowboy on his horse rode alongside us. Every now and then, we had to stop, as the parade got congested. One time, he asked Babette if she wanted to ride on the horse with him. She said, "Oui, Oui, I would like that very much."

She got on the horse and we kept on going, but he had to catch up a little, so he put the horse in a rough trot. That had Babette bouncing around a little more than she liked, I guess, and as they came by the Cadillac, she shouted, "Get me offa this goddamned horse!"

Her French accent was gone, too!

Those Maguire twins ended up having a rough tour. In Stampede, they would take vanloads of wrestlers to the next town. We had worked Edmonton and were headed for a big show in Calgary. That morning, we were packed in that van like sardines, and the van started to heat up. Bruce (Stu's oldest son) was driving the van and told the Maguire twins, "You two fatasses have to get out of the van! We're not going to make it into town. We'll come back and pick you up."

So they got out, and we left them by the side of the road. And then they forgot about them!

That afternoon, Stu asked Bruce, "Where are Benny and Billy?"

"Oh, shit!," Bruce said. "I forgot all about them."

So Bruce went back to get them, and when he got to them, they were just lying there on the side of the road, and they looked like two gigantic lobsters, or red whales! They were just roasted. Somehow he got them into the van, and they both just lay on the floor like two great big fat cells.

Another time, I stayed at the Hart House while I was in town. I woke up in the morning and went downstairs. I'd heard so many crazy stories about how Stu would cook breakfast for the guys and scoop up cat shit with the same spatula he used to cook the eggs, that I had my reservations.

But sure enough, I went downstairs (being very observant, looking for cat shit everywhere I went, because I'd heard those stories for years). Well, everything in the kitchen was spotless. Stu had eggs, pancakes, sausage and everything else you could imagine. Everything was just wonderful, and I was sitting there enjoying my breakfast, thinking, "What a bunch of crap! They spread all these stories about this guy, and everything's as clean as can be and just wonderful."

And I had a cup of coffee in my left hand. I took a drink and set it down. A few seconds later, I grabbed the handle in my other hand, which gave me a view of the other side of the cup for the first time. As I got the cup halfway to my lips, I noticed that there was a big booger, right in the middle of that side of the cup. I decided I had probably had enough coffee.

Another time, Stu had some of the wrestlers over for dinner, and he had a grand meal prepared—roast beef, salad and the works.

He asked us, in his unique growl, "Eh, eh, who, eh, eh, wants, eh, eh, salad?"

Several of us asked for salad and he turned to the large bowl, where Bo, the Hart family cat, was laying all over the salad. The big salad bowl was normally one of Bo's beds, apparently, and I guess he decided they had made a bed of lettuce for him to lay down on.

Stu shooed the cat away, "Eh, get the hell out, eh, of there, you, eh, damn cat!"

Bo scooted on out of the salad bowl, and then Stu grabbed the tongs and put batches of salad into smaller bowls.

"Eh, OK, now, eh, who said they wanted salad?"

But Stu was the greatest guy in the world, and we all loved him. In his day, he was one tough son of a bitch, and he was still putting submission holds on guys when he was 80! Of course, by that point he was tricking them, but it still hurt once he locked it in.

"OK," he'd say, "lay down here, and, eh, let me have your arm back here."

And the dumb bastards would do it! Next thing they knew, they were waking back up, and they'd pissed themselves.

But there was one NWA member I never did work for, and he knew better than to even ask. Even though Antonio Inoki's New Japan group had gotten NWA membership since the initial fight over which Japanese company to back, I never went there as champion. Inoki didn't even try to get dates on me, because he knew it would be a futile move. My allegiance was to Baba.

When it was all said and done, I had made more than $400,000 in my year as champion, which was huge money at that time. Sometimes I wish I'd kept it another year. Maybe I could have afforded to quit sooner. Maybe I could have done only one retirement match.

As NWA champion, I was paid 10 percent of the house. I tried to keep track of house sizes, but if I was getting the short end of the stick with a payoff after a match, what was I going to do? Even though I was called the world champion, I didn't have the power or control you might think.

I might make $1,500 working in the Omni in Atlanta, and then $750 in Kansas City the same day, yet they could afford to fly me on a Lear jet from one to the other. It was the kind of thing that made me think, "Something just doesn't add up right. They can afford a Lear jet, because I have that much importance, but I'm only making that much money."

The NWA president had historically controlled the champion's bookings, but Atlanta promoter Jim Barnett, officially the NWA secretary, handled bookings for me as champion. The reason was, after Sam resigned, the NWA members wanted to figure out a deal where they could have someone who knew what he was doing book the champion, but they wouldn't have to pay a percentage of their gates, like they'd had to with Sam. Besides, Fritz didn't have time to handle all the details involved in booking the champion, because he had his own territory to run. Barnett was willing to take on the job.

Barnett was great to work with, although one night, Dick Slater and I stayed out all night before a meeting I was supposed to have with him the next morning.

When I got to Barnett's office, I was so drunk I could hardly stand up. I still had the suit on that I had worn in the last town, for most of the last day and all night. That suit had booze, gravy stains, bits of eggs and God only knows what else on it from my midnight breakfast at the pancake house. It didn't smell very nice.

I walked in for my 11 a.m. meeting, and as I got close, Barnett said, "My boy! You know … I have another meeting right now! I'd love to be with you at this meeting, but I have to go!"

Off Jim went, and that was the end of the meeting!

In general, though, we got along, because I was doing good business, and I was always there.

But when I got the championship, I knew what I was going to do—I was going to run with it! I was going to wrestle as many times as I could with it, for as long as I could hold it. I didn't complain about the crazy travel or even the bad payoffs because the bad payoffs I got as world champion were still a hell of a lot better than any payoffs I'd gotten before, and better than the other boys were making.

There were exceptions, though. One time I wrestled Ronnie Etchison, in St. Joe, Missouri, and it was raining, snowing and just basically colder than shit. They had a $25 guarantee for all their guys, but the weather kept people away, so my 10 percent amounted to only $17.50 that night! Etchison and I wrestled for 40 minutes that night, in front of a crowd of a few dozen. I don't know how Etchison did it. Hell, he had to be around 60 years old at that point. And I remember thinking, "How could a guy that old still be wrestling?" Well, it doesn't seem so far-fetched to me now.

From the start I wasn't planning on holding it for three, four years or more. I knew better than that, and profited from seeing what people had done in the past and what it had done to them. I figured I'd be ready to drop it after two years, at the most.

I ended up lasting half that long. Vicki and I had started talking again, and she eventually agreed to get back together with me. It was just about the best news I ever got in my life.

I knew I'd have to give up the title, though. I just told the NWA I had a bad knee. I wasn't lying. My knee was terrible—still is, in fact.

As for Vicki and me, we're still together. My family has come first, which has been very difficult in the wrestling business. When I had gotten so obsessed with the business a few years earlier, there'd been a cost—my family—and paying that cost just wasn't worth it.

CHAPTER 11

Terry Funk, Ex-World Champ

My last week as champion was pretty typical, in terms of travel.

On Monday I was in Atlanta, wrestling Mr. Wrestling II. He was Johnny Walker, who also wrestled as The Grappler in Florida in the early 1970s. For Johnny, the greatest invention in wrestling history was the mask, because Johnny Walker couldn't draw 10 cents without a mask. I don't mean that as a knock on Johnny—I just mean he was plain-looking. If you saw him on the street, you'd never guess he was a wrestling star, but when he put that mask on, by God, he was Mr. Wrestling II and a hell of a draw. In the ring, everything he did got over with the people. You might think, "Well, he just got over in Atlanta because he was a local attraction," but when he went back to Florida later, as Mr. Wrestling II, he was over there, too. He didn't go many other places, but he didn't need to. He stayed over where he was. He would cock his head to the side and do his wiggle strut, and people went crazy. I truly think if he came out today and did that, it would still get over. The guy could just get over.

On Wednesday I was in Tokyo, facing Jumbo Tsuruta.

On Friday it was Saint Petersburg, against Dusty Rhodes.

On Saturday I was in Austin, Texas, wrestling Ivan Putski. Ivan was a hell of a football player. As Joe Bernardski, he played fullback for Southwest Texas State University. One thing about Putski's Polish strongman gimmick—it fit him, and he did it well.

Finally it was Sunday, February 6, 1977, and I was in Toronto, Ontario, Canada, where I was going to lose the belt to Harley Race. The only people who knew this would be a title change were the NWA board member promoters, the referee, Harley and me. Those things were always kept very secret. Even the other guys on the card didn't know.

The match ended when I submitted to Harley's Indian death lock. I had wanted it to be a submission finish, because I thought people wouldn't be expecting it. I thought it would be healthy for the business to have a submission finish. I wasn't really worried about losing the heat by submitting. I knew I could get myself over again. I could always work my way around it. Even if I didn't like a finish, I'd do it.

I never cared about doing jobs, and that one, in particular, was about doing what was right for the business.

And that was the approach I'd taken in deciding how I wanted to drop it to Harley. When the time came to drop the title, I had wanted to see it go to Harley because I felt obligated to him. I was the one who wanted it to be that way. I didn't give the NWA a lot of notice that I needed to lose the belt, and they hadn't really prepared anyone else by that time.

The closest they had to another candidate besides Harley was Ric Flair, by now a top star in Crockett's Mid-Atlantic territory, but I felt like Flair would have another time, and Harley deserved a good run with it. I knew Flair would be champion someday, but if it had gone to Flair, I'm not sure Harley would have gotten another chance at it. I'm not sure I could have said I was a good, fair man if I hadn't helped the championship go to the man who came close to getting the votes when I ended up with it. I wanted to do something to see that things were done right by Harley. It was a pretty damn big deal for Harley, who started wrestling when he was 14, to be able to be the top dog in his business. I felt like it was important to Harley. I talked to Junior about it, and he felt the exact same way—that I needed to do right by Harley.

I never was approached about being NWA champion a second time, and if I had been, I never would have taken it in a million years. I was at a point, and it was a point I was lucky to stay at for pretty much the rest of my career, where I could pick my own dates instead of letting someone else set them for me. With my ability to build up an issue, I think I could have gone into any territory and been a good draw, even if I'd never even held the world title. Besides, I had gotten back a much better prize than any wrestling championship.

Fixing my relationship with Vicki was probably the most important thing I ever did. She had remarried since our divorce, and I didn't figure that there was any chance of us getting back together, due to me. I was the one who'd been making things difficult. But she ended up leaving her second husband, and we did get back together. I guess after all our battles and fights over the isolation I created after my father died, we had just reached a point where we needed some distance for those issues to settle down.

And if I had to give up the NWA title to get her back, well, hell, that was the best trade I ever made.

CHAPTER 12

Everything Changes

After I came back to Amarillo regularly, the territory was running fine. Having two former world champions in the area was a huge plus for the territory.

In 1979, I noticed something new—cable TV, in particular a wrestling show coming out of Atlanta. I knew there was a change coming in the professional wrestling business.

And once that change with national television hit, I knew that we would have fragmentation of this once-mighty alliance as everyone fought to be the national power. Sure enough, that's what ended up happening, first with the WWF and then with Crockett, who ended up in 1985 on TBS, where I first saw *Georgia Championship Wrestling.*

Even in '79, I knew the day of the national wrestling promotion was coming. I also knew how much work it would be for Junior and me to keep Amarillo running. I didn't want a repeat of what happened after my dad died, when I became obsessed with the business to the exclusion of all else, including my family. I knew that had been a mistake, and I would be damned if it was a mistake I was going to make again.

Junior and I talked and decided to sell the Amarillo territory to Bob Windham (Blackjack Mulligan) and Dick Murdoch. Before the deal was done, though, I told them both that I didn't think the future was too bright.

"Gosh, guys, it's going to be tough with the TV going the way it is," I told them, and they knew it was a possibility, but they decided to take their chances. Junior and I decided to take the $10,000 apiece upfront from them for the territory and be on our way. They got five or six rings and the existing TV and arena deals we had. They were supposed to pay off the remainder to us over a period of time if they were successful. Unfortunately for all of us, times were changing and they weren't successful.

The Amarillo territory had been a big part of my life for almost all my life, but it didn't feel strange not to be in it, because I realized that with the way things were going, there was really no such thing as an area anymore. In this new era, it was the United States that was going to be the territory.

Junior and I did work some matches for Murdoch and Mulligan, but the bottom line at that time was that I wasn't making a promoter's money anymore, and there were areas where I could make a lot more money as a wrestler. I had just bought the ranch here, and I needed to pay for the thing, so I had to go where the best opportunities were.

Still, I sometimes think of all the talent that came through Amarillo. There are more names than you'd probably guess. Some of the names I came up with.

Not all of my names were successful. Some of them had no greater purpose than to entertain me. We had a guy come in to work one time, and his name was Joe Pelardy. Well, I told him, "No one's going to pay money to see Joe Pelardy. Let me come up with a new name for you."

He went to the ring and found out his new name, when they introduced the wrestling fans to Amarillo's newest star … Joe Chit!

Sure enough, the fans soon started chanting, "We want shit! We want shit!"

The next night, he came to me and said, "I don't like that name! I want my name changed!"

"OK," I said. "I'm sorry you don't like it. I'll change it, and you won't have to be Joe Shi--, I mean, Joe Chit anymore."

The next week, he came to the ring and the announcer introduced him under his new name … Mike Chit!

And the chant continued, "We want shit! We want shit!"

Boy, he was mad. But it was just a rib!

I spent my time doing short stints in a number of territories, making sure to leave myself plenty of time for Japanese tours, and plenty of time at home.

It was kind of like the sentiment I saw another guy who I consider a great heel receiving. Earlier, I talked about Mr. Wrestling II. Well, there was a masked heel who was every bit as hated as II was loved—Don Jardine, a.k.a. The Spoiler. The Spoiler was actually very influential in the wrestling business. He was a big, tall man, but incredibly agile and able to put on a great match. He wasn't just size, and no ability—he could move! He would go on to teach a kid named Mark Calaway the way to walk the top rope during a match. Mark used that knowledge in the 1990s, to help get him over as The Undertaker, working for Vince Jr. I watch the Undertaker today, and sometimes think I'm looking at Jardine himself.

Jardine was that rare big man who could do anything in the ring. Truthfully, though, and I think Don Jardine would agree with this, Don Leo Jonathan was the man among big men, and he always will be. As mentioned earlier, he was about six foot eight, and he wrestled as the Mormon Giant. He was also one of the most agile men I ever saw. He was so good and so spectacular that in some territories there was a problem with fans believing there was no one who could beat him.

Whether I was working with Dusty Rhodes or the Briscos, Florida crowds could be rowdy. Those people brought knives and everything else, but the worst fans might have been in Puerto Rico, home of the World Wrestling Council (WWC).

The Puerto Rican fans were nuts. They hated me with a passion, and they threw stuff. I don't mean beer cups, like they threw in the States. I mean rocks, bricks—dangerous stuff. Every time we went there, Junior and I had to battle them, not fight, but battle them, all the way to and from the dressing room. When I got close to the dressing room, I knew they had rocks, so I'd arm myself. I'd take beer cans, about five or six of them, and pop a couple open. Then I'd throw them, and with the beer streaming out they looked like grenades flying across the arena, and the fans would scatter to get away from them. I saved my last couple of cans for when I was about to get to the dressing room, and I'd haul off and throw one of the full cans I had left right at one of the nuts' heads, if there were any fans left blocking my path. A full can of beer right in the head would stop a man.

But a lot of the guys really enjoyed Puerto Rico. Pampero Firpo, a crazy-haired man who wrestled as "The Wild Bull of the Pampas," used to love gambling at the casinos down there. He'd get going on the slot machines, and call out to me, "Terry! Terry! Come stand here!"

I would stand in front of the machine, and he'd take off running. He had to take a piss, and he did it as quick as he could. He was afraid someone was going to put in a quarter and win while he wasn't there. There were times he spent his entire payoff in a casino. I mean he spent every nickel he earned in Puerto Rico, plus every cent he could borrow, or get his hands on in whatever fashion. He used to collect pop bottles and turn them in for the recycling deposits and then gamble with that!

The Puerto Ricans weren't the only fans I whipped into a frenzy, though. I have two pocket knives on the wall of my office. Both of them came out of me after fans stuck me. One was from San Antonio, where a fan stuck a knife in my neck one night, and the other came from Florida. I never did miss a day. Hell, I wasn't going to let a little puncture wound keep me from earning a buck!

In a strange way, I took being stabbed as a badge of honor, the same as when the cops had to take guns from the fans. Those people were really giving me an award, even though they didn't realize it. They were telling me I had done my job, as a heel, and done it pretty well.

Aside from getting stabbed in the neck, I did like working in San Antonio for promoter Joe Blanchard.

One of Blanchard's top guys, Manny Fernandez, also came from West Texas State.

Manny was a super worker and crazy as a March hare. Manny once got into it with a guy outside a bar in Amarillo, and ran over his legs with a car. Then he backed up and ran over the guy again. He was a wild man and another tough guy.

Manny made quite a name for himself in Florida in 1979, when Eddie Graham got crosswise with his top babyface, Dusty Rhodes. Eddie elevated Manny to that top level for a time, and Manny did well. I worked almost every night with him, and we drew a lot of money. Everybody thought the territory would go to hell without Dusty there, but I drew well with both Manny and Skip Young, who wrestled as Sweet Brown Sugar. The fans were willing to accept some other favorites. Skip, in particular, was a guy who never really made it anywhere else, because other promoters just didn't see it in him, but Eddie Graham did. He saw him as a money player, and as a result Skip Young did a lot of business in Florida.

Vicki and I had come to Florida because we had just bought a ranch in Canyon for a couple hundred thousand, and we were having to pay 18 percent interest on it, so we had to go out to make money. We had a pickup truck that was so damn ugly that I didn't want to be seen in it, because people would look and think, "Well, that guy doesn't have shit."

But I ended up making myself an eccentric, because I put a cow's skull on the front, almost like a big hood ornament, when I drove it to the arenas.

I also wrestled quite a bit against Mike Graham, Eddie's son. Mike was a unique case, as second-generation guys went. Eddie never pushed Mike to the moon, to make him a top superstar. You have to understand, it wasn't that Eddie didn't love Mike. Eddie loved his son,very much. In fact, I think it was that love that caused him to handle Mike the way he did, by making him slowly work his way up and only rarely putting him into the main-event picture. Eddie saw throughout his life what happened to the second-generation guys who hadn't deserved their big pushes. He didn't want that kind of resentment for Mike. He wanted Mike to be deserving of whatever push he got.

When Eddie passed away in 1985, Mike was not that old, and there's still a chance Eddie would have eventually pushed Mike at that top level. But Mike, once he had control of the company after Eddie's death, really didn't push himself to the moon, either.

I also got to see a little of David Von Erich's heel work in early 1980s Florida. He had been a lifelong babyface, but he was a great heel. He worked a lot with my brother, and I thought Junior did a great job of helping David attain a whole new dimension of his wrestling persona.

If David hadn't died so young in 1984, I think he would have been a great choice as a long-term NWA champion. I know his name came up, at least in discussions of possible champions, and he would have been very successful. He was a good talker and had great ring psychology. In terms of being a pro wrestling performer, he had it all.

It would have been interesting to see what could have happened with the Von Erich boys if the drugs hadn't been there. We might have a completely different wrestling business today; it might not be Vince McMahon running it. It might be the Von Erichs as the major power. That's one of the many sad things about that situation—that tragic moment when David died could have been a major moment that changed the course of the business.

I had an NWA world title duplicate belt made by Reggie Parks (probably the best belt-maker around—I paid him $500 for it), and went on San Antonio TV to declare myself the real world's champion.

I'm sure there was a little heat in the NWA office about that, but I could have cared less. I mean, the whole thing was ridiculous, but it worked! In fact, it worked so well that it not only got over with the fans, it got over with the boys and the office in San Antonio! They got so goofy about it, they decided it was a real world's title, and held a tournament for it! I'd just created it as something to get me a little heat, a little controversy.

I even went up to New York City and Bill Apter (editor of the biggest wrestling magazines) took pictures of me with the fake belt. That's what you call self-promotion! That's what you have to do in this business, and it's what I've always managed to do, one way or another.

Soon after, though, the belt disappeared from the locker room. In 1984, several months after the tournament for my duplicate NWA title belt, the belt showed up around the waist of Dick Slater! Slater was on Mid-Atlantic TV, doing an angle with then-world champion Ric Flair, where Slater had declared himself the real world's champion (sounds familiar, doesn't it?).

Throughout the 1970s, Junior and I were hated heels in much of the country, but in 1977 we popped the Detroit territory as babyfaces in a feud with The Sheik and Abdullah the Butcher.

The night of our big, final match, we had the biggest crowd Detroit had drawn in a long time. However, that night we also got some bad news. Eddie George, Sheik's son, came in the dressing room and said, "Daddy! Daddy! There's been a robbery at the box office!"

Honestly and seriously, I loved Ed Farhat, and I would have gone there for nothing. Hell, I went there several times for nothing. And who knows? There might have been a robbery. Who am I to say there wasn't?

I actually got to spend time around one of the toughest, craziest characters in wrestling while in the Detroit area. Dick Afflis was a stocky powerhouse of a man who wrestled as Dick the Bruiser. With his roughhouse style and flat-top haircut, he was huge box-office. He loved getting into bar fights with pro football players, or whoever else he could find. Dick was married to one of the city's more famous ex-strippers. She was a pretty good-sized woman and wore these fancy wigs onstage. Sometimes he'd come home drunk, put on one of her wigs and one of her fancy dresses, get on his motorcycle and drive up and down the yards on his block, tearing up the lawns in his very exclusive neighborhood in the middle of the night. His neighbors would look out the window and think his wife had gone crazy, because all they saw was this burly figure with a long, blonde wig on a motorcycle.

Bruiser also seemed to go to a lot of weddings. Whenever a promoter or booker would ask him to "get some color" (bleed), he'd always say, "Can't. Going to a wedding."

Farhat came out with a movie about Detroit wrestling and The Sheik, called, *I Like to Hurt People*. I am in it but I never saw it. I don't watch everything I've been in, that's for certain. And the older I get, the more I try to avoid my own matches, because I have memories of doing beautiful moonsaults and I don't want to watch the match and see what they really look like. Even when I am doing the things I do in the ring today, they feel like wonderful things I am doing.

It's like my memories of Dusty Rhodes talking about a finish with his opponent (of course, the discussion always ended with how Dusty was going to win). He'd say, "I'll go ahead and I'll climb up to the top rope before you can move, thinth you'll be down on the mat after I thlam you. I'll graithfully FLY off the top rope and land on yo' body and cover you, one-two-three! And the crowd will go wild!"

Of course, that was not what happened. Dusty would climb up to the top rope, taking quite a long time to get there. Then he would fall, like a 300-pound sack of shit, onto the other guy's body and get the pin. You know, there's a great deal of difference between graceful flying and falling like a sack of shit.

But Dusty believed he was soaring like a damned eagle! And that's why I don't watch my matches—because I have occasionally watched a match of mine, and I know that I don't look like what I think I look like.

Florida was always a good territory, before I won the title and after. Starting in 1975 and for about a decade, Dusty was the top star there. It was hard to believe this incredible star was the lisping baseball player from West Texas State.

Dusty had become a really big babyface—a 350-pound one! At five foot four! When he was born, Dusty was 14 pounds, eight ounces, and he was only 11 inches long! The intern dribbled him out of the delivery room and slam-dunked him into the incubator! I actually used that one on Dusty on TV once.

Seriously, he was incredibly over. What was so surprising was that the guy had a lisp, and he utilized it! He took every single hindrance he had, from his speech impediment to his physique, and turned them to his advantage. In college, Dusty could be very difficult to understand. I mean, you'd seriously have a problem communicating with him. That's how bad it was. He self-corrected that to a large degree and did it because he knew he had to be able to talk on TV in order to make a buck in the wrestling business. The lisp he still had he made into part of his character.

I can't say enough about the guy, because he was smart enough and tough enough to turn weaknesses into strengths.

He was a classic, and he was another one of those who was very real. He really hurt, and he really meant it when he told the people, "I am the American Dream!"

I also wrestled Scott Irwin in Florida. Scott would be better known as The Super Destroyer later on, but he died of cancer in 1987. He was tall and weighed about 280, but could move around like a much smaller man. His brother, "Wild" Bill Irwin, was also a very good worker, but just never seemed to find his niche in the wrestling business, which happened to a lot of people.

I also loved working for Paul Boesch, in Houston. I was there one night in 1977 to wrestle Nick Bockwinkel for the AWA world title. Harley was supposed to be on the card, too, defending the NWA world title against Jose Lothario, but didn't make it. I still don't know why Race wasn't there, but I know it happened again in 1981, and Boesch was so mad about Harley no-showing a second time that he pulled out of the NWA over it!

Again, I don't know why Harley wasn't there, but I do know Boesch was utterly elated to see the Funker that night, even though he was pissed about the no-show. Bockwinkel ended up wrestling twice that night, once against me and once against Lothario.

That was a big night for me, and not just because I had a good match with Bockwinkel. I brought Sylvester Stallone to the matches with me, and those crazy wrestling fans helped me out a lot that night. We were walking into the arena, and here came about 100 fans running up. Stallone thought they were going to attack him. He had bodyguards with him, and they were saying, "We have to get out of here now!"

But those fans ran right up to me for autographs, not paying any attention to him. I think that was when he realized, "Hey, this wrestling is really something."

CHAPTER 13

The Art of the Promo

Week One ...

(I walk into the camera's view—I am in a pasture, with a sign reading "Funker's, Texas" behind me.)

"This is Funker's, Texas, on the Double-Cross Ranch! As far as you can see to the left, that's my property. As far as the eye can see, that is my property. I have a gated entrance, so I can keep anybody out that I want to. And believe me, I live a life of solitude.

"All except for one individual. Jerry Lawler has taken up residence in my mind, and he's been in my mind for the last 20 years! Over two decades since he destroyed some of the vision in my right eye.

"I had a call from Memphis, Tennessee, in the hospital. It was from Corey Mac. He was blabbering and blubbering and bawling like an idiot, and he said to me, 'Oh, Terry! Oh, Terry, I need your help! Please come down here now! Please come, Terry!'

"And I said, 'Why?'

"He said because Jimmy Hart and Jerry Lawler had beat the hell out of him! I said to him, 'Corey, don't worry! I will be there, like I said, on the 28th of August, in the Mid-South Coliseum!'

"I will be there! Not because I love you, Corey Mac—because I hate Jerry Lawler! Not because I love Memphis, Tennessee, or the people of Memphis, but because I hate Jerry Lawler with a passion! Take a look at the man! Look at his face lifts that he has! He looks like Bob Barker!

"What I am going to do is, I am going to give Lawler an extreme makeover on the 28th! I am going to give him a two-fisted makeover!

I'm going to lower his eyes! I'm going to widen his nose! I'm gonna fatten his lips, and I'm gonna realign his teeth! And then I'm gonna pull every transplanted hair out of his head! I'm gonna put my foot so far up his … so far up his … so far up his *poo-poo*, he'll have to go the hospital to get it out!

"Lawler, there has to be a finality to this, and it's going to be the night of the 28th—I promise you this. Bring that wimp Jimmy Hart with you!"

On August 28, 2004, Jerry Lawler and his manager, Jimmy Hart, battled Corey Macklin and me in Memphis. We drew nearly 5,000 people—one of the biggest crowds for a non-WWE show in years! We had no exploding cars, no fancy fireworks shows, no elaborate backstage skits. Hell, I wasn't even in Memphis until the night of the show! How did we do it? With a tape I mailed to Memphis, containing four promos. We did it with carefully crafted promos— one a week, for a month of Memphis TV shows, leading up to our big match.

Throughout my career, there were places I could always go for a short, but successful, run. Memphis was one of those.

Florida was another. I could always go back to Florida and work with Dusty Rhodes. It was a feud that never lost steam. It'd had steam since the day we started. Some of the angles we did were silly, but our feud always had believability to it, because I would make fun of his family, his weight. Everything I said was strongly derogatory. People bought it because they thought no one would allow anybody to say that kind of crap about them.

I hate to admit it, but I really don't think Dusty is a slob. It's hard for me to do. It hurts me to write this, but I really like him. And that's a horrible thing to admit. I sure wouldn't want to be married to him, though, the fat asshole.

Seriously, it worked because I borderlined on him, and he borderlined me right back. He'd rip on my family, my athletic background, everything. Borderlining is cutting a promo and just coming as hard as you can at the other guy.

When I cut a promo on Dusty, I would say things that were true, to make people look at him and think, "God, that's *got* to bother him!"

And the same thing with the things he said about me. That was a key to being successful in our business. It's a combination of believing, and the suspension of disbelief, for fans. And we have to say things that they can suspend their disbelief on. You have to say things that are cutting, and you have to be clever about it, too. That way you get not only the fans who are going to buy into what you're saying and believe it, but the ones who view it differently, who can think, "You know, that's some sharp shit they're doing there."

And talk about a creative promo man, Dusty Rhodes was sharp! He was one of the truly great talkers—he could, as they say, talk those fans right into those seats.

And when I cut him up verbally, he knew that it meant we were going to do some big box office. And believe me, he hit hard on me, too. Our promos and knocking each other bordered on being shoots, from time to time, and I think that's why ours was such a successful feud.

For most of my career, we had an assortment of people watching wrestling, from true believers to people watching for an entertaining show, and we wanted to open up that whole audience and grab up what we could. That was what I tried to do with the cleverness of my promos, but it had to be with a grain of truth. Building up to my August 28 match with Lawler, I took our famous 1981 empty-arena match, where he took a wooden chair to my eye for the finish, added in a real-life tragedy at home and made what I think was a very solid promo.

Week 2 ...

"This is my horse's tail. I loved that horse. You talk about omens, no more than two weeks ago, my horse was in this pasture. Lightning came down and struck old Copus. He was 25 years old, Copus was, and when the lightning hit him, it went ahead and caused him to start turning in circles. It also paralyzed his lips. Well, that doesn't sound too bad, but when you think about it, a horse has to eat, and Copus couldn't hold the grass, or the grain in his mouth, so I had to do what a man has to do. I had to get a gun, and I had to put Copus down.

"Do you realize how I got that horse? My wife got me that horse after Jerry Lawler injured my eye, to give me solace! And now that horse is in the ground, and now, I am going back to Memphis, Tennessee, to find Jerry Lawler. That horse lay there, and I thought about it, and I thought about it, and I took that gun, and I thought about putting it to Jerry Lawler's head at that moment, and pulling the trigger! But I know that I can't do that to Jerry Lawler. So, Jerry Lawler, what I'm going to do, is I'm gonna bring you back something that you gave to me over two decades ago! And I've got it right here, in my back pocket!"

(I pull out a sharp piece of wood)

"Here it is, Jerry Lawler! The stick that you stuck in my eye—I have kept it for 25 years! If you look at it, it's worn. You've heard of a worrying stone—it's supposed to make you not worry. Well, this here, I rub it and I worry about you. It brings more worry to me—if I am going to have finality with you, Jerry Lawler, before I even die!

"I want you back in the ring, and I am going to bring you this stick! And, oh yes, I'm going to give it to you, Jerry Lawler, but it's going to be like an Indian giver! I'm going to give it to you in your right eye, and then I'm gonna take it back! Then I'm going to give it to you in your left eye, and I'm gonna take it back! And then your right eye, and take it back! Left eye! Right eye! Whichever eye! Lawler, we're gonna have some finality to this, and it's going to be on the 28th in the Mid-South Coliseum!"

Florida was where I learned about promos, from Boris Malenko. He was the father of Joe and Dean Malenko, but back then, he was the best damn promo man I ever heard. I would watch him constantly, because he did such a wonderful job with long promos that had such intensity. I also saw the amount of time he put into his promos. He would head off to the side, way before he ever went on TV. He would have his notes there, and he would be thinking out exactly what he was going to say. His philosophy was that if he had a 30-second promo, that meant he had 30 seconds to improve the attendance of the show, which meant it was time he needed to put a lot of effort into. Those 30 seconds could be the difference between a fan coming and not coming.

Two of the other greatest heel promo men were Curtis Iaukea and Mike DiBiase. They were both such great heels. Curtis made me understand the value of each word. You have an audience out there, and even one word can make a difference whether someone in that audience buys a ticket, or not.

Hell, King Curtis was so good that Mark Lewin made an entire career out of going from territory to territory and booking himself against Curtis! He was smart, and that's how effective Curtis was.

Some guys just seemed to be naturals for one role or the other. Take Nick Bockwinkel—he spent years as a journeyman babyface. He was better than average, but in terms of drawing money he just didn't have it as a babyface. After turning heel, he was AWA world champion for years, and he was money in the bank. He found his niche, as a condescending heel.

One guy whose name hardly ever comes up in discussions about great promo men is Jose Lothario, but he was an amazing talker. He would cut these very serious promos, half in English and half in Spanish. Between listening to him talk and working with him in the ring, I probably learned as much from Jose in 1966 and 1967 as I did from anyone.

People remember good promos. On his radio show Rush Limbaugh mentions Terry Funk on occasion. Why? Hell, he doesn't ever talk about wrestling. But he listened to me in the past and remembered me cutting a promo where I was out with a gun, looking for Jose Lothario at the city dump. I ended up shooting at what I said was a rat, and claimed I'd gotten him! That brought up the question, was I saying Jose was a rat, or did I think all Mexicans were rats?

Things like that are vital to being a good heel, because the heel has to create the controversy, and the babyface has to feed on that controversy. And there must always be a reason for the heel to be doing what he's doing. With me and Dusty, it went all the way back to college, when he was "jealous" because he was playing second team behind me and "couldn't stand it." He quit football because of me! As a heel, I always had to relate it to something like that.

Junior and I also had a long feud with the Brisco brothers that played off of the same type of thing. It went back to our families—we claimed they were trying to dominate wrestling, and that we were the one, truly great family in the profession.

The same thing holds true today—as you'll read, when I wrestled Lawler in August 2004, I called him a baby banger on TV, because of his legal problems in that area (he was cleared of all charges, by the way). What would create more believability than that? Who didn't know at least something about that story? Lawler knows the truth, and he knows the truth doesn't have anything to do with what I'd be saying. The people fed on what I was saying and knew Lawler would truly hate that.

Good promos are half-shoots, all the time. In order to do a good promo, you have to be ready to damn near shoot. There's an artistry to it—you have to live, breathe and believe what you're saying and doing. Some people might think that this concept of a "shoot promo" is a new development over the last few years, but it's not. That idea has been around forever.

And heel promos take a great deal of thought, because you want to get people hot, but you also want to be somewhat clever in doing so. Of course, you had to be able to follow that up by being clever in the ring.

And a good heel has to know the difference between true heat and cheap heat. Cheap heat is pulling a gimmick out of your tights and hitting the other guy with it. True heat is working hard for it, building up to a spot that's going to infuriate the people. Cheap heat is doing a promo where you say, "All you people have no teeth." True heat is doing something clever, something that gets people mad without having to directly insult each and every one of them.

Even today you see guys come out and just rip on the fans every week, or on the local sports teams, because they know it will get a pop, but that's just cheap heat.

I'm not saying don't *ever* use a cheap pop, but it is an easy way to get a reaction. It becomes a bad thing when you see a guy come out and use the microphone, and he does a cheap heat job. Then, here comes the next guy, and he goes for the cheap heat. Then, the next guy does the same thing. Well, that's horrible, and it's stupid on their part, because that first guy might get a pop, but each one after him doing the same thing is going to get less and less of a pop. If nobody had ever said that the local baseball team sucks, then that would be the greatest thing in the world to say, but it's been overused.

I guess the best way of explaining it is that cheap heat is when you say something and it's obvious to everyone that you're only saying it to get a heated reaction. I always thought it was better to be derogatory toward my opponent and toward the people who favored him, instead of just making a blanket insult to all fans. With Bob Armstrong, I might jump on his family because he has sons who wrestle, and fans know that family.

Of course, we can talk about good heat and cheap heat all day, but here's the bottom line—good heat is the kind of heat that leads to a sellout crowd. Bad heat is the kind of heat that leads up to a show with lousy attendance. It's really just that simple. I can keep being profound with all this bullshit about what cheap heat is, but it boils down to what draws money. And if it draws, it's good heat.

Another way of saying it is that good heat is when *I'm* saying some stupid thing on TV, and cheap heat is when *somebody else* says something stupid on TV.

I put my real life into those interviews, and I think people picked up on the emotion in those promos. Those promos, and some similarly great ones by Lawler, led to us drawing those 5,000 people to the Mid-South Coliseum.

And no team of writers could have come up with any of those promos, because Jerry Lawler and I tapped into what made ourselves, and each other, tick. I don't care how creative a writing team is, that team can only draw from the same pool of creativity, over and over, whereas, if you left the promos to the individual wrestlers, they would be able to bring the variety of their personalities to it.

When I cut promos, I wanted not only to borderline on the opponent, but on the paying customers. At the same time, there's a right and wrong way to do it, so you don't just offend the paying customers.

Here's another example, again using the Briscos. I would talk about playing ball at West Texas, and how we would have kicked the shit out of Oklahoma State, where they went to school. Well, a fan can see how petty that is, because West Texas is not at that level anymore. Also, it gives an opening for Jack to come out and confront me, at which time I take it all back, only to turn around and say, "We would only beat you by two points."

You not only want to stimulate the people buying tickets when doing a promo, you alsowant to stimulate the person you're working with and talking about. A lot of people don't realize that. When you're cutting a promo, you're feeding that other guy openings, for lines he can get in on you.

In the 1980s, Roddy Piper gave some great promos. He really talked people into those buildings. He had a fiery personality and was not a dummy when it came to knowing what to say. Ric Flair was no dummy, either. He doesn't just get on the microphone and start screaming bloody murder. He is headed somewhere constantly.

The good ones are the ones who observed the ones who came before. I always tell young wrestlers, "Watch the best, copy and steal. It's all done in a sense of admiration, anyway, and it's the way you're going to learn to put asses every 18 inches. You should also watch the worst to learn what not to do."

Week 3 ...

"HEY, JERRY! I hate your ever-loving guts! I hate you with a passion! Jerry Lawler, I hate you!

"I can't believe that a wrestling fan came up to me, right in the middle of Texas, Amarillo, Texas, and he said to me, 'Do you know who my five favorite wrestling legends are, Terry Funk?'

"And I said, 'No, who are they?'

"And he said, 'Hulk Hogan, Ric Flair, Mick Foley, Dusty Rhodes...'

"And I said, 'Don't go any further! And me, Terry Funk!'

"And he said, 'Why, no, Jerry 'The King' Lawler!'

"JERRY 'THE KING' LAWLER? I DREW BACK AND I KNOCKED HIS LIGHTS OUT!

"Hulk Hogan? I can understand him, even though he's an egomaniac! I can understand Ric Flair being in there, too, even though he's a banana nose! I can understand Dusty Rhodes, even though he's an egg-suckin' dog! I can understand Mick Foley, even though he's a satchel-ass! But I can't understand why he would put Jerry Lawler in there! Does he know who he's talking about? Does he know the Bob Barker look? Does he know about the hair transplants? Does he know that Jerry Lawler is a baby banger?! A BABY BANGER! A BABY BANGER!

"And do you know that his partner, Jimmy Hart, is nothing but a cheap thief? He was my manager in New York, and we shared rooms. So I would share a room with him, and in the middle of the night, he'd sneak into my pockets and steal my change! Later on, he was Hulk Hogan's manager, and Hulk Hogan said he insisted on staying with him. And in the middle of the night, he'd sneak into his pockets, and steal his change! And now he's back with you, Jerry Lawler, and I'll tell you one thing for certain that I know, and that you know, too! Jimmy Hart is sneaking up on you, putting his hands in your pockets, in your front pockets. But he's not looking for change! And what's worse than that, you know what he's looking for.

"Lawler, I've hated you all of my life! And I'm going to continue to hate you, until we have finality! That's why I am bringing this..."

(I hold the stick up again)

"It's yours, and I am giving it back to you, at the Memphis Coliseum! That's right, I'm giving it to you on the 28th! And Corey Mac, help is on the way! HELP IS ON THE WAY! ... I think I've heard that before. [referencing John Kerry's 2004 democratic convention slogan]"

These days, WWE has writing teams who script all the promos for the guys to say. The problem is, we are not actors. I like to think of myself as a capable actor, but you can't take a bunch of wrestlers and hand them pages and pages of dialogue 15 minutes before the wrestling match and then expect them to be thinking about their match and be able to do their lines at the same time.

And if you do, and you hold it against the ones who can't memorize dialogue on short notice, you might just be eliminating some of the better people who can create for themselves, the guys who might have better ideas themselves, just because they don't have photographic memories.

Also, when you script promos, you're taking away from those creative boys in the business, and taking away from their persona, not adding to it. I'm not saying there is nothing but creative guys who can do that, but there are several who I think could convey their points and get their personalities across. It's hard for a group of writers to write a guy's personality for him. Is this guy going to be able to do this promo by delivering 120 words a minute, or will he be better able to get his point across by talking at his own, natural, 30 words a minute?

And for the guys who aren't there yet, they need to be able to do their own promos, so they can learn about what's a good promo and what's not. If you take that guy and allow him some time to work on it, he might become able to deliver a better promo than what you or your writers could come with for him. But if he never has that opportunity, he's lost. A guy also learns to think about his in-ring character and how to develop it when he has to come up with his own promos.

And it's easy to say, "Well, then, we'll just find enough of them who can do it the way we want it done."

Well, yeah, you might find enough memorizers out there to fill your arenas halfway, but you might have someone sitting on the sidelines who's so creative he could be a great draw consistently, and you don't even know what you've got in that guy. Only by letting the guys do their own promos do you find out who is creative and who isn't.

That's what the business is missing right now, in 2005—that breakout star. And if you're keeping some creative talent on the sidelines because he's not good at memorizing scripts, then you're keeping him from making money for you, and that's your fault, not that guy's fault.

The result of all this scriptwriting and memorization is that the promos, for the most part, are godawful. As hard as the guys try, there's nothing fresh in the interviews. All the interviews are in the same realm, because they all come from the same group of writers.

I promise, no one wrote scripts for Wayne Coleman, who wrestled as the bleach-blonde, tanned and toned "Superstar" Billy Graham. He was a great talker. The Superstar, with his unbelievable physique and eloquence, was probably as influential a figure as anyone I can think of in the wrestling business. He certainly captured Jesse Ventura's imagination, not to mention another guy who made a pretty good living as a bleach blonde wrestling muscleman—Hulk Hogan.

Superstar Graham is the first to admit he's not the greatest in-ring performer of all time, but he had a great mind for what to say to get himself and his angle over.

I'll promise you something else. No one would write a script for Terry Funk! No writer could come up with things like having me just spend half my promo glaring into the camera, to show you how much I hate my opponent.

Week 4 ...

"I look through my good eye (I point to my left eye), and I see my lovely wife and family. And I look through my bad eye (I point to my right eye), and I see an ugly, yellow haze. I look through my good eye (I point to my left eye), at my lovely dog, and I see the dog. I look through my right eye, and I see Old Yeller, and he's a goddamned Jack Russell!

"Lawler, come closer! Come closer, Jerry—I want you to see the hate in my face!"

(I make a series of evil, hateful faces at the camera)

"Don't back away!"

(I scowl at the camera some more, and then break into a smile.)

"Do you see that hate, Lawler? Do you see that hate?"

(I make another series of faces at the camera.)

"Tonight, at the Mid-South Coliseum, I'll be in the ring with you, Lawler. We're going to have some finality to this. A closing—we're going to close it out, Lawler, and I don't mind if I die closing it out!"

(I make one last face at the camera, and walk off.)

CHAPTER 14

No Business Like Show Business

I met Sylvester Stallone in 1977, after getting this crazy letter that said, "Sylvester Stallone is doing a movie on pro wrestling and is looking for a wrestler to play a lead part in the movie."

I think everybody else who read it must have just thought it was a rib and threw it in the trash, but I read it and sent a reply back to them. They responded back and asked for a tape. I sent them a tape of me cutting a five-minute promo on Stallone, talking about him coming down from New York City, and just my normal bullshit.

He loved it.

He brought me out there, and I read for the part. He liked me, I guess, because he told me I got the part. He also needed someone to stage the action scenes, so I choreographed those. He also wanted someone to teach Lee Canalito how to work in the ring a little, and I did that.

Shooting a movie was a lot different than performing in front of a live crowd, more than I'd thought it would be. In that one, I was kind of in my element because I was playing a wrestler, but you still have to watch for overacting.

Most of the time, it's not easy for a wrestler to be an actor, myself included, nor is it easy for an actor to be a wrestler. There aren't as many similarities between the two professions as there might seem, and I found this to be true in everything I did in Hollywood.

The business side is also different. As a wrestler, promoters would try to find me. In the entertainment industry, I was having to find producers of TV and movies. Unlike in wrestling, the entertainment industry doesn't give a shit who you are. What matters is that you do a good job on the set. It's a profession of rejection. It would be like playing piano—if I started when I was three, by the time I was an adult, I might be able to play a concerto. Same thing with acting—if someone starts at age three, they can go along and do great later on. But to just walk out there and think you can play a part in a movie with heavy dialogue is like thinking you can play a concerto the first time you sit down to play the piano. When you get into dialogue, you'd better be pretty adept at what you're doing.

I've seen The Rock's movies, and he's good, but they're all action movies. You ask him to play a role on a show like *Law & Order*, where it's 95 percent dialogue, and he's going to find out it's all very long, hectic and heavy.

As far as I'm concerned, the best actor ever to come out of pro wrestling was Roddy Piper. He was able to make the transition to acting, and acting well.

You know who else turned in a pretty damn good performance? Andre the Giant, in *The Princess Bride*. And trust me, as you'll read later, I had plenty of chances to study that performance.

The toughest thing in acting is to play yourself, and that's truly what Andre did in that movie. A lot of people don't know this, but Andre was a very smart guy. He spoke something like six different languages. The first time I ever saw him, I was so in awe of the size of him that I didn't immediately notice the intelligent guy that he was. I certainly didn't assume he was a dummy. I'm not a prejudiced person, not the kind of person who's going to assume that a big guy must also be a dumb guy.

Even though Stallone liked me, Herb Nanas had his doubts. Herb was one of the executive producers of *Paradise Alley*, and was married to Helen Reddy, the singer.

I just drove Herb nuts. He hated me by that time, because I had gotten him with the old "Japanese flier" trick a couple of weeks before.

Canalito was there, too, and I stood up a package of cigarettes and had them on the edge of a table. The trick was to stand about 10 feet from the pack with your right side facing them, with your hand at your side, but one finger sticking straight out to the right. Then you'd step sideways without looking at the pack, but instead, looking straight ahead. The object was to knock over the pack with your extended finger.

I told Herb this was how the Japanese qualified their pilots.

"You had to pass this test before they'd even consider you for pilot training," I told him. "You have to pick yourself a spot before you look away, and concentrate on hitting that spot. I'll give $50 if anyone can do it."

Canalito tried, but couldn't do it.

Herb said, "Hey, let me try! I think I can do that!"

"Well, come on then, Herb! But don't cheat!"

"OK, I won't."

Herb stood sideways to the pack on the table and started moving towards it, while looking straight ahead. He couldn't see me from that angle, so just before he got to the table, I pulled down my pants and spread my cheeks. Before he knew what he was doing, he had stuck his finger in my ass!

Canalito and I were laughing, but Herb went out of his ever-loving mind. He went absolutely nuts! He was convinced Stallone had brought a nut onto the set after that.

Paradise Alley went well and got great reviews, and I thought, "Well, this is great! I'll just go home and wait for another job."

Another job didn't come. It took me a while to figure out why.

Who the hell was supposed to know me? How the hell were they supposed to call me up? I didn't even know to have an agent. That's how ignorant I was.

I just happened to be at a friend's house in Amarillo a few years later, when Vicki called. She said Arthur Chobanian had called the house looking for me. He was one of Sly Stallone's best friends and associate producer of *Paradise Alley.*

He told me, "We've had people calling, looking for you."

He told me about a part that was open on a new Western series called *Wildside* for the ABC network.

Tom Greene, who'd written episodes of the shows *Knight Rider* and *Magnum P.I.,* among others, was the show's creator. Chobanian told me to send Greene a tape, so I did.

The tape I sent Tom was a cornball thing, with me telling some stupid, five-minute joke. I filmed it right in front of a caboose on the ranch, a spot where I filmed a lot of wrestling promos over the years.

They had me come out and do a reading, and they offered me the part of Prometheus Jones, a former outlaw and lasso expert. Greene had really pushed for me with the Disney people.

Working on a series was difficult, because there's new dialogue to learn every day. It changes every week, just a constant deal. You can't just walk out there unprepared.

I thought the show was a pretty good series and could have had a long life if not for the competition. We were right up against the second season of *The Cosby Show.* Cosby just smoked us. But we had a great cast—Meg Ryan, Howard Rollins, J. Eddie Peck, Bill Smith and John D'Aquino.

I thought I'd learn from my *Paradise Alley* lesson and stay in California for a while this time, and I did pretty well. I ended up doing a number of commercials, and I also realized I could get health insurance with membership in the Screen Actors' Guild.

It was very beneficial, because in wrestling it was hard to get insurance at all. Every year I started going back just long enough to qualify for my Screen Actors' Guild insurance. You have to make a certain amount of money through acting each year to be a qualified member.

Those commercials did really well for me. I did one for Lipton's Cup-A-Soup and picked up $45,000, and all I did was take a a bite of a sandwich and a swallow of soup! The residuals worked out to where I got $35 every time the commercial aired, and it was playing on afternoon soap operas. I did Wendy's commercials and a ton of other ones.

That was one thing that made acting completely different from professional wrestling—the money. Filming *Road House* in 1988 took 17 weeks. It was an action movie about barroom bouncers, with Patrick Swayze, who was still a hot star from *Dirty Dancing*. It was only supposed to last four weeks, but it kept on running over. Well, hell, I was making $10,000 a week, which was a lot of money to me, *huge* money to me at that time, for sitting on my ass! I never had it so good!

Just to show you how times had changed, for *Paradise Alley*, where I had a much bigger part, I made $7,500 a week. And that was big money! I even cancelled a Japanese tour to do *Paradise Alley*, and I got in terrible trouble over it with Baba.

Before I really started making money, I used to save a few bucks by booking my flights from Amarillo to Albuquerque for $35, but I would always book it on a flight that was continuing on to Los Angeles. I would pay my $35 and get on the airplane. Then, when it got to Albuquerque, I'd be laid back, like I was asleep. I made it all the way to Los Angeles like that. Coming back, I'd do the same thing—book a flight to Phoenix for $27 and "sleep" my way to Amarillo. That was just what I had to do to make ends meet. They weren't paying me to do readings, auditions and all that other stuff.

I also took a page out of crazy Roger's book from the Boys' Ranch. I would stay at the same hotel in Los Angeles over and over, and never would turn in my key. Once I had about five or six of them, I'd get into town about 9 p.m. and call the rooms I had the keys for. As soon as I found one where there was no answer on the phone, I'd go up into the room and sleep in the bed. The next morning, I'd get up early, make up the bed and sneak on out of there! Whenever I did that, I always left all my bags packed, just in case. Sure enough, one night, I was in bed, and this guy opened the room door.

He said, "Oh, I'm sorry, I must have the wrong room."

I jumped out of the bed and said, "Oh! I don't know! I don't know!"

Then I grabbed my bags and ran out of there.

Road House was a heck of an experience. It was, among other things, the first and last time I ever worked for producer Joel Silver.

At the wrap party, once the movie was over, I told Roger Hewlett, another actor in the movie, to suggest that I go up and sing a song.

He went up there and told the M.C., "Hey, I've got this friend. Now he gets embarrassed very easily, but if you coax him up here, he's a heck of a singer."

The guy asked, "Well, who is it?"

Roger said, "It's Terry Funk."

The guy told Roger he'd be sure to invite me onstage. Pretty soon, here came the microphone.

"We understand we've got a singer in the house! Would Terry Funk come up here, please? "

I just sat back, motioning them off with my hands and saying, "Oh, no, no, I really don't want to do that."

"Aw, come on up, Terry!"

I finally said, "Well, all right."

I finally made my way to the stage and the guy asked me, "We understand that you might be willing to sing a song for us."

I took the microphone and the cast and crew who were now my audience, "Well, yeah. I wrote this song myself. In fact, Willie Nelson and Merle Haggard tried to buy the thing from me, but I just wouldn't sell it to them. I wrote this many years ago, in Abilene, Texas, on Peach Street and Avenue A. I was walking down the street, came to the stoplight at Avenue A, and there was a little, old lady sitting on the other side of the street. I walked over and said, 'Ma'am, what's your name?' And she looked at me and said, 'My name is Lucy.' I said, 'Lucy?' And she said, 'Yes, Lucy.' And I looked down at her, and the words to this song just came to me."

I paused for a second and began singing a touching little song.

"OH, LUCY'S GOT A PUSSY LIKE A JAVELINA HOG! LUCY'S GOT A PUSSY LIKE A HAV-A-LEE-NA HOG!"

Several filthy verses later, I was finished, and you could have heard a pin drop. I thought they'd think it was extremely funny, so I was disappointed. I thought it was a very funny song. But it was just dead silence. It was the strangest thing.

Vicki laughed a little, but she tends to think I'm rather funny. Joel Silver didn't seem to think it was as funny. Joel Silver has produced a lot of movies since then, but I've never been asked back to work on one. I wonder why?

I also did a lot of low-budget pictures. I did one called *Mom, Can I Keep Her?* with Gil Gerard, who had played Buck Rogers on TV, and one called *Active Stealth* with Daniel Baldwin.

In 1992, I got hired for another series, *Tequila and Bonetti,* a police show where I played a police sergeant who worked with the main character. It lasted a full season, but that was all it lasted.

The producer of that show was Don Bellasario, and he had liked me enough to get me a shot on this show after I'd made a guest appearance on another show he had created, *Quantum Leap.*

On the show, Scott Bakula played a guy who travels through time, inhabiting other people's bodies. On the episode I was on, Scott was playing a wrestler, and I was his main opponent. Bakula was just great, a great actor and a great gentleman. He must have had a photographic memory, because the dialogue he had was just amazing. He could go right from one scene to another, day after day, becoming a completely new character every week, without missing a beat. I had followed *Quantum Leap* since it first came on the air, so I really enjoyed being a part of it.

Looking back, working with Stallone was the best thing I could have done, because I ended up doing some stunt work on one of the *Rambo* movies. I acted with him again in 1987's *Over the Top* and was the stunt coordinator for *Rocky V.* The whole time I worked with him, Stallone never changed the way he treated me, even though he was an even bigger star by now than he'd been when we were filming *Paradise Alley.* Stallone is a good guy to me.

CHAPTER 15

Japan's Wrestling War

Junior and I spent a lot of the 1970s and the early 1980s as top talent and as bookers for Baba's All Japan Pro Wrestling, and the war with Inoki was going strong by the end of the decade.

In 1981, out of necessity, I had what would prove to be one of my most successful ideas ever. Inoki, at the time, had just debuted Satoru Sayama as Tiger Mask. Between his moves and his character, which was based on a cartoon show, he was a junior heavyweight who was as hot as anything that had ever happened in Japan. Add that onto Inoki, and they had a hot show going.

Killer Karl Kox had been working for us in Japan, and I met him at the airport. I was heading to Japan, and he was coming back.

I said to Karl, "How's business?"

"Terry, I'll tell you the truth," he said. "I don't think we can keep on going. The other side is really hot, and we're just dying out there."

We had TV the first night, and I thought, "Damn, I'm not going to let us die. I've got to do something."

As soon as I got to the hotel, the night before our scheduled match, I got together with Abdullah and I told him, "Abby, we have to do something, something extreme and different tonight, something that'll get the people off their asses. Inoki's been nipping at our heels, and he's got us damn near dead."

We swapped some ideas, and between us, we came up with the idea to do something in our match that the people hadn't seen before.

I went ahead and had my singles match with Abdullah, and during the match, he took a fork to my arm, making it bleed heavily.

To this day, I don't think they've had 4,000 people at the hotels to see the wrestlers who were staying there, but I had that many trying to find out where I was, and how I was doing.

That angle really captured the imagination of the Japanese fans. It might not sound very historic now, but at that time in 1981, nothing like that had ever been seen in Japan, and I never heard about anyone doing it in the States, either. Doing this angle wasn't exactly a pleasure, but I did it out of absolute necessity for the company. It wasn't done to help me, but to help the company by giving the fans there something to buzz about. It was meant as an act by a good soldier.

My bleeding arm was also the birth of hardcore wrestling to a degree. In Amarillo, we always had the occasional gimmick match—chain matches, death matches and the rest—and they were always violent matches. We never killed the territory with them. A chain match was only used as a blowoff to a feud, the climactic match between two longtime foes. So I was always in violent matches, but the more hardcore brawling style grew out of this angle.

Japan didn't transform into hardcore matches. It stuck to the physical style of wrestling. Full-fledged hardcore wrestling wouldn't hit Japan for about another decade, when Onita formed Frontier Martial-Arts Wrestling shows. But Baba was smart enough to ride the brutality of that fork angle for years.

Hell, Paul E. would have come back the next night and had two forks, if it had been ECW! The next week, he'd have had an eight-man fork match!

Just a few months after the fork-in-the-arm angle, Inoki really went for the jugular when he took Larry Shreeve, a.k.a. Abdullah the Butcher, right out from underneath us. I understood why Abby was doing it—more money for him. But it was a terrible blow to us, so we decided to hit back.

In 1981, Stan Hansen was working in Japan for Inoki, and in the States for Vincent J. McMahon's World Wide Wrestling Federation, based in New York. Vince Sr. and Inoki were still working together, and had been for years. Well, I'd known Stan ever since his West Texas State days. Now he was working for the other side, and he was very strong in Japan.

Junior and I got hold of Stan, and I met with him, without anyone knowing. I offered Stan a deal Junior and I had put together with Baba, to work for All Japan for a period of years, and we made the deal official when the two of us met with Baba in Hawaii. It was a big-money deal for Stan. He ended up making more than Junior or me. He got a bonus, plus $15,000 a week for 12 to 15 weeks a year. That was the biggest money deal in the country, and as I recall, he had a clause in the contract to cover inflation that called for a 10-percent increase every year. That might not sound like a lot, until you get to the point where Stan's been there for 20 years. That's why Stan's shitting through silk drawers, and I'm still wrestling for Joe the independent.

No one knew about it, not even the wrestlers on the card that night, except for Snuka and Brody. We wanted it to be a surprise to everyone, and that was important to Stan, too, because he had to finish up a New Japan tour and then immediately come over and appear with us. That made New Japan a snakepit during Stan's last days there, because he wasn't going to do a job before he left.

They wanted him to do a job, even though they didn't know he was going. He wasn't going to do one, because we wanted him to be strong coming in. It put him in a very precarious position in New Japan, because the promotions in Japan didn't pay the wrestlers until after the last match on the tour, and he had to be very careful so no one would know what he was going to do.

We knew the reaction he'd get when he came out with Snuka and Brody, for their match against Junior and me, in the finals of All Japan's 1981 Real World Tag Team Tournament. And he certainly didn't disappoint. The finish involved him giving me a clothesline and leaving.

The buzz over Hansen's jump spread through Japan's wrestling world.

The final move was to pull Stan out from under Vince Sr., when Stan was in the middle of a main event feud with his champion, Bob Backlund. That was actually Stan's second big run in New York. His first one was in 1976, when he was wrestling Bruno Sammartino. During one of their matches, Hansen accidentally dropped him wrong on a bodyslam, and Bruno suffered a broken neck.

Stan was sick over what happened to Bruno. Hansen never wanted to hurt anybody. He just worked solid. And working solid was Stan's path to success in the business. And Bruno knew that Stan wasn't trying to injure him. I'm sure he told him something along the lines of, "Be more careful, dammit!"

Bruno was pretty messed up and was unable to wrestle for a few months. Truthfully, it's a testament to Bruno's physical conditioning that a broken neck didn't have a much more serious impact on him.

Not long after Stan made his debut, I was sitting at home, reading at my desk one day, when the phone rang. It was Vince McMahon Sr.

"Why did you do that? Goddammit, Terry, why did you do it?"

"Well, dadgummit, Vince," I said, "you guys took Abby."

"But you stole Hansen from me."

"Yeah, and next time, we'll take your kitchen sink, if it happens again."

We both laughed. It was actually a very casual conversation.

Stan Hansen could have been a huge star in the United States, if he had not decided to focus on working in Japan as his top priority. Stan could talk, he could move, and he had a great look. He used his stardom in the States to build a successful career in Japan. The Japanese always had their pick of the best American talent because they could pay more per week than anyone else in the world. That held true for years, although I don't think it's the case today. For guys like Stan Hansen, Bruiser Brody and Steve Williams, it was a better life, because they earned six figures and only had to work 15 to 20 weeks a year.

Some of the guys, Hansen and Brody in particular, got reputations in the States for not wanting to do jobs. It was a combination of the Japanese office not wanting them to do a bunch of jobs in the States, and Hansen and Brody themselves not wanting to do jobs and using the office as an excuse.

I think Brody would have made an excellent NWA world champion. He had a good head for the business, and he did what was going to produce the most money for him. The way it turned out, the best thing for him was to be strong in America, to build himself up for Japan. However, if he had been champion, he would have been one of those champions who damn near got beat every night, because that was what he would have needed to do to build for a strong return.

One thing was always true—Bruiser Brody was in business for himself, but if you knew that, you knew everything you needed to know about Brody. He found early on that in the wrestling business, you have to push at times. Brody pushed, and sometimes he pushed too hard, but he had a lot of success with it.

Those guys didn't need to do jobs. They were making big money. I can't blame them for saying, "I'm not doing that! They don't want me to do that!"

Well, of course they were going to say that! "They don't want me to" sounds much better than "I don't want to."

Right after Abdullah left, we were giving Bruiser Brody the big push, but an untimely injury (a broken ankle) made us change plans for a tournament he was supposed to win, which led to a one-time-only match on April 30, 1981.

Junior ended up winning the international championship by forfeit over Brody in the finals, and we knew we had to do something to make up for the Brody match that was supposed to happen, since he had broken his ankle.

We're sitting there, knowing this is all going out on TV, and we had very little time to come up with something special to put on, to keep the fans from feeling shortchanged, so Dory's first title defense was against me. It was the only time the Funk brothers wrestled each other.

It was probably the toughest match I ever had. I think by then either of us could have had a match with a broomstick, but wrestling my brother was another thing entirely. I don't think the fans were very interested in seeing us against each other, either.

It would have been like us feuding in the U.S. There are certain times and places where that would be accepted, but the Japanese fans at that time weren't buying that two brothers would fight for a title. It did produce some interest and was the right thing to do, but when they saw it, they didn't quite accept it, because of the way we were portrayed over there. Once the match started, the fans realized they didn't want to see Junior beat me, or me beat Junior, because they liked both of us.

However, years later, it's become almost the Japanese equivalent of the empty arena match in Memphis—something remembered as greater than it was. People say, "Wow, you wrestled your own brother? That was something!"

One thing never changed, even in Japan—wrestlers were as goofy on bus and plane rides as they were in cars going up and down roads in West Texas.

During one of the first tours of Japan I was on, I was on a plane with my brother, plus Moose Cholak with Brute Bernard. Moose had a horrible case of hemorrhoids, and if you ever saw Moose Cholak, you know how horrible that must have been, because his ass was gigantic. Moose was just bound and determined to show people his hemorrhoids (they looked like a damn fist sticking out of his ass), and as you might imagine, Moose was not in a very good mood.

We were flying from Fukuoka to Tokyo, when one of the jet's two engines went out. They turned around, back to Fukuoka and jettisoned all the fuel, which looked like a big funnel of smoke flying out of the plane.

Junior saw it and said, "Hey, look at that!"

"I don't want to look at it, Junior," I said.

"Look at it!"

He was about to shit his pants and I was, too, and Brute Bernard decided at this time that it would be really funny for him to stand up in the aisle and sing, "Bringing in the Sheaves."

Moose stood up and said, "I don't want to hear that shit!"

Brute kept singing, so Moose shoved him, and they got into a shoving match right up there while all this was going on.

I remember thinking, "That's all I want to see—those two idiots fighting, as my last memory on this Earth!"

Luckily we landed safely.

As goofy as he was, Moose Cholak could really wrestle. All people remember is that big, goddamned moose head he wore. Sometimes that thing would go over the ropes before he could get through them. He had a hell of a problem with that moose head.

Moose was ornery, too. If he didn't like you, you were going to have a problem in the ring. I used to pump him up all the time, just for the hell of it.

"Moose, goddamn, you're a big, tough bastard, you are," I'd tell him. Then, he'd get to the ring, and whoever he was in there with couldn't do a damn thing with him.

I truly believe, although Stan Hansen might not agree, that my brother and I, in the 1970s, established a much more physical level in Japan than what there had been to that point. That was some of the work I was most proud of in my career, and I think Stan and Bruiser Brody saw our success with that style and took it onward, but I don't think that style really existed much before Junior and I did it there.

We wanted to establish a closeness to reality, like the realism my father wanted to portray in Amarillo.

Sometimes, some of our opponents stiffed us a little in the ring, which, as I've said, I've never understood. Brody's partner Buck Robley, in the seat in front of me, turned around to face me on a plane after a 1982 match in Tokyo and said, "Boy, did we ever fuck you on that last match."

Buck was a good guy, but he had been drinking too much and just decided to start smiling at me and talking shit.

"Yep, we really stiffed you on that match," he kept on.

"Buck, shut your ass up and turn around right now, or else I'm going to beat the living shit out of you."

He kept going, so I went ahead and beat the shit out of him, right there on that 747. Afterwards, he was back in his seat in front of me, and every three or four minutes, I'd haul off and just kick the shit out of his seat. And, every time I did, I cussed him.

"Goddamn Robley, you son of a bitch!"

The stewardess never even said anything about it. The plane was completely silent, except for every few minutes, when I'd kick Buck's seat and cuss him out again.

When we were landing, he asked me to carry some of his payouts for him, because he was carrying a lot of hard cash, and he was worried someone was going to rip him off and take it.

So in one trip, I beat him up and then helped him get his money through, and we're still friends to this day.

We had some wild times, but the promotional war was very serious. My whole life, I've been in competition, whether it was wrestling, football, or whatever. I learned that you constantly had to motivate yourself to compete. You almost had to think of your competition as enemies.

The guy who played ahead of me on the West Texas football team was someone I liked, but I was always envious of him, and I worked my ass off to get where he was. Same thing in the wrestling business—when someone got ahead of where I was, I wanted to be where he was.

Is that healthy? I don't know, but I think it's necessary, and Inoki was the competition, which made him my adversary and my enemy. He was an enemy I respected, though, and still do, to this day.

Would I have fought him? You're goddamned right I would have, and I'm sure he felt the same way. If he'd wanted to fight in the street, we'd have fought in the street. If he'd wanted to fight in the ring, we'd have fought in the ring. It was that serious.

One thing I'll say for him—the Japanese fans were always more appreciative of what they saw in the ring, because both Inoki and Baba were very smart about keeping the evolution in check, advancing things slowly, unlike the States, where everything was always getting wilder.

Inoki and Baba limited what was done in the ring, and therefore people in Japan appreciated wrestling itself more. They had finishes in the middle of the ring. There were no "screwjob" finishes in Japan for as long as I could remember, until the modern era.

Now, that's not to say they didn't have disqualifications, or countouts, because they did. But we never did one of those crazy finishes where the referee is knocked out and misses one guy pinning the other, or half the locker room coming out to interfere.

They usually had winners and losers. When you have winners and losers, each match takes on a greater degree of importance, as opposed to the States, where things got to the point that the importance was with the stipulations of the match. If there was some sort of gimmick or bizarre finish, it would typically be in only one match on the card, and even then it only happened a couple of times a year, which made each angle stand out and be something really memorable.

And those two booked that way on purpose.

CHAPTER 16

Working the Territories

I spent a lot of my time in the U.S. during the early 1980s bouncing around the regional territories. I would come in, do a few weeks' worth of matches, and then I was out. It was a good way to make some money and still get to spend extended periods of time at home, between tours of Japan.

In Memphis, having a main-event feud meant wrestling Jerry Lawler.

I agreed to go there in 1981 after they promised not to steal me blind. That was always necessary when dealing with the promoters in Memphis. Jerry Lawler, who had part-ownership there, was a friend, but he wasn't the man making the payoffs.

I had a good feud with Lawler in Memphis, culminating in the first "empty arena" match. I had the idea for the match, but I couldn't tell you where the idea came from.

It was so absolutely absurd, so ridiculous, that it became a cult favorite. Hell, people don't remember that I was gone from Memphis two weeks after that!

The idea of the match was that I had been saying Lawler always played to the fans and drew strength from them, so I wanted a match where there would be no fans. We had the ring set up and all the chairs set up, but the only people in the building were Lawler, Lance Russell, the camera guys and me. The only way the match could end was with one guy giving up, a variation of an "I quit" match.

That thing continues to live to this day, I think because of the sheer foolishness of it. They introduced us, as we walked down the empty aisle, surrounded by empty chairs. They even played up that they started the tape before announcer Lance Russell was ready, and Lance had to put out his cigarette!

And then I came in and started ranting about Lawler, giving a profanity-laced promo, which doesn't seem like much today, but was a very unusual thing back then.

They bleeped me for TV of course, but I was on a tear, and when Lance asked me not to cuss, since they had to be able to show this on TV, I looked at Lance and said, "I don't give a shit!"

A few seconds later, here came Lawler. And the main thing I remember about that whole match was Lawler walking through the curtain, with his crown tucked under his arm and his robe on, as if there was a full house there. It was the most absurd thing I ever saw.

As for the match itself, it was very strange to be wrestling when there was no one making any noise. The only sounds came from Jerry Lawler and me. I figured, since no one was making noise, that I'd go ahead and provide the noise.

Every time Lawler would hit me, or start to come back, I would yell, "Oh no! No! Oh God no, Jerry!"

I don't know how Lance Russell could have announced that thing with a straight face.

It ended when I submitted, with Lawler grinding a wooden stake from a broken chair in my eye.

I called Lawler a few more nasty names and screamed, "My eye! My eye!"

It was an absurdity, but I wish I had the tape to put out—"The Empty Arena Match from 1981—First Official Release!" Hell, I could sell it at video stores and everything! Mick Foley and The Rock did one in 1999, during halftime of the Super Bowl, which might have been even sillier than mine with Lawler.

Lawler and I were also set to do a match in Florida, and I did a promo for it that became rather famous in wrestling circles.

The shot opened with me standing in a shower stall, holding a can of motor oil.

"Jerry Lawler wants to become a Floridian. Not a transplant—the King wants to become a real Floridian. Well, I would like to know exactly how it feels to be a true Florida cracker, so I have Quaker State Super Blend Motor Oil," I said, pouring the oil over my head, "and I am going to show you people how it feels to be a true Florida cracker. And right here, I have five pounds of dirty, filthy dirt, and that's exactly what it is!"

I started dumping the dirt on my now oily head, as I continued, "and I have got this dirt entirely over my body, and now, I know what it feels like to be a dirty, stinky, greasy Florida cracker, and it's something I never want to feel again!"

And all that oil was an incredible pain in the ass to get out. I got that shit in my eyes, too, and I nearly got blinded. I washed and washed my hair. I went home and went to bed, and the next morning, my damned pillowcase had oily splotches all over it, and Vicki had to throw away the whole pillow!

I thought it was an original idea at the time, but it didn't make the match a particularly big draw, so it became another one of my deals that didn't work.

Now that might seem like a contradiction to what I was talking about earlier, about not wanting just to insult the fanbase, but the difference is, I was never one of those who went out every week and just ranted about how lousy the people were, because I had more focus on my opponent and how to cut a promo that best fit that situation.

I was always throwing ideas out there. I guess I figured eventually something would work. I was like a weatherman—if I kept talking, eventually I'd say something that was right! And the beautiful thing about people is that they tend to remember when I'm right and forget how many times I've been wrong.

Later, in 1983, I came back to Memphis as a babyface, teaming with Lawler! We had a TV match my first day there, against a team managed by a young manager named Jim Cornette. I chased Cornette around the ring and ended up tearing his clothes off. He had no idea. There was nothing pre-planned about it—I just disrobed Jim Cornette for the hell of it! Cornette went on to become one of the all-time great managers and mouthpieces in our business, but I'm proud to say I was the first one to tear the pants off of him on television. And if I see him today, I'll do the same thing. Next time I see him at the Cauliflower Alley Club reunion, his pants are coming off!

Memphis had Lance Russell as an announcer. Lance was right up there with Gordon Solie. They were probably the two best announcers in the country. He had believability with the people. They took different approaches, but they had a lot in common, in that they were like good whiskey—they had the age and maturity behind them.

Junior and I also did an angle in Florida in 1982 involving our uncle, Herman Funk. Uncle Herman came out to back us up and ended up getting beaten up by Mike Graham, as part of the story. He was on vacation in Florida and was with us in the dressing room, and somehow he got talked into coming out with us.

Around that time, one of the young up-and-comers was a kid named Barry Windham. Of course, I had known his dad, Blackjack Mulligan, and Barry himself was another West Texas State boy! Dick Murdoch got hold of him and ruined him, too! Barry was a great athlete and was doing all right for himself on the football field. He was big as a house and probably could have gone pro, but Murdoch got hold of him, and down the road he went!

Seriously, I always loved working with Barry, because he was from the old school. And he was a big, tough kid who didn't take shit off of anybody.

In San Antonio in the 1980s, I became a beloved babyface after years as a heel. It was the only time I ever babyfaced there. Blanchard really had the place popping at the time.

Southwest had a very talented crew, including Gino Hernandez, who was a great performer. I'd met him when he was 16—by then he had two years in the business! This teenager already talked and acted like a seasoned wrestler, because he was one.

Gino could get heat like no one else. He was just a natural-born heel. Joe put him in a tag team with Joe's son, Tully, and they were a damn good team. I loved Gino Hernandez, and I liked his work. I never saw a kid who achieved success in the business and adapted that quick. I mean, here was a kid who was 17, 18 years old in the late 1970s, and he already carried himself like an experienced wrestler. Hell, he *was* an experienced wrestler! He could do great promos and everything, as if he'd been around for 10 years. The way he could do things, and do them well, was just unheard of for a kid that young. And with all his talent, he didn't have the big head! He got along with all the boys in the locker room. Gino's success was always something that was hard for me to understand, because I'd always believed in maturity. I always believed it took three or four years to really understand what you were doing in wrestling, but Gino jumped right in and took off.

Joe Blanchard had been working with Fritz Von Erich in Dallas. Fritz had been doing the booking, and Joe felt like he could do a better job at it, so they just had constant problems. It wasn't even that they both had wrestling sons they wanted to push, although there was some heat between Tully and the Von Erich boys. Joe just got tired of paying Fritz a percentage of his houses as a booking fee. They also couldn't agree on which town belonged to whom.

Joe was also working with Houston promoter Paul Boesch, until 1982, when Boesch started working with Bill Watts's Mid-South Wrestling to bring talent in.

My sympathies were with the Southwest guys, but as Boesch started easing Blanchard's guys out and Watts's guys in, I just kind of backed away from the whole deal. I could see where things were headed, and I knew if I wanted to keep working in Houston, I'd have to go work for Watts's territory. There was no reason for me to want to work there. Bill would have had me running from town to town seven nights a week.

Even though I'd sided with Blanchard, I certainly wasn't trying to screw Paul Boesch around.

A few months later, Joe decided to promote a show, with a world title tournament, in Houston, against Boesch, who ran a show the night after ours. In the tournament, I beat Bob Orton Jr. in the first round, but then we did a deal where Abdullah the Butcher injured me in the second round, knocking me out of the tournament.

I don't know what plans Joe might have had for running Houston, but the tournament was just kind of a one-time deal for us in Houston after the split with Boesch, and the aspect of competing against him never even crossed my mind.

Orton was a very, very talented wrestler. I had seen his father wrestle, and now, I watch his son, Randy, on the WWE shows. They remind me of each other, and I promise, Randy has never, or hardly ever, seen his grandfather wrestle, but all three of them wrestle alike. They all have that same, great psychology.

I still get a call from Bob Sr. every Saturday morning. He calls to talk to me about how Randy's doing, and to warn me about the latest activities of the communists, or the terrorists, in his gravelly growl.

"Hey, kid, you gotta watch those airplanes. Goddamn, I don't want to get on those airplanes anymore. You don't know who you got sitting next to you. They might have something in their shoe, or wrapped around their leg, or some other damn thing. You can't take any chances, kid. You got them broads walking up and down the aisles, taking drink orders. Hell, could be the pilot's drunk—you don't know! Anything can happen up there, kid!"

And every few seconds, I say, "Uh huh."

And that's my weekly conversation with Bob Orton Sr. I love him, but he's always been nuts! This isn't like some creeping senility, some new thing brought on by old age. We used to ride together, 30 years ago or more, and he'd bundle himself up in blankets and tell everyone, "Now, don't breathe on me, kid, there's goddamn germs everywhere! And turn that air-conditioning off! You don't know what the hell's coming out of there!"

Bob Jr. never wanted to be like his dad, but damned if he didn't turn out exactly like him! In the late 1970s and early 1980s, Bob and Dick Slater were one of the truly great teams in wrestling. There was a real crop of incredible wrestling talent that came out of Florida, educated by Eddie Graham into the business, and many of them became dominant performers. Steve Keirn, Bob Roop, Bob Orton Jr., Dick Slater, Paul Orndorff—a great many wrestlers came out of Florida who could really work their asses off during that time period, and I'm just scratching the surface. Eddie impressed the importance of that background and education in pro wrestling on them as children viewing the product, and it greatly influenced their desires, and even the types of performers they became.

Bob Jr. and I worked a tour of Germany for promoter Otto Wanz, which turned out to be a nightmare for poor Otto.

I was always something of a nightmare for Otto, but I had nothing on Bob Orton—he was just a maniac over there. Bob was laying into Germans on the street, executing wrestling takedowns on them; it was like he thought the second world war was still going on!

I liked Otto. I went 40 minutes with Otto once. We did a big match right before he retired. Over there, they did matches in three- or five-minute rounds, and I don't remember how many rounds we went, but we tore the house down because of Otto's ability to get over to his fans. As an in-ring performer, he was just amazing. I'm not saying whether he was amazingly good, or amazingly bad—just amazing. But I'll tell you this—big Otto was over like a son of a gun over there, because he understood what he could do, and he understood what the people wanted. He gave it to them.

There were some great European workers, like Tony St. Clair and David "Fit" Finlay, over there. And there were also some real crowbars, too, some guys who I thought shouldn't even be there.

I used to think the same thing about some of the guys my dad brought in to work Amarillo.

"Dad," I used to say, "why do you keep that guy around? He can't do a thing."

"Son, it's my company, and I like the guy. I want him to be able to make a living," he said.

He kept guys just for that reason, which was a perk of being a promoter, and it was something Otto did, too, for the same reason. Even today, you can see examples of Vince McMahon doing the same thing. He takes care of people, just because he thinks they're good people.

I loved going to Germany because I had relatives in the little town of Krauthausen. They treated me like my family had never left there. Two of them were teachers, and they had children who played the cello and piano, who were highly educated and refined. It made me wonder—what the hell happened when Adam Funk crossed the seas to get to America?

Germany was a great place for guys to work. It's a real shame that the promotion isn't there anymore. Otto would bring guys in, and we'd work the same building every night, the whole summer. They'd change the matches, but we were in the same building every night. It really taught guys how to be creative because you had to be in that situation. You had to change up your match every night.

Having to work that more scientific German style and always adapting helped give a guy a sharper wrestling mind, because you always had to adapt and change. Plus, you had to be real enough that they came back the next night.

One of my favorite people to work with was in San Antonio around that time—Dick Slater. I've heard from a lot of people over the years that I had a big influence on Slater's wrestling style. Well, Slater wore trunks like me, but there wasn't anything wrong with that.

As long as I knew Dick Slater, he worked like I did. He worked like me before he ever saw me. We just had a lot of the same ideas about what would get over. We became good friends, and I don't think he changed his walk or anything for me. I think he walked like a goof, because he was half-goofy, and he did some pretty wild things.

Hulk Hogan once told me the first time he ever saw Dick Slater was on Clearwater Beach, Florida. Slater had a cat by the tail and was swinging it around over his head while running down the beach, according to Hogan, and the cat was on fire.

Slater was one of the toughest guys you'd ever want to meet—just hard-nosed. There was a promotional war in the Tennessee area, with a bunch of guys claiming on TV that the Fullers couldn't wrestle, and neither could anyone on their roster. Well, Slater was booking for the Fullers when he went to the bar where the other company's boys hung out, and he beat the hell out of Bob Roop. Now, Roop was no slouch—he was a national AAU amateur wrestling champion and represented the United States in Greco-Roman Wrestling, in the 1968 Olympics. You don't get those distinctions unless you are tough and can handle yourself.

As I went through the territories, I also got to see a lot of young talent that was on the rise. One young wrestler was Paul Taylor, who decided to name himself after his favorite wrestler and called himself Terry Taylor. I wrestled him in Georgia and thought he had a lot of wrestling talent. Plus, he had good taste in his choice of favorite wrestler! I always thought he had a lot of sense, too, and it looks like he had a lot more sense than I did, because he got out of wrestling in the ring full time and went to work in the office end of things, working behind the scenes in WCW and the WWF. I think it's a hard job, and Taylor is a guy with a good mind who added to whatever company he worked for.

Another couple of impressive talents were Don Kernodle and Sgt. Slaughter. Junior and I wrestled them once in the Mid-Atlantic territory, where Junior was booking in 1983. Junior brought me in for a shot so we could work a tag match with them.

Slaughter and Kernodle were both excellent. I really think a lot of Don Kernodle's work, and he really doesn't get his due. Slaughter was great, too, a really great-moving big man. Putting those two together was a great idea, and those two did a great job with it.

There was almost the sense that they were the new big heel team, taking over from Gene and Ole Anderson, who had been one of the top teams in the area in the 1970s. The Andersons were another good team, and they drew some money. As far as work and style were concerned, it seemed to me Gene was the bigger influence. The original Andersons team was Gene and Lars (Larry Heinimi). Ole became Lars's replacement on the team, and Ole went from being Alan Rogowski to really being Ole Anderson in those years. I don't know what he would have become if it wasn't for Gene Anderson and the style Gene did.

One of Gene's last runs as a wrestler was him being managed in the Carolinas by Sir Oliver Humperdink, who later had a lot of success in the 1980s in Florida. I loved Oliver, but he was one goofy bastard. He had a sign on the back of the old van that he drove, which said, "Onward through the fog." I don't know that any phrase could have fit someone any better than "Onward through the fog" fit Oliver Humperdink.

One night in Tampa, he went through the fog … and a stop sign, and a dead-end barricade, and the side of some family's house. I think that was a very foggy night, and yet, the weather was clear.

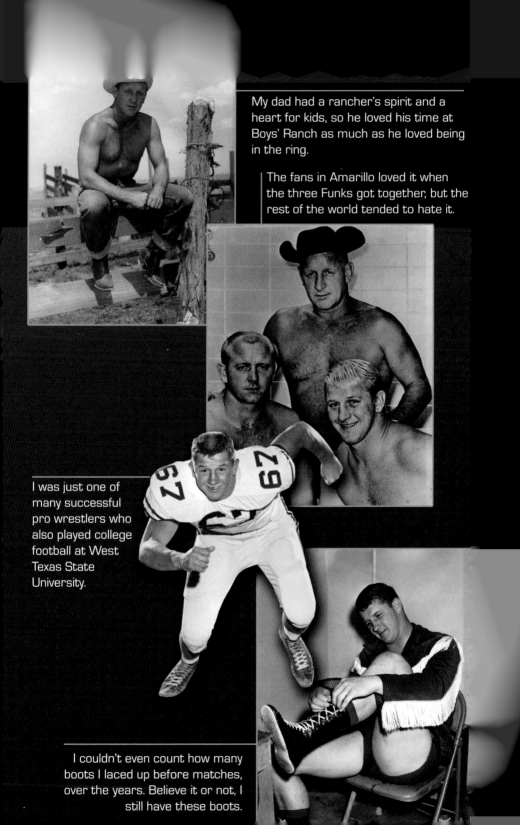

My dad had a rancher's spirit and a heart for kids, so he loved his time at Boys' Ranch as much as he loved being in the ring.

The fans in Amarillo loved it when the three Funks got together, but the rest of the world tended to hate it.

I was just one of many successful pro wrestlers who also played college football at West Texas State University.

I couldn't even count how many boots I laced up before matches, over the years. Believe it or not, I still have these boots.

The Sheik was a truly scary individual, and wrestling him was always an exciting (and frightening) proposition.

Teaming with Jose Lothario in Florida, in 1966. Jose was one of the most knowledgeable and truly great workers in the business.

The Western States championship, pictured here, was one of my first titles.

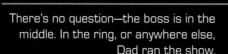

There's no question—the boss is in the middle. In the ring, or anywhere else, Dad ran the show.

One of the most memorable moments in a lot of fans' minds was when I piledrove Ric Flair onto a table to start our big feud in 1989.

Holding the world title was a great thing to me, but I was not the first champion to be worn down by the grind of the travel.
(Photo by Dr. Mike Lano, wrealano@aol.com)

In 1977, I dropped the title to Harley Race, a truly tough guy.

Dusty Rhodes was always one of my favorite opponents, but I must admit—I have no concrete proof that he actually does suck eggs.

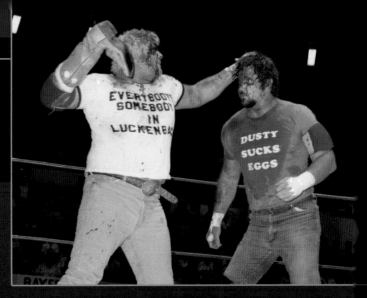

Our 1977 tag-title win, after a brutal match with Abdullah the Butcher and The Sheik, helped solidify my brother and me as two of the most popular wrestlers in Japan.

Wrestling on independent shows was not a piece of cake. It could be a tough road. Here, I'm diving onto Sabu, one of the true innovators in the wrestling business.

The legendary Abdullah the Butcher was a superstar in Japan, and one angle we did changed the course of Japanese wrestling.

It's pretty clear to see the fear in Hawk's eyes as I strike my fighting pose.

Some of the brutal matches in Japan required serious mental preparation and some hard thinking.

I'm slowly crawling into the ring, trying to keep from getting snagged, for a barbed-wire match with Atsushi Onita, a revolutionary figure in Japan,

For years, my wife Vicki has accompanied me on wrestling trips, and that has made the travel a lot easier.

Enjoying time with my family at the Double-Cross Ranch is something I am going to do forever, and I mean forever.

I might have stayed in Mid-Atlantic, but Jimmy Crockett, who owned the territory, didn't want too many Funks there. He was enjoying a lot of success and felt like his way was the right way of doing things. Junior and I actually brought Hansen and Brody in to work there, and they were one of the hottest teams in the world at the time, based on their work in Japan. Jimmy thought they would be too much too handle, and he might have been right.

I don't know that me staying there would have helped their business, because their business was great at that time. Why did Jimmy need me, Hansen, or Brody down there?

Crockett did a good job of protecting his area. He ran the Carolinas and Virginia, and it was a very isolated area. If you thought about the places for big money in wrestling, you might think of Chicago, or Detroit—one of the major metropolitan areas. Yet, that Carolinas territory, with all those small towns, was kicking ass and taking names in 1983, making more money than anyone else in the country! They were doing much bigger business than the World Wrestling Federation that year, and the WWF territory back then included New York, Philadelphia, Boston, Washington, D.C.—some of the biggest cities in the world!

I didn't just travel around to wrestle. I also traveled around for about six years trying my hand at rodeo.

My daughters got into rodeoing while they were in school, and I think between them, they won more than 50 saddles. My younger daughter Brandee was a natural, but she got burned out on it before she finished high school. My older daughter Stacy won a scholarship to West Texas State in rodeo.

Whenever I was out on the road, hopping around territories, and they had a rodeo event, I would always try to squeeze in a short trip home to see them. Vicki, God bless her, would pick me up at the airport and drive the pickup truck to the event while I slept in the bed of the truck. It was the greatest thing in the world to watch my kids compete and do well. Those girls were incredible, and that's not just "Proud Papa" talking, either. They were both state champions in barrels and pole bending.

We also got the girls a good horse. His name was Lightning, and he was a little albino horse, about half the size of a regular horse, but he had a huge heart and would just win for them, time after time. And the kids knew exactly how to work with him, to get the most out of him.

CHAPTER 17

My First Retirement Match

I announced my retirement in Japan in 1981, two years in advance of my planned 1983 retirement show. It was around the same time as the Abdullah angle with the fork to the arm and was born out of the same sense of necessity to compete with Inoki.

I wanted All Japan to have something that the fans could follow along with for a long period of time, and my idea was to announce my retirement that far in advance and then build to it slowly.

I discussed the idea with Baba and Junior, but it was my choice and my idea, and it was my idea to have it for two years. I thought we'd have something built up by then, and at that point, All Japan would have some other things with momentum to carry the company from that point.

Things kept on peaking, and the company was really rolling by the time we did my retirement match. The match was Junior and me versus Stan Hansen and Terry Gordy.

If I hadn't done what I did when I did it, I truly believe Inoki would have eaten All Japan, and the company wouldn't have existed much longer. New Japan was leaps and bounds ahead of us at the time, in 1981. My retirement was an enabler; it enabled All Japan to have some long-term programs to build to the future while it was going on. I'm not just patting myself on the back when I say that I unselfishly gave that company three years to get back on track and then willingly gave up my position as one of its top attractions. I would call that being a good soldier. Give me a medal, please?

The night of the show I had a tough time. It was very emotional for me, because I truly had no intention of ever going back to Japan. Baba certainly never said anything that night, or in any of the nights leading up to it, to make me think there was a plan to bring me back. I had gotten close to a lot of the wrestlers there, and even a lot of the guys in the press, and I was very much taken aback by the whole thing.

The point of the match was almost as much to show Gordy in a new light, with more of a main-event feel, as it was to spotlight my retirement. I think the match really did a lot for Gordy. He was a hell of a hard worker and had unbelievable natural talent.

After that retirement match I was done. That was it. I still got paid a meager amount as a booker, but I had no involvement with the company. And they had programs going so strong that things just kept on rolling for the next 15 months, and I just stayed retired that whole time.

Now, we must be clear—I said I was retiring *in Japan*. I never did say I would never wrestle again, and it was never my intention to stop wrestling everywhere. I didn't lead Baba, the fans, or the press to think that was what I'd meant. I had worked a handful of matches by early 1985 in the United States, but I really did stay out of the ring for most of that first year after the retirement match.

And the retirement ceremony that night was very real to me. It was very, very emotional to me and, I think, for the whole audience. My kids were there and they were crying. It really wasn't a work. I was really retiring, and I felt I could. I felt I had the knowledge and fortitude to survive in the real world of business.

In 1984 Baba asked me to come back and referee a match in February, in which Jumbo Tsuruta would win the AWA world title from Nick Bockwinkel. Several months later, Baba asked me to come back on a tour, and I did. Coming back in Japan after retiring hurt me somewhat in the fans' eyes there, but it wasn't like I could tell them that it wasn't me who had asked to come back. And it hurt me personally, to know that my return hurt the fans, but there was a financial reward to returning that I could not ignore.

I must have been some kind of idiot. I had paid off the Double-Cross Ranch, and had a good chunk of money in the bank. I thought, "My gosh, we're finally going to be all right, for life. I can probably make more money in the States than I was making in Japan, anyway."

Only a fool would think something like that.

Somehow it never came out that Baba asked me to come back. It always seemed to the fans as though coming back out of retirement was all my idea, but it wasn't. I knew when I agreed to come back that I wouldn't be as hot as I'd been. But it must have worked to some extent, because otherwise you wouldn't be seeing 101 Japanese wrestlers retire and then come out of retirement, over the past few years.

The company I came back to in late 1984 was somewhat different than the one I'd left.

All Japan scored what was considered a major coup in 1984 when Riki Choshu, one of Inoki's top stars, and 12 other wrestlers from New Japan jumped to our side. Well, it *was* a coup, but after they got to All Japan, it became a chaotic coup. I really don't think getting them was a smart thing to do, and never did.

We ended up with too much of a crew, more than even Baba could handle. What we got were more guys vying for main-event positions than we had main-event positions, not even counting the main-event guys we already had. There is strength in numbers, but Baba got the numbers a little out of balance there. I think the proof of that is that almost the whole group jumped back to New Japan a few years later.

They were a clique, and cliques can cause chaos because they start from a stronger position than a single individual. I was glad to have Choshu because of his stature, and Yoshiaki Yatsu (one of the wrestlers who jumped with Choshu) was a good guy who I liked, but Choshu wanted more control over the matches than Baba wanted to give him, so Choshu wasn't going to be happy. And when Choshu wasn't happy, none of those guys were happy.

Baba also had a tough choice to make—which of his two top stars, Tsuruta or Tenryu, would get the shot to work the feud with Choshu? It was a big slot—imagine what it would have been like if Vince McMahon could have gotten Goldberg from WCW in 1999. That's what Baba getting Choshu was like, and the person getting to feud with Choshu was going to work a lot of main events.

Choshu and Tenryu had been friends from their days before All Japan, but I don't think that played into Baba's decision to give Tenryu the slot. Tenryu used the octopus, which was also Inoki's hold, so it was a natural to put those two in together. I also think that since Tsuruta was Baba's main boy there was a desire to keep him from Choshu for a while. I know he didn't trust Choshu enough to take care of Tsuruta. Now, I'm not saying Tenryu was a sacrificial lamb, because he wasn't. But it didn't hurt Tenryu to be beaten by Choshu, whereas it would have hurt Tsuruta. And to have Choshu beat Tsuruta would have given Choshu too much power, which Baba wasn't about to do. But whatever the reason, Choshu and Tenryu made for a very successful feud.

I mentioned earlier about Choshu stiffing me in a match, but it was really the office stiffing me. I honestly think he was under orders from Baba not to give me too much out there. I think Baba decided, after getting me out of retirement, that he didn't really want me back there after all, and the Choshu match was his way of sending me that message. Maybe Baba thought I had too much power. He wanted the total availability of Terry Funk, and I was not going to give him that availability, because I wanted my family to have it.

In addition to the $7,500 a week I got for *Paradise Alley*, the movie also helped me in Japan in terms of exposure. When I was filming the TV series "Wildside" in 1984, I got $10,000 a week. And I was getting that huge money for not wrestling. Compare that to the $7,500 a week I was making in Japan, for helping book and for killing myself every night in the ring.

I loved Baba, loved Mrs. Baba and loved Wally Yamaguchi, one of Baba's right-hand men. But the fact that I loved those people didn't keep me from seeing that I wasn't getting everything from All Japan that I probably could have.

Case in point: Wally Yamaguchi would bring me this stack of 12-by-12 cards, which I'd sign. I'd sign 25 or 30 of them, "God bless, Terry Funk," or whatever, hand them back to Wally, and he'd take them to be sold. During the big shows, Wally Yamaguchi would sit in the back of the locker room, and he'd be like a machine, signing my name on those cards, in what I would have sworn was my own handwriting if I didn't know better! He could sign those things at a clip you wouldn't believe—he could actually do an exact duplicate of my signature, and do it faster than I could sign my own name! They were selling these for 2,000 yen apiece. Guess how many yen I saw out of those? Not a one. Was Wally the pirate profiting from my name? Of course not.

I didn't complain. I looked at it as part of the package. But All Japan also took a cut out of everything I did outside of wrestling, whether it was the record album, or whatever.

And there was always the unknown in Japan. The unknown part of the business is what goes on behind the closed doors, and it's a very big part of the business. Gaijins have very little understanding of that part of it. I'll probably never know how many opportunities for commercials or other ventures I lost out on because Baba shot them down.

Baba didn't make many bad moves, but bringing in Choshu's entire crew was one of them. And that move set a precedent of doing more Japanese versus Japanese main events. I saw it happening, with fewer American wrestlers involved in the big matches, which I knew wasn't going to be good for any of us.

A better move was when we offered some good money to Tom Billington, the Dynamite Kid, the most famous opponent of the original Tiger Mask in New Japan. Dynamite came to work for us in 1984 with his cousin Davey Boy Smith. They were a great team, but there was no question Dynamite was running that show.

Dynamite was a guy who would go out there night after night after night and physically destroy himself in the ring. I've seen him go into the ring with a melon-sized swelling on his lower back, barely able to walk. He would still work the match and take some ungodly bump. Then he'd get on that bus with the rest of the boys. He really needed help to get to his seat, but he wouldn't accept any. He'd make it all the way to the back by himself, because he was too damn tough to take help. He'd get to one of those seats, get himself a beer and do the same thing the next night. Dynamite loved to have the respect of the boys, and he certainly had it, but it would just kill you to watch him climb onto that bus.

Sometimes I think of Dynamite and some of the insane things I've done in my own career. Why do we do that stuff? Why do we shorten our careers, and maybe our lives, physically? Why did I drag my 50-year-old ass up to the top rope for a moonsault? Why do I hurt myself on small shows where there's not a lot of money to be made? I have absolutely no idea what drives us to do some of those things. Maybe guys like me are just queer, but in a different way. Instead of being queer for guys, maybe I'm queer for wrestling.

In 1985, Junior and I got to work with two guys who had become probably the top-drawing tag-team in the world—Mike Hegstrand and Joe Laurinaitis, better known as Hawk and Animal, The Road Warriors. At that time, they were probably the best box office attractions in the world, aside from Hulk Hogan. I always loved working with them, except for one thing. Mike Hegstrand, Road Warrior Hawk, loved to imitate me, so every time I saw Hawk, I'd have to listen to 30 minutes of him doing Terry Funk before we started talking about the match. He really loved me, but I think that might have just been because he could imitate me so well!

I actually hurt my back badly in a match against them in Puerto Rico. They stormed the ring, and I bailed out, but when I did, I misjudged my landing, thinking that there was an elevated platform outside the ring, like on the other three sides. I took a nasty fall and could barely finish the match. I was in a tremendous amount of pain.

The Road Warriors were also sharp businesswise, and I think their manager, Paul Ellering, was a real boon to them. Hawk knew that he needed that solid platform that Ellering provided, and Animal (Joe Laurinaitis) knew that he needed Ellering there, because he couldn't handle Hawk all by himself. Hawk was a wild man, and Animal was a stable person, but I don't think he could have handled Hawk like Ellering could. And I'm not talking about in the ring.

CHAPTER 18

1983: The Wrestling War Begins

As I ended my full-time Japanese career in August 1983, the industry there had changed a lot. On my first tour there, in 1971, it had been me, Dominic DeNucci, Bruno Sammartino, Jerry Kozak, Mike Paidousis and Junior. That was the crew, along with Baba and his boys. We had TV, but the houses weren't always great, and it was a struggle.

By the early 1980s, business had grown and grown and was just phenomenal by 1983. It's a funny thing. When business is going strong, the strong points infect the rest of the promotion, and it gets healthy all the way through.

Baba had some great talent and was about to steal Inoki's thunder a bit by buying the rights to the TV cartoon character Tiger Mask and giving the gimmick to a young wrestler named Mitsuharu Misawa. Baba really ingratiated himself to the creator of Tiger Mask and capitalized on the relationship he had cultivated to get that license.

The new Tiger Mask created interest, but I don't know that Misawa was the best choice to be the new Tiger Mask. Misawa might have been better just as Misawa, all those years, and he was (and is) a great performer, but Misawa was Baba's protégé. Baba felt like the gimmick would be an instant success.

Misawa wrestled in a style that was very reminiscent of Jumbo Tsuruta. He was brought along slowly and taught the heritage of his wrestling. I truly think that his training and education were the reasons he was so successful in the long-term. He was taught to respect his business and take it seriously, and wrestling was his life.

Hell, Tiger Mask wasn't the only character who existed in both the wrestling and cartoon worlds at that time. Years before, a popular cartoon magazine strip debuted called "Terry Boy." In the story, Terry Boy wrestled, and he looked awfully familiar, but I never saw a nickel from it. He even became a TV cartoon. Ol' Terry Boy did all right!

Meanwhile, in the States, the wrestling business was shaping up to change more than ever before.

Up to the 1980s, the NWA was the power in pro wrestling. In 1983, Vincent K. McMahon decided to challenge the territorial boundaries and try to establish his World Wrestling Federation as a national promotion.

The NWA was not strong enough to stop Vince McMahon Jr. from expanding his company into a nationwide promotion. They hated him in the 1980s, and I'm sure some still do today, but any one of them who thought he could pull it off would have done the same thing. Everybody knew that opportunity was going to come.

Hell, Vince wasn't even the first person who tried it. In the mid-1970s, Eddie Einhorn stared a group called the International Wrestling Association which included Pedro Martinez.

Einhorn was a sports guy who helped create the NCAA tournament and the "Final Four," a great concept. This was before cable came out, and he put the promoters in the position of trying to keep a national program from taking over. Einhorn's idea was to make wrestling a nationally syndicated show.

I actually got sued over that deal.

It happened while I was NWA world champion. Pedro Martinez was on an airplane that Dusty Rhodes and I were also on.

Dusty spotted him and said, "Terry, you thee that goofy thun of a bitch back there? That'th Pedro Martineth!"

I wouldn't have known him if Dusty hadn't pointed him out, but I did know that the IWA had gotten on TV in Odessa, Texas It was just one small town in our territory. Who gives a shit, right?

But it was serious business to me, so I asked Dusty, "Where is that son of a bitch?"

Dusty said, "He'th thittin' back thayuh," and motioned his head toward the back of the plane.

I said, "Well you just point him out to me when we land."

After we landed and were walking in the terminal, Dusty pointed Martinez out to me. I walked up to him, touched his collar, grabbed his lapels, got right in his face and said, "Keep your goddamned tapes out of Odessa, Texas."

He said, "What are you talking about?"

I guess he had tapes going in stations all over the country and didn't know every single city he had. I told him he'd better stay out of our area, and to be ready for a fight if he didn't.

I let go and Martinez took off.

I went back to Dusty and said, "Well, I guess I showed that son of a gun."

As we were passing security, there was Pedro Martinez, only now his lapels were ripped and torn, his shirt ripped open and his belly hanging out. He was pointing me out to the two police officers with him.

They put me under arrest and took me to jail.

I got right out, but soon after that I found out Martinez was suing me for $18 million and Eastern Airlines for $1 million. I went to court, and Martinez passed around a picture of a testicle that had swollen to the size of a basketball. He said I kicked him in the nuts.

I never *touched* his nuts! What happened was, he'd found another wrestler who had a swollen testicle, took a picture of it, and they found me guilty off of that! It wasn't even his nut, the dirty son of a bitch!

I appealed, but I ended up settling out of court with him for $5,000, but that was $5,000 I shouldn't have even had to pay for another guy's testicle!

The NWA, Jim Barnett in particular, wasn't very happy with that situation. I thought they'd be very pleased. Hell, I thought the entire wrestling industry would be proud of me handling Pedro Martinez for them.

The entire NWA ran from it. Anytime you had a lawsuit, you had no friends. Even Eddie Graham would run from me when he saw me, if there was a lawsuit! Here I was, doing the right thing to help protect their business, and they ran from me!

I've dealt with a lot of lawsuits, but I have to say, what's wrong with our country today is that we say you're innocent until proven guilty, but the fact is, in a lawsuit, you're guilty until proven innocent, and it can be very costly.

Someone once told me about an old curse: "May you be involved in a lawsuit in which you are in the right."

Einhorn ran out of money and closed up a few months later in 1976, but Vince and the WWF weren't going down as easily in 1984.

Months before the younger Vince McMahon started his national campaign, I saw something else that I knew would have an impact on the business.

This kid from California I had seen and talked to a couple of times at shows over the years gave me a copy of his typed wrestling news bulletin, called the *Wrestling Observer Newsletter*.

As I read it, I immediately thought that this thing was going to take off. There would be no stopping it. Instead of talking about the matches as if they were real competitions, like the newsstand magazines had done, Dave Meltzer wrote about the business behind the scenes. It had news and results from all over, and was obviously written about someone who understood the business.

A lot of wrestlers thought it would "expose the business" and ruin it, but I saw it as a thermometer of sorts, to see how different things were getting over in different places. For me, it was a fine tool to look at, to see some of the trends in the business.

CHAPTER 19

Working for Vince McMahon

By the mid-1980s, Vince McMahon Jr. was "the enemy" to every NWA promoter in America.

From Christmas 1983 on, McMahon was breaking all the boundaries and putting his wrestling shows in markets that had been exclusive to their respective regional promoters for years.

I knew it was coming. The day I first saw the TBS show, back in 1979, I knew the business was changing and changing fast. It was Jim Barnett's Georgia Championship Wrestling, and Tommy Rich was his big star. Jim stayed within his own area, and I don't know why, because he could have made a stab at it himself, since he had the national outlet.

I would love to say I was a visionary in this regard, but I wasn't even the first Funk to see this. My father always knew that someday, someone was going to get control of national television. It was no premonition, just a belief that someday someone was going to get on nationally. We didn't know who it would be, but we knew someone would. The best thing that could have happened, for the individual promoters around the country, would have been to have it run through the old National Wrestling Alliance. But that was almost an impossibility.

Nor was Georgia the first show to be shown far outside of its own territory. In the 1970s, we saw Los Angeles wrestling in Spanish on a Spanish-language UHF channel in Amarillo.

Vince Jr. first got people's attention when he got the USA Network slot for his WWF show, from Joe Blanchard's Southwest Wrestling group. There was a money dispute between Joe and the network, and USA pulled Joe off the air. I don't know exactly what the dispute was, but I do know that it wasn't Terry Funk's idea of dumping cowshit all over Bobby Jaggers. Yes, that *was* my idea, but that was not the reason the show went off the air.

And if you think about it, that would be such a mild angle today. And we poured real shit on him! We had to be "real," so it had to be real cowshit—wet, runny cowshit! Now, why we had to do that, I don't know, but the ammonia, the shit and the piss that was in that stuff damn near blinded Jaggers.

But at least we were being real!

McMahon's early shows on the USA Network featured his stars, but also featured stars from other groups. A lot of the NWA promoters thought at first that he was being cooperative, but it was a façade. I knew what his game was as soon as he took that USA slot from Blanchard. He was featuring the guys he wanted to take from the different promotions.

I think ultimately McMahon ended up succeeding where Eddie Einhorn (and that no-good, phony-testicle-showing son of a bitch Pedro Martinez) failed because of a few reasons. First, he was able to create a perception that his product was hot, and because he surrounded himself with the right people. Einhorn's IWA was a similar effort at national expansion, but was doing no more than selling a product. Einhorn made a lot of wrong decisions, including on talent. Johnny Powers was a good worker, and he could draw money in limited areas, but he was not someone who could be a national franchise.

Neither was Mil Mascaras, Einhorn's champion. He was someone the wrestling world nationally didn't know. He was a draw with Hispanic audiences, but you move him up into Minneapolis, and people weren't going to give a shit about him. Einhorn also had Ox Baker, who was a hell of a character, but as a national star he didn't work, either. There's a difference between being able to be over in one area and being able to get over everywhere.

Vince also had location on his side. If something doesn't come from New York or Los Angeles, it's not considered "in." And coming from New York gave the WWF the legitimacy for the national push. If Vince had been heir to a wrestling promotion in Oregon or Oklahoma, I think things would have turned out very differently for him, and for this business.

The other thing Vince had going for him was Vince himself. I'm not just saying this—Vince McMahon is the smartest man in wrestling, or else he wouldn't be in the position he's in now.

When Vince started his national push in late 1983, he pulled the top talent out of Gagne's Minnesota territory, which was the top territory in the country at that time. He took their top wrestlers right out of there.

It was the right move, because Vince's original Northeastern territory already had a large population, and when he took Gagne's top talent, he effectively added Minneapolis, Chicago and Gagne's other top cities to his list.

In retaliation for Vince's expansion into his area, Verne Gagne tried promoting in the Northeast, Vince's stronghold, under the guise of working a cooperative deal with alliance members in opposition to the WWF, but it was an unworkable approach, because someone was going to have to be boss, and those old promoters couldn't agree on who that would be. Junior and I even worked a couple of shows for the group, which was called "Pro Wrestling USA," but we knew it wouldn't last.

Vince went about it the right way, but the main thing he had going for him that Eddie Einhorn didn't, was that Vince was willing to risk all the money he had on it. Vince backed his plan up with big bucks, paying the wrestlers more than they could make in their territories. And once he started to roll, it was over, and no one could catch him, although it took some of the other promoters years to figure that out.

Vince's traveling show made the regional guys less of a big deal. If you're a regional promoter running a town every week, and there's now a traveling show coming through only periodically, your show is now ordinary. That traveling show becomes the big thing.

In the past, when someone had promoted in an NWA area in opposition to the NWA promoter, the other alliance members would send in top talent and help squash the opposition. And some of the old promoters had made rumblings about running national. Verne Gagne talked about running from his strong, Midwest base, and the California promoters, Mike LaBell and Roy Shire, made some noises, but the other members stepped in before they got going. But that approach wasn't working this time, because Vince had succeeded in making his wrestling seem like the big time.

Some of those NWA promoters were very good friends of mine. When I decided to go to work for Vince Jr. in 1985, some of them viewed me as a traitor.

They said, "You're leaving us! You're supposed to be an NWA member and loyal to the NWA!"

Hell, there was no NWA at this time! By 1985 it was gone. Vince had already won. As soon as I saw the angle he had in 1984 with Hulk Hogan and Cyndi Lauper, I knew he had won, because he had found a wider appeal than any company had before.

I don't remember who called who, but I'm pretty sure I called Vince, trying to get in. I do remember the show I debuted on. It was also the first show for Randy Savage and the British Bulldogs.

Randy Savage was Randy Poffo, son of my dad's old friend, Angelo Poffo. I'd actually been one of Randy's first professional opponents. He wrestled under a mask while playing for a minor-league team of the St. Louis Cardinals. I knew even then that he had a lot of talent, but I had no idea he'd hit as big as he did. That whole family is so tight-knit, and I've always marveled at their ability to stay close through the years in the wrestling business.

Somehow we all ended up in the same airport and flew into Poughkeepsie for the TV taping. I have to tell you, I was thoroughly impressed. I had been around all the territories, but this thing was organized and run on an entirely different level.

It was a high-end production, with the people working for Vince all doing their jobs like a well-oiled machine. It was a first-class operation, built and designed to run the country, and by 1985 it was a matter of when, not if.

It was a match with Savage's brother, "Leaping" Lanny Poffo, after I'd started in the WWF, where I lost an entire pectoral muscle and a tricep muscle from a neck injury. In the match, I gave him an airplane spin, stopped and dropped his throat across the top rope. I'd do this by dropping him to the mat with him across my shoulders. This particular night, I was too far from the ropes, when I tried it. When I landed on the mat, Lanny's entire weight came down on my neck, and I lost all the tone and control of that pectoral and tricep.

I had actually talked with Vince's father, Vince Sr., in 1980, about me coming into what was then the New York territory to work with his champion, Bob Backlund, but we just couldn't make it work.

I would have enjoyed working with Backlund. He was an NCAA Division 2 amateur wrestling champion and one hell of a performer. He was over very well with those fans. A lot of people underestimate how over Bobby Backlund was. Backlund actually came through Amarillo in the mid-1970s. He had been a job boy (a wrestler who gets squashed every week, to make the stars look good) in Oklahoma, and after a few months here, we contacted Eddie Graham and got Backlund booked in Florida, where he did very well, until he finally ended up with Vince Sr.

We recommended him to Eddie because he had a great athletic background and was easy to work with. We saw a lot of potential in him, and I think he learned a lot here. He learned a great deal more from Eddie in Florida, and Bob was a great fit for his place and time.

Now, there was a new champion. Terry Bollea, better known as Hulk Hogan, had taken the belt from The Iron Sheik on January 23, 1984 and was the face of Vince's promotion, which was breaking all boundaries and going nationwide.

I had worked with Hogan before. In 1981, we worked in Sun City, South Africa. And the adage was true—don't go to Sun City, especially if you're wrestling on a show run by a bunch of Pakis!

I'd set the whole thing up for Hogan—$35,000 cash, which was certainly more than the $8,000 I was getting. Good thing I had a big run on a blackjack table! I set him up with a better deal than I did for myself. But I went directly to Hogan with it and around Verne Gagne, and I was happy about that, because I wanted him to make the money from it and not have to share it with Gagne.

We really had a great match, and then Terry asked me, "Would you pick up my money?"

He said he was due to wrestle in Japan, so I told him getting his money would be no problem, but when I did, I had to do all the money changing. I had to ride with the Pakis, and they took the worst roads I'd ever seen. There I was, riding in a Mercedes, with one idiot to the right of me, one to the left and three in the front seat.

Sun City was technically in South Africa, but everything in the city was done in Botswana money, including our wrestling payoffs. We had to change our Botswana money into South African rands. To do that, we had to go to this remote outpost in the damn jungle, where there were baboons, lions and every other goddamned animal you can think of.

The Pakis were not happy. They only drew a crowd of about 300 for the show, and they'd laid out all this money, so I was telling them what great guys they were and laughing at their shitty jokes.

After getting the money in rands, I had to take it to a South African bank and have it transferred to my bank in the States, my money and Hulk's, because I couldn't change it into dollars there. They said the transfer would take 10 days to two weeks.

About two days after I got home, I got a call from Hogan's mama.

"Where's Terry's money?"

"Well, ma'am," I said, "it's gonna be here. It's gonna be a little while."

It finally came, though, and I sent it to him.

The mere fact that we actually got paid made that trip better than my other excursion into Africa a couple of years earlier. That one was a trip to Nigeria, the true asshole of the world, for wrestler/promoter "Power Mike," the most rotten son of a bitch in the world.

Junior and I should have known something was wrong on the plane over there. We were nearly there, and all the natives in their suits got up and went to the bathroom. They came out wearing all their crazy-ass African costumes. I swear, they had bones in their necks and all that shit!

We stayed at the Holiday Inn in Lagos, Nigeria. We would turn on the TV and see the "picnic at the beach," which was where they had 30 or so people, criminals I guess, tied to posts. People would be having lunch in this field, while soldiers would walk by the people who were tied to stakes in the ground, and shoot them. It was public execution while people were dining.

Frenchy Bernard was on the tour with us. He was the referee, and we were going to a small town called Katana, about 70 miles from Lagos. It was an all-day trip. We were in this bus, and about halfway there, Frenchy said, "My God. Look out there. It's a body!"

I looked, and sure enough, there was a dead body.

I said, "Hey, there's a body on the side of the road!"

The driver didn't say a word. He just kept on going. On our way back, two days later, I looked out the window when we got to the same spot, and there was the damn body, except by now, someone had stolen the dead man's clothes, and some animal had eaten a big chunk out of his torso.

At the Holiday Inn, we'd sit back and drink beer when we weren't working. When you had a bottle of beer outside there, you had to put your thumb over the opening when you weren't drinking, because that was the only way to keep flies from flying down into the bottle!

I sent my clothes off once to be washed, and the dirty bastards stole my clothes! They sent back what they didn't want.

One night, we went to eat, and they brought us a plate of hors d'oerves, with little toothpicks in these small pieces of meat.

I said, "What is this?"

The waiter said, "Oh, it's very good! Bush meat!"

"OK," I said, and tried one.

"Well, this is good," I said. "What is it?"

"Oh, in America, you call it 'rat.'"

Goofy sons of bitches!

One time, I asked one of the locals, "So what do you do for fun?"

The guy told me, "Oh, we have betel nuts and palm wine. Very, very crazy, but you chew the betel nut too much, and your teeth get black."

"Well," I said, "Give me some of that betel nut, and some of that palm wine. Let's try that shit out!"

I went to my room, locked myself in and secured the windows, in case I got all goofy and decided to climb out, or something. Then, I chewed the betel nuts and drank the palm wine.

The next morning, I woke up to find I had chewed a hole in the mattress the size of an orange.

The big show had drawn something like 90,000 people, or some ungodly number, in a soccer field, and so we were looking forward to a good payday. Well, the naira had to be changed into pounds, and the pounds had to be changed into dollars, but Power Mike was going to handle all of that. Every damned dollar managed to get lost in translation, though. Power Mike did nothing, except live well!

And then when the tour was over, we had to leave through the Lagos Airport. Try getting out of that son of a bitch sometime!

But all in all, I thought everything went well in Africa my second time, especially for Hogan. But when Hogan got to Japan, he did some interviews that really kind of pissed me off! He was telling the reporters he had beaten me in two straight falls! I thought, "That son of a bitch!"

Keep in mind—he was working for Inoki, so he was on the other side from me. Not long after, he and I were in Japan at the same time and I went looking for him in his hotel room. I ran through the door and nobody was there.

Looking back, I'm kind of glad no one was there, because I might have been the one who went out the window, 30-something stories above the ground. It's funny how you can look back on stuff like that and laugh. I was not happy at the time, but it's just the kind of shit that takes place in this business.

I actually was the one who connected Hulk Hogan with Sylvester Stallone for the part of "Thunderlips" in *Rocky III*. Stallone called me up and said he needed a huge wrestler for the part of, well, a huge wrestler. I gave him a few names, and it came down to Sly choosing between Hogan and Gorilla Monsoon, whom Vince McMahon Sr. suggested. Gorilla was a tall mountain of a man, but Stallone wanted a more muscular guy, and so he went with Hogan. I tried in 1985 to get Kerry Von Erich the part of the Russian boxer that Dolph Lundgren eventually got. Sly was in love with the guy, but Kerry couldn't memorize any lines.

But Hogan made the most out of his stardom.

When we had our match in late 1985, on the fourth NBC *Saturday Night's Main Event*, we worked together fine, and I never had anything but a good relationship with Hogan when we were both in the WWF.

I got the *Saturday Night's Main Event* assignment because nobody else wanted to do the job, and Vince wanted Hogan going over cleanly for the TV audience. A lot of guys felt like getting beaten in front of such a big audience would hurt their personas.

There were no volunteers, except for the Funker. They asked me to put him over on national TV, and I said, "No problem at all."

Most of my early matches in the WWF, however, were part of my feud with Sylvester Ritter, the Junkyard Dog. On my debut, they had me attack black ring announcer Mel Phillips to set up my feud with Junkyard Dog, a black super-hero of sorts.

The Phillips deal and the ensuing feud had some racial overtones. I've never been a prejudiced person, but I didn't have any qualms about the racial angle. Believe me, I have been on the receiving end of prejudice. I know what it's like not to get the fair shake. The biggest misconception among the American wrestlers when I wrestled in Japan was that we were on equal footing with the Japanese from a business perspective. I have a lot of friends over there, but not everyone was equal in Japan. They felt like it was their country, and they were going to take the lion's share of the money, and the lion's share of the matches, and they did. And I'm not talking about the public, because the general public there was wonderful, but in business that was the way it was. So I have experienced prejudice, and I know it's an awful thing.

But a racial angle could be a wonderful thing, if it was handled properly. You had to have your minority hero overcome the racial overtones for it to work, though. Now in the year 2005, it would be utterly ridiculous to do an angle like that, because the whole issue is in a different place in our society. In those days, and back to the 1960s and 1970s, a well-executed racial angle was probably one of the better things pro wrestling could show our society. The guy would come in with the strong racial overtones, whether against Hispanic or black people, and then gets the crap knocked out of him. That sounds funny, but people weren't that used to seeing a black man beat the crap out of a bigoted white man.

In our Amarillo territory, Thunderbolt Patterson, a charismatic black wrestler and an amazing talker, had more heat than anyone else when he was a heel for us in the late 1960s. It took a lot of guts for him to do that, because almost every night he had a riot. One night we were in Albuquerque, and the place was packed to the rafters. We had a hot finish planned, with him going over my brother in a tag match.

When his hand was raised, the riot started. Thunderbolt tried to get through, but the fans kept closing in more and more. Junior and I were even trying to make room for him! Finally we were closed in, so Thunderbolt reached into his tights, pulled out a Derringer, fired twice into the ceiling and screamed, "All right, back up, motherfuckers!"

Those fans parted for him like he was Moses and they were the Red Sea.

He and Ernie Ladd were the first prominent black heels in the United States, and I thought my father was very innovative in positioning Thunderbolt that way. He carried heavy heat, but when he finally turned, he became one of the biggest heroes the territory had ever seen.

When he fought racist heels like J.C. Dykes and the Infernos, or the Von Brauners, it was like everyone in the crowd was with him, wanting to see him beat the bigots. I think it helped black Americans, because the heels knocked the black babyfaces but always got their comeuppance. And the white fans would even pull for the black man, because the white heel was so rotten, at a time when acceptance of a black athlete by white fans was something that wasn't usual.

My series with JYD did some good business. At that time, there was an "A" crew and a "B" crew, with Hogan always heading the "A" shows. JYD and I were the main event for the "B" shows, and we held our own.

Shortly after I got to the WWF, they put me with Jimmy Hart as my manager. I didn't think I needed a manager, because I could do my own talking, but almost all the heels had managers at that point.

And one of the longtime heel managers, Lou Albano, was now a babyface as a result of the big MTV feud with Hulk Hogan, Roddy Piper and Cyndi Lauper. That feud went a long way toward putting WWF on the map.

Albano ended up managing George "The Animal" Steele, who was a Michigan high school teacher named Jim Meyer who only wrestled in the summer. George was one of the true geniuses of the business, because George "The Animal" Steele convinced everyone that he was a teacher pretending to be an animal. In reality, he was an animal pretending to be a teacher! That's what I accuse him of every time I see him.

Steele was feuding at the time with Nikolai Volkoff, a big Russian wrestler. Here he was, the terrible, brutal Russian, doing all his power moves on his opponent. And then, out of nowhere, here came a cartwheel! He'd be working along, getting heat, and then out of the clear blue, he did a cartwheel. It had nothing to do with the match. I don't know what crossed his mind. Maybe he had hopes of joining the Cirque du Soleil. Maybe he knew where wrestling was headed and was determined to be the pioneering WWF acrobat!

I saw a lot of my old friends in wrestling while I was in the WWF, including tough guy Adrian Adonis. He was an absolute maniac. I had known him for years, and he always wanted to ride with me.

Jimmy Hart and I had been riding together to a town in New York, and when we were getting ready to head to Newark, N.J., Adrian said, "Hey, can I ride with you guys?"

I said, "Sure. Come on."

Boy, he was happy about that, so he got a case of beer and a five-foot submarine sandwich. I remember thinking, "What in the hell does a guy need with a five-foot sandwich?"

He put that thing in the car, propped on a board, and it reached all the way from the dashboard, back into the back seat. It was sliced in four-inch sections, and I ate one four-inch piece and drank two of the beers. Jimmy Hart ate one four-inch piece of the sandwich and he didn't drink.

Adrian Adonis ate all 52 inches that were left of that sandwich and drank the rest of the case of beer.

Then he decided he wanted to drive! Before that, he had me pulling over every 10 minutes, because he had to take another piss, so I had gotten to where I was too tired to drive. Jimmy Hart was asleep in the back seat.

I was too tired to argue, so I said, "OK, Adrian, you drive."

He was going down the damn road at 105 miles an hour, when he passed a Connecticut police car, waving at the damn cops as he drove by!

They pulled him over, of course, and ended up putting him in the back of their car.

One of the officers told me, "We have to take him in."

They took Adrian to jail, and I drove to the jailhouse to get him out.

They were giving him a drunk test at the police station, and Adrian was farting so bad it was awful, but the cops were all thrilled to meet the WWF star Adrian Adonis. His farts were godawful—they smelled like those Chinese eggs that are 2,000 years old, or whatever they are, but those cops were lining up to get his autograph, and they didn't even seem to mind his gas!

But they still had to test him, so Jimmy and I sat there, waiting, and I thought, "Damn, we are going to be here forever. He's gonna be in jail, and I don't know how we're gonna get him out."

A few minutes later, here came Adrian—he'd passed every single one of their tests. All I can think is that the bread from the 52 inches of sandwich he ate absorbed the case of beer (minus my two) that he drank.

God bless him, he was a slob. Sometimes we'd be in a restaurant and he'd have his plate cleaned off within minutes, and he'd start reaching over and eating off of my plate!

Adrian really kept me on my toes, too, even though I never wrestled against him there. I was never sure if he was admiring my work, playing a rib on me, or trying to drive me nuts, but every night, he would watch my match. The next night, he would do all of the spots he had watched me do the night before, so I had to come up with a completely different match with the Junkyard Dog that night. The next night, he'd do all the new spots I had done the night before, and I'd have to change all of my spots again.

Adrian's gimmick changed in 1985, when he went from being a leather-wearing tough guy, to an obese cross-dresser, wearing a dress, makeup and everything. You might think he hated that gimmick, but I think he was utterly elated. That nut absolutely loved that, because if anyone was misanthropic, he was. Adrian didn't care to fit in anywhere.

Adrian was a tough guy, but he found out the hard way that he wasn't as tough as Dan Spivey. They ended up in a beef over a match they had, where Adrian wouldn't sell for Dan. And Dan didn't do anything about it in the ring. He worked the rest of the match like the true professional that he was, but he sure did something about it in the dressing room. When they both got back there, Spivey beat the living crap out of Adrian. Spivey busted him up and just beat on him until he didn't feel like beating on him anymore. It didn't take long, either. It was a pretty short fight.

I actually had wrestled Spivey in his first match for the WWF, in a little town in New York. I had to show him how to do every damn thing. Boy, he was green.

"Spivey, take the headlock."

"Loosen up a little bit, Spivey."

"Now take me over, Spivey."

He was such a nice guy, too, although Adonis probably wouldn't have agreed. Everything with Spivey was, "Yes, sir, Mr. Funk."

Spivey was a tough guy and a phenomenal athlete. A lot of people forget that he was an All-American football player as a sophomore at the University of Georgia. He probably could have played pro ball if he hadn't torn up his knee in college. He was still a good hand in the ring, though.

Later on I helped him get into Japan, and he really proved himself there. He worked his ass off for All Japan, absorbed a lot of physical punishment and was one of the company's harder in-ring performers (and that was quite a statement, in that company). As a result, he became very successful there, but the punishment cut his career short, and he was out of the profession by the mid-1990s. But he didn't let wrestling rule his life, and he ended up becoming a big success in the construction business in Florida. He went down the road, which is a tough thing for a lot of wrestlers to do. He still stays in touch with a lot of the guys, including me, but he doesn't look back. He doesn't linger, and I find that very admirable about him.

Spivey's tag partner, Mike Rotunda was another one—a smart guy and a great athlete. He made a lot easier transition than a lot of people have, from being a great amateur wrestler (at the University of Syracuse) to a very good pro. He also watched his money very well over the years. I can promise you, if Mike's not working right now, his family's not going hungry, because he's been very smart with his money.

Paul Orndorff was another nut, and tough on top of it, as his car found out one day when he got caught in traffic on the way to a show. He got in such a rage that he ripped the steering wheel right out of the car. Then he started reading The Bible. He said it calmed him. Paul was also the kind of guy who'd fight anyone. He didn't care if you knew more wrestling than him—he was going to beat your ass. Don't get the wrong idea—he was a great guy, but everyone knew you didn't mess with Paul.

Don Muraco was another crazy man, and another guy you wouldn't want to meet in a dark alley. He was a true Hawaiian and didn't care about much. Muraco was such a great worker, but he had that island attitude, and when he was ready to go back to the island for a while, he went back. He never let anything get to him, because he knew he could always go home and go surfing if he wanted to.

Like with the NWA championship, the thing that finally wore me out was all the travel. If anything, the travel with the WWF was tougher than it was when I'd been champion a decade earlier. The WWF schedule had us taking a plane and going to a town, taking a plane, going to another town, and so on, constantly. When I was NWA champion, there were many times when I'd go into a territory for a week at a time. If it was Florida, I might do a night in Tampa, then work Jacksonville and drive back to Tampa. I could work several cities but head back to Tampa each night, sleep in until noon and then head out to the next show in Orlando, or wherever. Each territory had a base. The WWF had no base. It was everywhere!

Between the big paydays and the crazy travel, it was too much for some. A lot of the boys practically exploded from the combination of money and pressure. I saw a lot more drug use than I'd ever seen by the guys, on the whole. It was a situation that no one alerted Vince to that I know of. It stayed among the boys, and it got heavy at that time. And Vince was insanely busy, trying to run every aspect of this huge show. Would Vince have intervened, if he'd seen a problem? I don't know, but I'd like to think so. Vince had road agents, guys who went on the road who were supposed to keep the guys in line. I think they were the ones who slipped, who maybe weren't as observant as they could have been.

The road agents knew of some of the issues and instances involving drug problems, but they tried to handle those things themselves. I think they were afraid if they told Vince, he might think they weren't doing their jobs controlling the guys on the road. When they were asked, it was "all clear" on their front. Except it wasn't.

You can talk about drug testing, and I think there's a point where it becomes necessary, but in 1985 we were a couple of years into a thing that was red hot, and everyone was blowing and going. I'd been around drugs, seen them, and had partaken of them a little bit earlier in my life, but certainly don't now. My drug use had pretty much been confined to that time in 1973 right after my divorce, when I weighed 195 pounds and went to Florida. There were drugs everywhere there. The whole state was running amok, on cocaine, marijuana and everything else. And even then, I was never a big drug user.

I went to parties and all that shit, but when I became NWA champion, there was no time for drugs. And when I got back with Vicki, there was no way that stuff was going to ruin my life. Even if I had wanted for it to, it wasn't going to happen.

In the 1970s, not long after we got back together, I got back home from several dates I had been working. I had some pot in my bag, and I said, "Hey, Vicki, you want to smoke some pot?"

She said, "Terrence, you really have some pot, do you?"

"Yeah, I sure do."

"Let me see it."

So I handed her my little plastic bag with the marijuana in it. She opened the bag, sniffed it, then walked into the bathroom and dumped the bag's contents into the commode.

As she flushed it away, she yelled, "Don't you ever bring that stuff in my house again!"

And I damn sure didn't.

Besides, once our family was back together, I truly realized life was the greatest trip of all. I think that's one of the reasons that I'm still alive and a lot of the boys I worked with, including guys younger than me, are not.

There were several guys on steroids, but I guess I was lucky when it came to steroids. Actually, I was lucky in a lot of ways—I was born into the business, and my father knowing the other promoters gave me a two- or three-year head start.

My first experience with steroids was in college, although I didn't know what they were. In 1964, we were playing for West Texas State and the doctor said, "We've got this stuff called dianabol. It's supposed to make you stronger and gain weight. Do you want to try it?"

Now, no one knew then the harmful side effects of the steroids, so hell yes, I wanted to try it! So did most of the guys on the team. It wasn't illegal, and there was nothing wrong with it, as far as we knew.

I took them for about five days, and I thought, "Geez, I'm not any stronger. This shit don't work."

I threw them away. Some of the guys who stayed on them got stronger and bigger, but that's how unknown steroids were back then. Later, when I got into the business, hell, we were too busy shooting jackrabbits and drinking beer on the side of the road to think about steroids or anything else.

I'll be honest, if I'd been 20 years old when steroids became better known and someone told me they were my ticket to getting into the business and having a good 15- to 20-year run, but it might cut some time off my life, I would have probably taken them. Fortunately, I was a little older, and pretty well established by the time all these other guys were taking them, and I just didn't have any interest.

There was only one other time I took steroids. In 1989, I broke my sacrum in a match with Sting, and it was the most painful thing I'd ever felt in my entire life. One of the NWA wrestlers (who I won't name), a good friend of mine, gave me some tablets and said, "Terry, I really think these things will promote healing."

I ended up losing them a few days later, in a North Carolina airport, after airport security found them. The police asked me about them, and I told them the truth, without naming the guy who gave them to me. I just said I had been given the pills to heal my injured sacrum.

One officer looked at me and said, "You sure don't look like you take them," and they let me go, without the pills, of course.

But getting back to 1986, my time in the WWF was coming to an end. It just got to the point that I was working on a run of God-only-knows how many days without a break, without getting home even once, and there was no end in sight. The travel had gotten to me, and I'd finally had enough.

One night I was splitting a room with Jimmy Hart. He was in one bed, and I was in the other, and I set my alarm for 6 a.m., hoping Jimmy would go right back to sleep. I snuck in the bathroom, packed my bags, shut off the light in the bathroom and started heading out of the door with my bags.

Just then, Jimmy sat up and said, "Terry? Where are you going?"

"Jimmy," I said, "you caught me. I can't take it anymore. I'm going home, going back to my girls."

CHAPTER 20

Terry Funk, Part-Time Wrestler

After leaving the WWF in 1986, I spent a lot of time at the ranch, only leaving for brief stints of wrestling.

One of those turned out to be my last trip ever for the World Wrestling Council, and my last trip to Puerto Rico until 2002, when I went in for a shot for the IWA. I wrestled Barry Windham and Carlos Colon, and even in 1987, the fans where still crazy.

It ended up being my last WWC trip because of what happened to my old West Texas alum, Frank Goodish—Bruiser Brody. In 1988, Brody was stabbed to death in a locker room bathroom by WWC booker Jose Gonzales. Jose was eventually found not guilty by reason of self defense, which surprised me. I did not believe he would be acquitted.

The thing that still haunts me is, what brought Gonzales to the point of doing what he did to Bruiser Brody? Was it fear, or was it hatred? I'm not knowledgeable enough about the situation, even after talking to the wrestlers I knew who were in the locker room when it happened, to really have an answer to that. But it is beyond my conception that someone could take a life in anything except a completely self-defensive situation.

I had always enjoyed my trips there, and it was always a good place to make a buck, but what happened to Brody took the fun out of it.

I was never someone who made a point of saying publicly, "I'm never going down there again," but I just didn't want to.

A year before he died, Brody ended up back with Giant Baba, in All Japan, after a tumultuous split.

Brody had ended up burning his bridges in Japan, by jumping to Inoki's side in 1985 and then wanting to jump back. When he returned, he went back for the same amount he had been getting when he left in 1985. He talked to me about it, after starting to work for Inoki, and he felt he had made a mistake by going there. He realized he would have been better off just staying where he was.

Junior and I both talked to Baba, trying to get him to take Brody back. Bruiser was talented, and I don't think he felt that they were pushing him as well as they could have. I agreed with Brody—Inoki didn't really have any plans to make Brody a top superstar. His main benefit from having Brody was just that he had taken him from Baba.

I truly believe that if Brody hadn't been killed, he'd have made one hell of a run in the WWF, for Vince Jr. He certainly had shown no signs of wavering up to the end of his life.

Brody was coming back in just as I was making my last shots as one of Baba's soldiers in 1987. After all that time, Baba felt it was time to de-emphasize me, and I knew it. I wasn't going to allow them to take me back to absolutely nothing. I felt like I'd paid my dues, and it was just time to go. My relationship with Baba had really grown strained over the years, from when I was on "Wildside" at a period when he wanted 100 percent of my time. Also, since Stan Hansen had started there in 1981, he had pretty much become the leading American for Baba. Baba felt like he could do without me, and I felt that I could do just as well without him.

And I had been instrumental in bringing Hansen in, along with my brother, and when we did, there was no doubt in my mind that the route we were taking would be to make Hansen the superstar, and that was all right with me, so I never had any hard feelings for Stan, or for Baba, for that matter. But at the time, I didn't feel I was ready to be put to pasture. Baba felt like I was just an old dog, and I felt like the old dog had a few tricks left.

Around the time all this was going on in All Japan, something happened in New Japan that changed the course of the business.

After a couple of years with Baba, Choshu (and most of the crew that went with him) had come back to New Japan. In a tag match, Akira Maeda kicked Riki Choshu full out, cracking his orbital bone. Maeda was fired, but ended up starting a group called UWF that worked a slower style that looked more like a shoot.

The UWF was actually a restart of a similar promotion that popped up a few years earlier. This time, though, Maeda had convinced people he was the real deal, and he and the UWF were box-office magic for a few years.

We'll never know what went into that kick, but I'd guess Maeda decided that Choshu just needed to be kicked. And he damn sure kicked him!

What surprised me was that Choshu never went after him. That was the thing I never understood, because getting kicked full in the face would anger me. I think I would have had to have a second time around with that boy. When my bones mended, I think I would have gotten right out of bed and gone looking for that son of a bitch! And Choshu was a tough guy.

A couple of months before that happened, in August 1987, I found myself working one last WWF show. It was in Houston, for a show commemorating the retirement of Paul Boesch. A few months earlier, Boesch had switched from Watts' Mid-South (which had become the Universal Wrestling Federation in 1986, not to be confused with Maeda's UWF) to McMahon's WWF. But now, he was calling it a career.

Halfway during the show, they had a ceremony in the ring for Paul, with a lot of his old friends. One of them was Verne Gagne—a bitter enemy of the WWF, standing in the WWF's ring! It took a hell of a man to get him there.

Verne Gagne, Gene Kiniski, Lou Thesz, Danny McShain and the rest of them were there because they knew it was the end of something special, something they only had a chance to deal with on occasion in their careers—an honest man. And Paul was an honest man, to the penny, throughout his entire career, and he took care of people when he really didn't have to.

CHAPTER 21

On the NWA's Side

After I finished up *Road House* in late 1988, I was working out every day, several hours a day. I'd been doing 1,000 crunches a day, every day for years. And I was ready to get back into the ring.

Here I was, 225 pounds, in the best shape of my life, and Dave Meltzer, in his *Observer* newsletter, said I was "too skinny!" Skinny, hell! I had well-defined muscles—hell, I had abs, for the first time!

I also started back into wrestling, first in Dusty Rhodes's group in Florida. The old Championship Wrestling from Florida office closed down in late 1987 and a year later left Dusty the promotion on TBS that used the NWA name, although the old coalition of promoters using that name was no more. Dusty formed a new Florida office in 1989 and asked me to come in and work some shots with him and his son, Dustin, who was a rookie wrestler with a lot of promise.

We did some pretty creative stuff. On one spot, I was about to drag Dusty behind my pickup truck, but he somehow got himself untied and got away. I wish he hadn't (just kidding, Dusty!).

Working with Dustin was an experience, because I'd known him since he was a child. He would turn out to be an excellent worker, and although he was a little green in 1989, his potential was obvious.

For Dustin, overcoming the shadow of the American Dream was always difficult. With me, I went out from Amarillo, where Dad tended to stay, so it was easier for me to overcome the image of my father. With Dustin, his pop had worked on top in all the areas where Dustin found himself now trying to get over. It was hard for Dustin to overcome his dad's notoriety and force of personality. It wasn't a matter of ability, because Dustin was damn good in the ring.

If Dustin had been able to come along when his father was at his peak in the late 1970s and early 1980s, I think he would have melded a lot easier. Sometimes it's easier when you're with the legend than it is to follow the legend. You get the rub from being with that legend, and there's also not the same type of comparison. You're not trying to live up to people's gilded memories of what the legend was like. But when people saw Dusty for years, and then Dusty was gone, and then Dustin appeared, the comparison was inevitable.

Dustin bleached his hair like Dusty's and had a lot of the same moves, but could not become a duplicate of his father, and the best thing he ever did in wrestling was to quit trying to be a duplicate of Dusty. In 1995, Dustin went to the WWF and became Goldust, a really flamboyant character that was totally different than anything he had portrayed previously. I truly believe Goldust was one of the greatest characters in wrestling, and I don't think people realize that this guy was doing something quite special. I give Vince McMahon credit for creating the idea of Goldust, but it was Dustin who brought Goldust to life, and it worked because he was good enough to make it work. A lot of people think that was a stupid, absurd character, but I thought it was great. And he did a great job with it. I think that character could have gotten pushed to greater heights than it ever was, but Vince put limitations on Dustin's push, because of what the character of Goldust was. If Goldust, as the exact same type of character, had debuted in late 1997, instead of late 1995, I think he would have been a huge deal from a box-office perspective. But in 1996, just as the character was taking off, Vince just didn't want the kind of flak that character was getting, and he toned it down.

Not long after I finished up with Dusty, I got a call from Jim Herd, the TBS executive running WCW (still calling itself the NWA) after TBS bought it from Jim Crockett, to come in for a Clash of the Champions show on April 2, 1989, where they wanted to honor past NWA world champions. I also announced the main event of Ric Flair versus Ricky Steamboat, with Jim Ross.

Steamboat was a world-class pro wrestler and a hell of a guy. He was one of the few guys I know of who never turned, over the course of his career (Bruno Sammartino was another). I think he would have made a hell of a heel, because it is the guy who grows to learn babyface crowd psychology who can become a great heel by doing the opposite, or depriving the people of what they want to see. But he was a career babyface, and I think it was because he was such an asset as a babyface to whomever he worked for that it just never crossed their minds to turn him. That also says a lot about Steamboat's ability to get over and stay over. A lot of guys have to be turned, or have to leave an area, so they can be fresh, either in the opposite role after turning, or in their new area. But Steamboat was able to stay over, to the extent that he spent years in the Carolinas in the 1970s and 1980s as a top babyface, and I think he was more over when he first retired in late 1983 than he was in 1977, when he got his first huge push.

A month after the best-of-three-falls match, they wanted me back to "judge" the last Flair-Steamboat rematch on their "Wrestle War 89" pay per view, with the storyline being I would help determine a winner of the match if it was a time-limit draw. They also wanted me to do an angle with Flair, and they wanted me to serve as a member of the booking committee. That appealed to me, because I thought it would be a chance to use some creativity.

The booking committee was me, Ric Flair, Jim Ross, Kevin Sullivan, Jim Cornette and a few other guys. They didn't exactly work together, though. There was a lot of division and conflict within that committee. I had no idea I was walking into a loaded situation, because the committee wasn't in agreement with Herd. I walked into my first meeting, completely unaware of the problems. When Herd talked to me about coming in, he'd made it sound as if things were as smooth as glass. I ended up being the outside individual, almost alone, compared to everyone else in there. What was asked of me ended up being damn near nothing. It was a pretty shocking situation.

The conflict seemed to be a power struggle between the committee and Herd. The members of the committee, all of whom had put in years in the wrestling business, felt Herd was inept. Herd, a former St. Louis TV station manager and executive with Pizza Hut, was fighting to show he was boss. If everyone had been on the same page, I think we'd have had a much stronger product.

Jim Herd was as qualified to run that company as anybody whom Turner would have put in that position. Anybody put in that position was going to have problems. Especially a non-wrestling person is going to have to be led. Because of the shape the thing was in by the time I got there, I don't know if they had tried to lead him in the right way and educate him into the business, or if they just tried to muscle him around, or if he had tried to muscle them around. To this day, I don't know what happened between those people before I got there.

All I knew that on one side was Jim Herd, who had just signed me to one of the better deals I've had in my life, and on the other was people in the business I knew and respected.

Not long after I started, Kevin Sullivan approached me before a meeting and said, "I just need to know one thing, whose side are you on?"

I said, "What? I'm on the NWA's side!"

He said, "No, that's not what I mean! Are you on our side, or Jim Herd's?"

"I'm on the NWA's side!"

I thought that was the most ridiculous question I'd ever heard, but my answer was not the politically correct answer. But I'm not a dummy. I saw that the best thing I could do, for myself, was to keep from falling into one side or the other.

And there were some very creative guys on that committee! Kevin Sullivan was one of the greatest idea men I've ever known. He had a gazillion creative ideas and could go one after the other, never running out! Here's an idea you wrestling fans might not know was Kevin's—Goldberg. The undefeated streak was Kevin's idea, and it was the last thing in WCW that really got over like a million bucks. It was a very basic thing, but something that really worked. That idea made a ton of money for WCW before they found a way to screw it up, although that wasn't Kevin's fault.

The thing about Sullivan was, someone had to be there to separate the good ones from the bad. I'd recommend Sullivan for a booking committee anywhere, even today. He just needs to be regulated, is all.

There was such a mix of strong personalities on that committee that there was no one boss, no one steering the ship. Herd thought that booking committee was the way to go, because when he was an executive at Pizza Hut that was how they did things. For the wrestling business, a committee like that needs a strong leader, someone who can control and fire the other members of the committee and who could make the final decisions, instead of having eight people who wanted to go in eight directions. But you weren't going to fire Ric Flair, the world's champion (although Herd did just that in 1991). You weren't going to fire me, not in the middle of such a hot program with Flair. That concept just doesn't work in wrestling.

And again, you don't need guys booking who are working in the ring.

Here's an example of how little control over things I had. I brought in a talented young man to wrestle, and even though he put me over in his first match, I thought his talents were obvious, but they never brought him back. His name was Eddie Guerrero. Maybe you've heard of him.

I hadn't brought Eddie in just to do a job for me. It wasn't like I was sitting around one day and had the brilliant idea to bring in Eddie just so I could beat him up on TV. I knew he was a hell of a worker, because I had watched his early matches, and I told Herd and the rest of them, "This guy's got it. He's really good."

I thought the world of his work, and I was shocked that he didn't get an offer after our match. I did everything I could do to get him in there, which shows you how much influence I had as a member of the booking committee.

Eddie, of course, ended up making his own way, as part of a great tag team with Art Barr in Mexico, and then (after Art passed away) a great talent with ECW, WCW and WWE, where he finally rose to the top.

I also couldn't do much to help my old friend Dick Murdoch. Dick was working for the NWA in 1989, but he didn't last long after I got there.

We were having one of our meetings in the dressing room, with Herd trying to figure out what was wrong with the company, when Murdoch walked by. Herd had always liked Murdoch, so he called him in and said, "Dick, come in here and tell us what you think is wrong with the business."

Murdoch said, "Well, Jim, it's you. You don't know a goddamned thing about this business."

Well, hell, that was the truth! Jim Herd's idea of a good concept for professional wrestling was the Ding Dongs, a tag team that wore little bells all over their costume!

But for Murdoch, that was also the wrong thing to say. About a month later, Dick was let go. I still loved Murdoch, and he was probably right, but I couldn't blame Herd. Hell, that's not what you want to hear from one of your workers.

After Murdoch left TBS, he went to work for the Coors distributorship in Amarillo. He was the Coors goodwill ambassador, which meant his job was to go from bar to bar, buying Coors for people everywhere he went. It was the perfect job for Murdoch—$90,000 a year, and all he had to do was go to bars and say, "Hey, how are you, pal? You'd better drink a Coors. Here—let me buy you a beer. Let's have one together."

That was his job!

Coors sponsored a rodeo in Amarillo, and Dick was there. So was this guy who was a bit of an asshole. He was in the stands, cussing at everyone and just being obnoxious. Right in front of 3,000 people in the stands, Dick just beat the shit out of the guy.

Vance Reed, who owned the distributorship, was there. He wasn't thrilled, but Vance was a great guy, so he let that one pass. A short time later, Dick took his new pickup truck to the distributorship, where they had these huge delivery trucks. They also had a high-pressure wash system for the trucks, and Dick told one of the guys there to wash his truck.

The guy said, "We're not supposed to wash people's pickup trucks."

"Goddammit, wash my truck! Get the thing in there and wash it!"

So the guy washed the truck, and the high-pressure system blasted all the paint off of it. Dick took the truck and had the body shop repaint it. Then, he sent the $2,800 bill to Coors!

Needless to say, Dick was not the Coors goodwill man for much longer.

It ended up that just about the only thing I could affect was the stuff I was doing in the ring, although that was the program with Flair, which I was pretty pleased with. The program itself, after the initial attack, was my direction. It started when I came in the ring after Flair regained the title from Steamboat and challenged the new champion. When he pointed out that I'd been in Hollywood and out of wrestling for a few years and needed to work my way into contention, I went berserk and attacked him, piledriving him onto a table. It ended with Flair being carried out while I screamed, "He said I wasn't good enough!"

The story was, the attack would leave Flair injured for several weeks, and they would tease that the injury was serious enough that he might have to retire, before he came back and got his revenge on me. While he was out, I cut some really intense promos on Flair, including one where I brought out a skinny Ric Flair imposter with a yellow stripe painted down his back.

Flair was really bothered by this stuff, and I was told to tone it down a little bit. I didn't see the problem, because I was the heel—the ending was going to be that Flair was going to kick my ass! I sure wasn't going to say all these outrageous things, only to beat up Ric Flair and then go home and hang up my tights.

I don't know if Flair was upset because he was insecure, or because he wasn't there. You see, he was home, selling the injury angle, and all he knew about what I was doing was what he saw on TV. All he saw was me blasting him every week. With all the divisions in WCW at that time, I wouldn't be surprised if he thought I was working on behalf of someone else there to make him look bad. He had been having his problems with Jim Herd even then, fighting over his contract, which Herd thought was too much money for him to make.

All that stuff was done to create a heated atmosphere for our match. If it hurt him, that certainly wasn't my intent. I'm certainly not sitting here apologizing, because I didn't see any real damage that was done to him. I did it as a kick in the ass for business. I had certainly done heavy heel promos like that and had never hurt a babyface before. I never did hear about Dusty Rhodes being upset about the things I'd say about him, because he understood it was business to build up revenue at the box office. And while the Funk-Flair feud did very strong business, I think its box office was hurt by me having to tone down the heat.

I'd toned down promos a few times before when the heat got to be too much, particularly in Puerto Rico, but I had never before had to take it down a notch because someone's feelings were hurt.

I wasn't the only one Flair had a problem with that year. There was a lot of heat between Flair and Paul Heyman, known then in wrestling as "Paul E. Dangerously," manager of the Samoan Swat Team. What was Paul E.'s heat with Flair over? Hell if I know, but one night, they were screaming at each other in the dressing room, and not long after, Paul E. was out of WCW. It was a definite personality clash.

Paul E. was young guy who would play a big role in my professional life. I knew right away that he was nuts. The thing that really showed me that was when he rented a car on his credit card and let the Samoan Swat Team drive it on their own.

About $4,000 worth of damage later, the car was sitting in front of the rent-a-car place, and Paul E. realized he had made a mistake. Sometimes, Paul E. was not the genius many people think he is! But when it came to wrestling, the guy had a feel for it, a great mind and unlimited energy, as I would find out when I worked for him a few years later.

Regardless of how he felt personally about my promos, Flair was a pleasure to work with. I truly enjoyed every one of our matches. We had some very solid encounters. How could I not love a match when I was in there with one of the best performers in the world?

But I paid a price for those matches. One night I went over the top rope in a match with Sting and hit the rail outside, cracking my sacrum. It wasn't anybody's fault, just a bad landing. I ended up riding around on a plane every day going from town to town, and I couldn't sit on the plane, except for takeoff and landing. The only way I could stand it was to kneel on my seat, facing the person behind me.

I also had a nasty staph infection. I had torn my bursa, and my elbow swelled to the size of a baseball. I got myself some needles from a veterinarian in Amarillo and drained the damn thing myself, every night. I was thinking I was some kind of doctor, but I was almost Doctor Kevorkian, because I almost eliminated myself. While draining the fluid out, I was letting germs in, and the result was a staph infection. I just didn't feel like I had the time to go to a real doctor about it, but Dr. Funk ended up putting me out of action for a couple of weeks. He wasn't one of my better characters.

When I went into shock from it, Paul E. was the one who took me to the hospital. They operated on me, and it was quite a deal. But Paul E. was there for me, when everybody was gone, and he stayed with me. No one else did.

What heat was left after I toned down my interviews for the last couple of weeks built up to a main-event match at the July pay per view, the *Great American Bash '89*. And what I'd said must have done the trick, because the show was a sellout in Baltimore, and it drew the best gate for a live show the company ever had, until 1996.

I had announced a big surprise for Flair, which turned out to be Gary Hart as my manager. Again, I was given a mouthpiece, even though everyone in the company knew I could talk on my own. Why? Hell, I don't know. Ask Jim Herd—or maybe the booking committee!

Gary was a good manager, though. Managers have all but disappeared today, but there used to be a role for a guy who couldn't wrestle but who could talk for a wrestler with limited verbal skills. The best I ever saw was "Wild" Red Berry, who managed the Fabulous Kangaroos. They came through Amarillo when I was a kid, and I was fascinated by him. He threw around big words, half of which weren't even real words! Where he got them from, nobody knows. He mixed in a lot of condescension and made himself a very hated man among wrestling fans.

Another one who was really good was J.C. Dykes, who managed the tag team of The Infernos. The Masked Infernos, in their blue outfits, were Frankie Cain and Rocky Smith. They were really talented guys, and that gimmick was really over for a long time in Florida, because they knew how to get heat, and so did J.C. He did all the talking, which created a kind of mystique about the Infernos.

In 1989, Gary Hart was also managing Keiji Muto, who wrestled as "The Great Muta." He was a hell of a talent, but was kind of standoffish with me at first, since I'd been an All Japan man for years and years, and he was someone Inoki was grooming for stardom in New Japan. Maybe he had a sense of, "What is Funk going to do to me?"

But that soon disappeared, and we worked well together. They used him exclusively as a heel in his year from 1989 to 1990, but he could have been a big babyface, because he was doing flashy moves that no one had ever seen before.

Muto wasn't the only great, young talent I met that year with the NWA. I was also introduced to a young man who would play a big part in my life in years to come—Mick Foley, who wrestled as Cactus Jack.

He introduced himself to me at a company party in late 1989. My first impression of him as a wrestler had actually come about a year earlier. I can't remember where I was, but I was watching the World Class Wrestling show out of Dallas, and there was Cactus Jack. I immediately picked up on him as a major piece of talent. They weren't doing any business, but I saw him and thought, "Damn, that guy's got something," and I knew he wasn't going to wind up working preliminaries for the rest of his life. He really captured my imagination.

And as a person I liked him from the day I met him. He introduced himself at that party (he had only started working for the NWA at that time) and asked me what I thought of his work. I ended up telling him I really thought a lot of his stuff, but I had to give him a hard time first, so my immediate response was, "I think you're the shits."

He also had some serious questions about his work, and how he could get over better. His desire to learn and improve was obvious to anyone who would have taken the time to look at him.

I told him he needed to be more aggressive in the ring, because he'd been letting his opponents punish him in the match, which showed he could sell, but wasn't going to get him over.

He said, "Why?"

I thought, "What am I talking to this guy for? Jesus!"

"All you're doing is having the shit beaten out of you the whole goddamned time," I said to him.

And yet, 15 years later, I look back on wise Terry Funk advising foolish, young Cactus Jack, but who became the rich man first? Hell, maybe I should have been less aggressive! Maybe I'd be as rich as he is.

Another one was Brian Pillman, who would become a good friend.

He was a real character, from the first time I met him. He was a fun guy and never at a loss for words.

He was just a great guy, and he'd call me in the middle of the night and talk about the business for an hour or more.

When Vicki answered the phone, she'd hold the receiver to her chest and whisper to me, "It's Brian Pillman."

"I'll talk to him, honey."

"Terry! You're gonna be on the phone for an hour!"

And she was usually right.

I had a lot of heat with those NWA fans, almost everywhere I went. One night in Marietta, I was on my way to the ring to wrestle Flair, and a woman went after me with a butcher knife. Now, why would she defend a banana-nose instead of a good-looking Funker?

Now, if you'll notice, I did say *almost* everywhere. Flair and I had a match during our 1989 campaign in Amarillo, where no Funk had ever been a heel. Even if I'd wanted to be one that night, those people weren't going to let me. They booed the hell out of Ric Flair! He didn't get flustered, because he understood it, having been through the same kind of thing in the Carolinas. To this day, no matter how big a heel he is everywhere else, they still love him in the Carolinas, and that's how it was for me when he and I wrestled in Amarillo.

The truth was, when I went out to the other territories and played my heel role, that only made me a bigger babyface back home, because a big part of my routine was to talk about how great Amarillo and Texas were, and how crappy every other place was. There was no way I could have ever turned heel in Amarillo. The people just wouldn't have accepted it.

After we did a round of singles matches, we did a tag match at 1989's *Halloween Havoc* pay per view, me and Muta versus Sting and Flair, in a steel cage match with an electrified roof. Well, it was supposed to be an electrified roof, but it kind of went south on us. Our first problem was that there were these crepe paper Halloween decorations in the cage, and the electric fence caught the crepe paper on fire, so they shut off the electricity! It was the damndest pile of crap anybody ever saw in their lives. Nothing worked.

The finish was supposed to be that someone would touch a ball attached to the fence roof, and shocks would fire out and shock the hell out of him, but it didn't work. Actually, I'm kind of glad it didn't work, because I think it was supposed to be me!

They told me before the match that it would really shock me, "but not too bad."

Well, how bad is "too bad?" Fortunately, I never found out. We ended up doing another finish, where Ole Anderson (in Flair's corner) decked Gary Hart (in ours), forcing Gary to throw in the towel for us.

It ended up being one of the most ridiculous damn things I ever participated in, and that covers a lot of ground.

Fortunately, sometimes fans accept things better than you think they will. Cactus Jack and I found out the same thing a few years later, wrestling in an explosives match in Japan, and the damned explosives wouldn't go off! The fans knew it wasn't our fault and accepted it. Maybe the Havoc deal would have worked better if we'd just touched the damn electric ball earlier in the match, shown that it didn't work, and just gone on.

Leading up to the Havoc match, we had a deal where I attacked Flair by putting a plastic bag over his head and suffocating him. That deal could have been extremely hot if TBS had gone along with it. They ended up getting so many complaints about it, they never replayed it. People were calling in and complaining about it so strongly, you'd have thought I was really trying to murder Flair. Maybe the complaints were from Vince McMahon, because that angle did get over.

That was so tame compared to the stuff they do today. If you did that same angle today, they'd just laugh at you.

While all this was going on in 1989, the McMahons were testifying in New Jersey, and to get out of paying taxes to the athletic commission they admitted in public that wrestling was predetermined. Right after I heard about it, I thought it was lousy. Within a few weeks, though, I thought it was one of the wisest things they could have done.

Ultimately, what it did was make the business stronger, because it opened us up to the media. The big issue of whether it was a real sport was gone, and so the media didn't have that to harp on, which meant they could focus on the kinds of stories that could improve public awareness of his business.

It was the smartest thing he could do—not the smartest thing that *we* could do, but it was the smartest thing for him because of the ridiculous commission situation and because of the change in dealing with the media.

The Flair feud wound up with an "I quit" match, where the loser would submit and shake the winner's hand. It was time for me to get my comeuppance, time for Flair to finally go over in a big way, and time for the feud to be over. The idea of doing an "I quit" match was my idea. Actually, I'm the guy who created the "I quit" match in the 1970s, with Dusty Rhodes. We'd sold out the Bayfront Center in Saint Petersburg, Florida, with the match, and I thought it would be an exciting end to the Funk-Flair feud for the fans. This was one of the times I was right, because it was broadcast on WTBS and became the most-watched wrestling match in the history of cable television, up to that point.

In an "I quit" match, two men fight until one says those two words. I thought when I said, "I quit," I'd be quitting the match. I didn't realize Herd's idea was that I was saying, "I quit wrestling."

My age was one of the reasons they wanted to push me out, but the other was that I just did not fit. I didn't belong to one side or the other in those power struggles I described earlier. I wasn't for any group of the wrestlers, or for Jim Herd—I was for the promotion. I really was on the NWA's side.

I was never worried about being ruined by losing a big match, in part because I always believed I could get myself over with the people through my working ability and my interviews. Maybe that was foolish of me. Maybe if I'd been a more selfish guy, I'd have gotten a lot richer. But to me, my way was a successful way. Maybe it came from the way I grew into the business, as the son of a promoter, with the mindset that we had to do business to be able to keep writing checks to all the guys and making a living for ourselves. That sense of putting the company first and helping the company never left me.

After that match, they asked me to do commentary. I finished out my time there by calling matches with Chris Cruise, and then I went home.

They were building up Sting to be the main guy, taking over Flair's spot, but it was too quick of a switch. What ended up happening was, on the February 1990 Clash of the Champions show that was one of my last nights with the company, Flair, Ole and Arn Anderson turned on Sting. It was supposed to lead to Sting taking Flair's championship, but Sting ended up injuring his knee later on the show. He was out for four months, and when he came back that summer, he beat Flair for the belt in his first match.

But with Flair having been such a strong babyface and having that sympathy built up in our feud, Flair was in position to be more over as a babyface than Sting ended up being. It was a premature push for Sting. If they'd taken the time to build to it, then fine, but they rushed right into it. Their feud peaked in that first match, where Sting won, and that was that.

Chris Cruise was easy to work with. He knew his stuff and was a good announcer, and I think I taught him a fair amount. He always listened to me, because if he didn't I would kick him in the ass!

I'm just kidding. He was actually very good, and I was surprised he didn't have a long career behind the microphone.

I saw the writing on the wall, though. They wanted me to take a pay cut, to an announcer's pay, after my year's deal ran out, and I wasn't about to take a cut in salary for all the back-and-forth travel. I felt I could make more money doing other things, picking my shots.

CHAPTER 22

Back to (What Was Left of) the Territories

My next significant wrestling campaign was a return to Memphis in late 1990.

Once again I was working with Lawler, but by now Lawler's was one of the last territories left. Over the 1980s, most of the regions that had thrived for decades died out. The WWF had been gathering momentum as time went by. This is a hard thing for me to say, but not only were they like the circus coming to town on occasion, they also had great performers, better performers overall than anyone else had. McMahon had been picking off the best talent from around the country for years, and the other promoters were left trying to dress up whoever was left over. Well, you can cover a turd in chocolate, but it's still hard to sell. And I'm not talking bad about the other guys, but from top to bottom, Vince had the highest-quality performers.

One of them was Ted DiBiase, whom I'd known since he was a kid. The WWF picked him up in 1987 after they told him McMahon had a gimmick for him that would be McMahon's own, if he was a wrestler. Ted called me and asked what I thought he should do.

I said, "Teddy, make your move, because if he's got something that good in mind for you, you'll be able to set yourself up financially for life in a shorter period of time than any other way. You're not ever going to get another opportunity like this. You'd better get it while you can."

Ted ended up out of the business after hurting his neck in 1993, but he was financially secure because he had spent six years as "The Million-Dollar Man."

The first time I saw him in the role, he fit it like a glove, and I knew he'd made the right choice.

Memphis was the last surviving territory because it was the last one to keep its top star. Lawler had never been pulled out of Memphis because he was part owner of the Memphis promotion, and whether it was 1976, 1981, 1983, 1990, or today, Lawler never changed. I'll tell you something about Jerry Lawler—Lawler, right now, could step into a WWE ring, get on the microphone and cut as good a promo as the top 10 percent. Lawler could get into the ring and work as well as the top 10 percent, if he wanted to, and he can also throw a better punch than 99.9 percent of anyone working today. I worked a show in 2004 with Lawler, and he hadn't skipped a beat.

And there's none better to connive or manipulate than Jerry. Thank God he's never had a reason to put a dagger in my back. And that's a compliment to Lawler, because I've been around the best, the smartest and the slickest.

To be able to survive in Tennessee for as long as Lawler's been able to, you've got to be awful sharp. Hell, Cactus Jack should have taken Lawler as his mentor, instead of me—Mick probably would have ended up owning the wrestling business!

Lawler could also be a hell of an addition to the WWE writing staff. I promise, the only reason he's not doing that is that he has no desire to do that anymore.

In 1990 and early 1991 I was working a Texas versus Tennessee feud with Lawler, and I was teaming up with Eric Embry and Tom Prichard. Embry was a good worker, and Prichard was just great.

I wasn't in Memphis long, but it wasn't because I got sick of it or anything. The plan all along was for me to come in for a short time and help spice things up. It was Lawler's idea, and I think it was a good one.

Just as I hadn't worked in Memphis for some time, I had not worked for Baba in Japan for five years. Andre was also on the tour (one of his last in Japan), and it was one of the last times I ever saw him.

He was hurting so badly, and people would look at him all stooped over and say, "He's not so big."

Let me tell you something. When he was around in the 1970s, he was pretty damn tall. I don't know how tall, but I guarantee he was over seven feet, but that acromegaly that he suffered from made him stoop so badly that he was probably a couple of inches shorter than he'd been several years earlier. I think gravity also took its toll on the massive Andre.

One night, we were on the bus going from one town to the next. Andre brought out a jar and showed it to me. It had all these huge chunks of bone in it. They were pieces that had been taken out of his knee.

Andre was in a lot of pain, but he'd see me and say, "Terry."

"Yeah, hey, Andre."

"You wanna watch a movie?"

"Yeah, Andre. I want to see it."

"OK."

And he put *The Princess Bride* in the machine, and we watched it.

The next day ...

"Hey, Terry. You wanna watch the movie again?"

"Yeah, Andre. Let's watch that movie."

I had to watch that damn movie every damn day of that tour.

Andre would ask, "Hey, Terry. You wanna play cribbage?"

Well, what was I going to say to Andre the Giant?

"You're goddamn right I want to play! Come on, Andre! Let's play some cribbage."

And I stayed in touch with a lot of other people I had met in the business. Brian Pillman still called the house at weird hours, and we'd talk for 60 minutes or more. He was a fun guy, like I said, but he thought a lot about the business. If you didn't know Brian well, you might not know he was as enthralled by the wrestling business as he was. I mean, he really loved it. Maybe he loved it a little too much.

He was talking to me when he came up with the idea of the "Loose Cannon" character that he played on WCW and WWF, a character who was crazy and unpredictable, even by wrestling standards. And I wonder if he didn't fall prey to a hazard that a lot of guys did, of becoming his character. He truly became a loose cannon, just as Louie Spicoli became the crazy idiot who was a bigger nut than everyone else, which was his character in wrestling.

But Pillman was a sharp guy. In 1995, Pillman was working an angle where Eric Bischoff (head of WCW at the time) thought he and Brian were working everyone, including the boys in the locker room. The idea was he was in such a bitter feud with Kevin Sullivan that Pillman was let out of his contract. And they really did let him out! Turned out, the ones getting worked were in WCW, because what Pillman did was sign with the WWF, once he was free.

I thought it was a tremendous maneuver on Pillman's part! He knew where he was going from the start.

Another old friend, my fellow WCW booking committee member Jim Cornette, called me in 1993 to work a couple of shows for his Smoky Mountain Wrestling group. Cornette started the company after leaving WCW in 1990, and I think he guilted me into working for him by harping on the way I disrobed him 10 years earlier!

So he called me in to work with Bob Armstrong.

Cornette ran that company pretty well, especially for a guy who'd never been the boss before. The thing was, that company was a one-man show, and Jim Cornette was that one man. And he loved every minute of it, because he was everything to that company. He wrote the checks, he booked the matches, he set up the promos, he produced the TV—he was a one-man show. But that was the way Cornette liked it.

Cornette was also very creative. I think if WCW in 1989 had said, "OK, Jim Cornette, you're in charge, so bring in your booking committee, and we'll run this thing your way," they would have been a lot more successful than they were by having him as a member of the committee, but with no real power. He certainly could have put in people he could have controlled, and would have had things going in the right direction, because Jim Cornette had much more knowledge of the business than Jim Herd did. Of course, that would never have happened with TBS running things.

A couple of years after I was there, Cornette had to fold up Smoky Mountain Wrestling. As great a job as he did, Cornette couldn't keep that thing alive to see its fourth birthday. I hate to say it, but I wasn't surprised. Hell, at that point in 1995, I wouldn't have been surprised to see anyone go under in the wrestling business, and I still wouldn't be.

One, the TV costs are huge. If you can't get someone to pay for it, you're in trouble, and there's not many people with that kind of money. If you're not lucky enough to be born into a very wealthy family and don't have someone backing you with an extreme amount of money, you are going to fold up.

Two, you have to pick your location. As I said before, a big part of the reason Vince was successful when he took the WWF nationwide was because of his location—he was based in New York City, media capital of the world, and his Northeastern base had tremendous populations from which to draw. When Cornette started up Smoky Mountain, he based it in Knoxville, Tennessee, and ran little towns in Tennessee, Kentucky and West Virginia. Cornette went to his home area, the place he loved, not to the place he would have picked if he'd been thinking strictly as a promoter. His problem was, that area didn't have the population to make him a huge success, and he knew it when he went into the thing. He knew he was running a risk of seeing the demise of his promotion, due to the population in the area. It just wasn't enough people to support that company on a weekly basis in the 1990s.

To this day, Jim Cornette lives, breathes, eats, sleeps and walks wrestling. And he is very satisfied, being in his own world. His world revolves around professional wrestling, and Jim Cornette doesn't care if that world is in New York City or Yackumoff, Tennessee. In fact, I think he'd prefer Yackumoff. But it doesn't matter much, as long as Cornette gets to be creative in pro wrestling, something he's very, very good at, and have control over it. Cornette is one of the few in our business who truly doesn't give a shit about the money. He loves to create, and he loves to call the shots. The only way Cornette doesn't function well is if he's in a creative position, but can't have control. If he's subordinate, he has a tough time, because he's strongly opinionated. You're not too likely to convince Jim Cornette that your way of doing something is better than his.

CHAPTER 23

Getting Extreme in Japan

Atsushi Onita ended up being a very influential figure in Japanese wrestling, and it was a very unexpected event that started him on his way. In 1992 Onita took a few castoffs from the major two companies in that country and formed FMW, Frontier Martial-Arts Wrestling.

I had known him for nearly 20 years at that point. In the 1970s, Onita was full of energy, just a screaming banshee of a kid. He didn't know where he was going, but he knew he wanted to be a millionaire and he wanted to be a big star.

FMW was based around main events featuring Onita in pretty innovative, and pretty brutal, stipulation matches. Some involved electric fencing, or explosives. Most involved barbed wire. Hell, the referees in those matches looked like goddamned beekeepers with all the stuff they wore to protect themselves. You would have thought we were Martians, infecting the world with radiation, instead of wrestlers.

A lot of that wild style came from Onita being exposed to barbed wire matches and other crazy stipulations in Memphis, Puerto Rico and some of the other territories he was around, and some of it, I think, came from some of the bloody matches he saw with people such as myself and Abdullah the Butcher when Onita was working for All Japan. But Onita took all of it to another level, partly out of necessity. He knew when he was starting up that he wasn't going to be able to get a lot of top, big-name talent, because a lot of those names had allegiances with Baba or Inoki.

I got involved in FMW after Onita came out to the ranch and talked to me about it. He didn't have to ask for directions. He had lived here for a month or two, more than a decade earlier.

In 1980 Masa Fuchi and Onita had wrestled in the Dominican Republic for a guy named Jack Veneno. Veneno was also the champion, and Onita was brought in to wrestle him. The office there wanted Onita to drop two straight falls, but Onita refused to do it and stiffed Veneno in the ring. When they got back to the dressing room, one of the promoters said they wanted to talk to Fuchi and Onita in the office.

When Onita went through the door, about four Dominican wrestlers went in after him, and they shut the door behind them, locking Fuchi out of the office. They beat on Onita until they got tired of beating on him.

He was hurting when he called me, and he and Fuchi came here. And they stayed in Amarillo for a while in 1981. They didn't have a pot to pee in or a dollar to their names. They stayed until Onita was feeling well, and I got them booked for one shot in San Antonio, and then for a stint in Tennessee.

While they were staying with my family and me, Fuchi insisted on cooking, as his way of making a contribution to the household. Fuchi would go into the kitchen and drive my wife crazy! He'd get the biggest damn pot he could find, three or four gallons, and he'd fill it up with rice. He cooked pounds and pounds and pounds of rice, with all kinds of other things. It would take him an hour and a half, and he tore up the kitchen every time. He made Japanese soup with rice and all kind of ungodly things, which we had to have every night for supper. But he was taking care of us, in his own way.

My daughter Brandee became the biggest fan Onita ever had in the States during this time. She was hospitalized with the measles, and Onita had to go see her at the hospital, so Vicki took him. He asked her to stop at the grocery store first, though. He came out of the store with, literally, a grocery cart full of candy and brought it to her in the hospital. Of course, Brandee felt better after seeing that, and Onita got over with her like a million bucks.

I hunted around and bought Fuchi and Onita an old Chrysler I had found advertised for $400. As you can imagine, it wasn't a luxury vehicle, but it was a usable car, and they drove it for about a year and a half, until it was spent. Fuchi had an international driver's license and Onita didn't, but Fuchi was a horrible driver, so I took Fuchi's license and a picture of Onita, and used a copy machine to make Onita an international driver's license. He used it successfully for about a year and a half in this country, showed it to the police when he was pulled over and everything.

He came back several times in the 1980s, like when he tore up his knee in Japan, and Baba didn't want him anymore. Ironically, the match where he got hurt was supposed to be the start of his big push. After he won, he did this huge leap over the ropes and out of the ring, like he had done every night. On this night, though, someone had spilled some water on the floor pads that surrounded the ring. He slipped on the water and cracked his knee.

It tore ligaments, blew out cartilage and truly shattered his kneecap. They wired it back together at the hospital. I saw an x-ray of his kneecap, and it looked like a spider's web. He bawled like a baby that night, but I didn't realize the true reason for it, at first. He was crying because he knew his injury was so severe that he would not be productive, and Baba would let him go.

And Baba did let him go. Onita felt like the true love of his life, wrestling, was gone. What no one knew was, that injury would turn out to be a major turning point in Japanese wrestling history, because of what Onita would end up doing.

That leap, that moment of catastrophe for Onita, was the beginning of the end of Baba's dynasty in Japan. It was a moment that changed the course of Japanese wrestling history every bit as much as Vince deciding to go national changed wrestling in the States, because in that moment, Onita knew that he was finished with Baba, because of that injury. That knowledge led to him looking for ways to remain involved in wrestling, which ultimately led to the formation of FMW. And FMW was tremendously influential, not only in terms of the hardcore ring style it made popular, but because it was the first small group to really succeed on the major level. Once FMW took off, it showed others that smaller promotions could thrive, and that spelled the end of the total dominance that Baba and Inoki's groups had.

Onita stayed at my house, and he decided he wanted to import beef jerky, but that didn't work out. Then he tried to sell me on going into business with him selling portable telephones.

I said, "What the hell is this? No one's going to use these things over here! You're out of your mind! That'll never work!"

I guess I should have listened to the son of a bitch—hell, he had cell phones before anyone did!

Another time, he had one of my shotguns and told me he wanted to go hunting. Well, I didn't give him any kind of safety lesson, or anything. What I did was, I took him out on my property, far enough that he wouldn't hit the house, and just let him go. He was shooting up in the air at ducks flying around and whatever else caught his eye. I just went back in the house and wouldn't let my wife or daughters outside until Onita ran out of shells. He was out there for about 30 minutes and came in. He hadn't hit a damn thing, but he was very thrilled with getting to shoot a gun.

The times I went to Japan and he was there as a young wrestler, he'd always try to carry my bags. I always told him, "Don't you carry my bags. Just leave them there. I can carry my own damn bags."

Now, he was running his own company, and I was working for him!

He told me about the company and how it was doing, and then he told me he'd pay me $20,000 to work one match! That was really all it took for me, but I told Onita there was a call I needed to make first.

I called Baba, even though I hadn't worked for him in quite a while. I said, "Baba, I am going in for Onita, if you'll allow me to."

I knew he would, but making that call was a part of showing him respect, which was just how business was done in Japan, graciously and properly. I was always able to stay on good terms with Baba, because I busted my ass for him all those years. I never screwed him around, and I hope he never thought I screwed him around. I never jumped to Inoki.

Because of what I'd read about FMW, I was expecting a crazy, violent show, but Onita really put on quite an amazing show. FMW was not just bloody, hard-core matches. Because of the limits he had in terms of getting top male wrestlers, Onita had exceptional women wrestlers, like Magumi Kudo and Combat Toyoda. Those girls weren't just good—they were phenomenal! They were the best female wrestlers I'd ever seen.

He also had high fliers from Mexico, and his own high flier, Hayabusa. He had The Sheik at 65 years old, every bit as frightening as he'd ever been. He had great workers who could do some serious wrestling. He would have boxer versus kickboxer matches, even bringing in former boxing champion Leon Spinks, at one point. The mixing of wrestling and martial arts was done out of necessity, but it was a formula that proved to be successful and continues to be successful to this day in other companies.

Onita had a menagerie of different attractions, a wide variety with something for everyone. Yes, he had exploding rings and barbed wire, but he didn't have them every match, or even every night. He usually had one wild and crazy match per show, and it was a very well organized and well done show. It was no fly-by-night organization with nothing going for it but blood and guts, like some of the independent groups you see in the States today. He had no TV, but was a success in part because he booked it as "a big night." It was a night of entertainment for those people, with all manner of attractions for the people who came to the shows.

FMW also had a very tight-knit group of guys working together. Onita ruled the whole thing with something of an iron hand, but was also inclusive. Onita had girls on the ring crew, and it was brought to his attention that one of the girls was dating one of the men who worked on the crew, a big no-no.

Onita called a companywide meeting, explained the situation, asked what the employees thought he should do, and then took a vote! The other employees voted to let both of them go, and they liked those kids, but everyone knew they broke the rules.

Evidently, his promotional philosophy worked, because you don't put 41,000 and 50,000 people in Kawasaki Stadium without having a good game plan. Are you looking for a good booker? Call Onita. No one else in the world would have done what he did to get over, at that time.

And now he was the celebrity and millionaire he'd always wanted to be. Every time I would arrive in Japan and see him, the first thing he'd have to say to me was, "Terry, I am big star now."

Nowadays it's, "Terry, I am senator!"

Well, no shit you're a senator! I knew it before he told me, just like I knew he was a big star. But that didn't matter—he had to tell me. Every damn time.

To be honest, I wasn't surprised when he got elected to the Japanese House of Councilors in 2001. When he got a direction, he had a do-or-die mentality. The guy came from absolutely nothing over there. He was a nobody and worked his way into becoming a wrestler, and then had his knee torn up so bad that he had it wired, and he can hardly walk on the damn thing. And he came back from that! He wanted to be a star, and he became a star on his own. He started out without a pot to piss in, and made himself a huge success. I'll tip my hat to Atsushi Onita any day, even if he is probably embezzling the entire Japanese treasury, as you read these very words. Just kidding!

The only thing I ever really hated that Onita did was when he did an angle in late 1990, with Jose Gonzales, the man who stabbed Bruiser Brody to death. They staged an attack where Gonzales stabbed Onita to build for a match. The match never happened, though, because Brody had been a pretty beloved figure, and people in Japan were pretty pissed off about the whole idea. When I heard about it, I knew how it would be received. It turned out to be one of the few things he did that did not work. He had felt it would be really strong, and he couldn't have been more wrong.

I was pretty pissed off, too. I just thought it was pretty shitty for him to even conceive that it would work, and if it had worked, he wouldn't have abandoned it. I will never understand things like that. There are limitations to things you should do, even in wrestling, and exploiting something so tragic is on the list of things you don't do. I don't know how I could live with myself and look myself in the mirror if I'd tried something like that. Maybe he thought it would be OK since Brody was only a *gaijin*, an American wrestler.

I spent a week there for FMW in 1993. On my last night in, we did the exploding ring match with the ropes replaced by barbed wire with land mines strapped into it, at Kawasaki Stadium. I had no idea how powerful or dangerous these things were. I put my trust in the dynamite man's hands. The barbed wire didn't bother me, but the explosions did.

The first time Onita whipped me into one of the explosives, my first thought was how loud the thing was. Don't ask me what it was that blew like that, but the percussion from it also pounded me pretty good.

Those were some brutal matches, and I saw Onita take a lot of stitches, after they were over. He had a lot from other matches, too. The amount of stitches he had done was just ridiculous. Hell, I've glued together cuts, or taped them shut, and just went on down the road. I've saved tons of money doing that.

The fans in FMW weren't like the All Japan fans. In All Japan, when I'd been there, the fans would politely applaud and only got really excited on rare occasions, although the clapping became less as the crowd slowly got more Americanized, over the years. The FMW fans were wild. They were in love with Onita and the stuff he put on.

In 1995, I went back to Kawasaki Stadium for another group, the IWA. The group, run by Kiyoshi Asano, did a "King of the Death Match" tournament. The official attendance was 28,757, but it sure seemed like more than that when we were out there.

By that time, Onita wasn't working that many shows, and I was a free agent. IWA was willing to pay what I wanted, so I went.

Where Onita's shows were filled with top attractions from top to bottom, the IWA was a different story. There was a whole lot of blood, and a lot of crazy, violent matches, from start to finish.

There were some weird deals going on, too. There was a doctor in Tokyo who was doing circumcisions and offering two free "King of the Death Match" show tickets to anyone who came in and got one done on their kid, or themselves. All that stuff is paid for by the government, since Japan has socialized medicine, which meant the guy got paid by the government for every one he performed. I think he did pretty well. What a business! He probably didn't know what to do with all that foreskin!

But every ticket he had was counted as one already sold by the promotion, which was similar to how the Yakuza, Japan's version of the mob, used to contribute to a lot of sellouts for wrestling in Japan.

The Yakuza always had numerous ways of making money. They weren't involved in the drug trade back when I went to Japan regularly for Baba, and I don't know if they are now or not. Back then they made money from gambling—they ran every pachinko parlor in Japan. They also ran events, and the way they ran events was that they bought 2,000 tickets to a wrestling show in a 2,500-seat hall, almost "buying the show," in effect. Then they went to every business in town and sold tickets. Not buying tickets was not an option.

They were very fair about it, though. They would go to a big business, making a lot of money, and say, "You buy 100 tickets."

The next guy might be a mom-and-pop operation, in which case they'd say, "You buy two tickets."

And when they were done selling their tickets, the show was officially declared a sellout, which it was. There might be a few hundred empty seats, but the tickets were all sold.

The deal with the King of the Death Match was, every match in the tournament was a different kind of bloody stipulation match. I worked the semifinals with Tiger Jeet Singh, a big foe of Inoki's in the 1970s. Our match was a barbed wire/broken glass match. I knew Tiger well enough to know that even though I was going over, I would also be the one taking the bumps into the barbed wire, because he sure wasn't going to. What else did I expect? Tiger was Tiger, and I knew and accepted that before the match even started. As long as I accepted that beforehand, by God, we'd have a match!

After defeating Tiger, I moved into the finals against my good friend, Cactus Jack. By that time the show had gone from afternoon to nightfall. It was the Forever Show, but the fans were still there and still elated. They had known it was going to be a long one. Hell, some of them brought their lunches!

The final match, billed as a "barbed wire explosion ladder match," turned out not to be all it was cracked up to be, kind of like the electrified cage match from Halloween Havoc 1989.

The idea was, we'd have all this stuff in the ring, which would be surrounded by explosives. At the 10-minute mark in the match, they would all go off, causing an incredible explosion of the ring. Before the match, Cactus and I went to talk to Asano. We didn't care about the explosive force, the dangers to our own bodies, or any of that. We just wanted to know, "Is this going to work?"

Asano said, "Oh, going to work very well. I spend $20,000 on this."

We said, "OK, that's good, then."

We figured if he was spending that much on the damn thing, it would work.

They also had some explosive boards with barbed wire around them, and those weren't any pleasure. Asano had huge amounts of barbed wire rolled up onto a board, and hitting those was just atrocious.

Finally, the countdown started as Cactus and I kept battling, and the crowd was in great expectation of this tremendous explosion that was going to take place.

I said to Cactus, "We'd better be ready for this one."

Finally, the sirens went off, the lights were flashing, and Cactus and I figured we had them, as we both lay dead in the ring.

And then the huge explosion went, "Poof."

Poof! That's all there was! Hell, compared to the bombs they used in FMW, these felt like a puff of fresh air. There was nothing to them! They were half-assed explosions, from a half-assed promotion.

I looked at Cactus and he looked over at me, and we didn't know what to do. Finally, I stood up in the middle of the ring, put my hands out and said to the fans, "WHY?"

All those people had sat through all these matches for the big death match finish, and all they got was "poof."

But my reaction showed them I was as disappointed as they were, and they accepted it as Cactus and I went on and continued the match. Eventually Cactus tangled me up in another exploding barbed-wire board and beat me, but we both left the ring with some nasty burns.

I still had a name in Japan, and I felt that Cactus beating me in the finals of that tournament would help him a great deal, and I wanted to help him. When we first went over there, Mick was not looked at in Japan as a top wrestler. The first time Mick had gone to Japan, it was a few years earlier, and he had gone in for Baba. Baba saw nothing in him and wasn't willing to look at him as a potential success. That's nothing against Mick—it's just that Baba wasn't willing to try to make successes out of people who had not proved themselves in the States, in his eyes. Until the American companies started signing guys to guaranteed contracts, Baba had always been able to get away with his approach, because he could pick from the cream of the crop. Everyone wanted to work Japan, because that was where the biggest money was, so Baba could pick and choose who he wanted. Those contracts for Americans changed everything in Japan, because the Japanese had to make their own boys now. I'm not so sure shoot wrestling would even exist over there today, much less be as popular as it is, if the Japanese groups still had access to the top Americans.

What happened to Mick in his first trip to Japan happened to a lot of guys. You have to prove yourself in Japan, and Baba almost always reserved his big pushes to Americans for the ones who had already made a name for themselves in the States. If an American who hadn't made a name for himself in the States was coming into Japan, he was coming in to do jobs, and that was Mick's role in his first tour.

By 1995 in the States, Mick had already become someone special, in WCW and the independents. But in Japan, he needed a bump, a push, and I felt winning the tournament would be a good push for him. I think it helped him.

We ended up going to the hospital together, and the next day we got on the same plane. Neither one of us looked too good, but it was great money, and I would do it again.

Now you might ask, "Why would you do these things to yourself?"

Well, we were with an independent promotion, and that meant very little coverage and no TV, so Cactus discovered what I had learned a long time ago, in Japan. They have a great many newspapers and magazines covering wrestling, and if someone was entangled in barbed wire, or had a stick up their ass, that guy was much more likely to find his picture in one of those periodicals than if he had a headlock on someone. We endured the crazy spots to steal coverage in the weeklies and dailies for what we were doing.

One thing that got us a fair amount of press was the "fire chair." Cactus and I were wrestling on his first tour for IWA, when he lit a chair on fire, and proceeded to wear my ass out with it. Now we had discussed it, and he was only supposed to hit me once. He ended up hitting me about six or seven times, until I finally just tackled his fat ass and told him, "OK, Cactus, now that's enough of that shit! That's enough!"

But damned if the flaming chair didn't make a few magazine covers! And it should have—it looked like Cactus was holding the goddamned Chicago fire over his head.

The other thing about it that struck me (if you'll pardon the pun) was that when I walked by it on to my way to the ring for the match, I noticed the thing had been completely doused in kerosene. I could see it glistening, and I could smell it.

I thought, "You know, I was the one who was supposed to soak that thing, but I didn't soak it that damn much! Is that damn Asano trying to kill us?"

But the more time passes, the more I think my buddy Cactus might have been the one to come behind me with an extra gallon of gas.

Cactus and I represented IWA on a show at the Tokyo Dome, April 2, 1995, where 13 promotions were represented, each providing one match. The match was Cactus and the Headhunters against me, Shoji Nakamaki and Leatherface, who had wrestled for Vince Jr. in the 1980s as Corporal Kirchner, in a barbed wire match with baseball bats.

Weekly Pro Wrestling, one of the wrestling magazines there, was the show sponsor and was involved in getting me to come in for the show. When I first heard the idea, I thought it was utterly absurd! Thirteen different offices were going to be able to work together to put on a show?

We had worked out a spot where the Headhunters and my partners would be outside the ring fighting, and I would do a moonsault, crashing onto them. It worked out beautifully, with the Headhunters catching me.

The Headhunters were about the only guys who ever did. In another match in Japan involving Onita, I did my courageous moonsault off the top rope. Onita, Cactus and Mike Awesome somehow missed me. Nothing was there for me, except the floor.

I ended up with a hematoma on the side of my head the size of the softball, and for the rest of the match, I wasn't sure where I was or what I was doing. Onita tried to toss me back in the ring, and Victor Quinones, my manager, came running down to the ring to stop the thing because I was out on my feet, just knocked silly. After the show was over, I ended up taking another trip to the hospital. I am grateful to this day for Victor's help.

I sure hope those guys never get the idea to try to play baseball, because they damn sure can't catch!

But getting back to the Tokyo Dome match, Cactus and I came close to getting into some real trouble. During the match, Cactus was going to set fire to a board. We had talked about it earlier, and were both in agreement that we needed to do something special to call attention to our match, which was only the fifth match on the big card.

One of the Japanese officials apparently had seen some of the things we had done before, because he said to us, "No fire. You use fire, fire marshal close down whole Dome."

But Cactus and I felt like we'd get some great publicity out of this and decided to light the board anyhow. We got to the spot in the match, and Cactus and I were the only ones in the ring. He squirted fluid all over the board and got out the lighter, while we were both lying on the mat. He kept flicking and flicking the lighter, but wasn't having any luck, mainly because he was holding his hand upside down and was trying to light the board as it lay on the mat. He kept on burning his hand, and then he'd drop the lighter, pick it up and repeat the whole process.

If he'd thought to raise up the board and light it on its side, it would have gone up beautifully, and I guess we would have closed the show, because after his fourth failed attempt, the fire department guys saw what he was doing and started going nuts! The referee was trying to stop the thing, but all that kept it from happening was that Cactus kept burning his hand and dropping the lighter. If we'd closed that show down, we'd have been immortal in Japan, and that was what we had in mind. Of course, we never would have been asked back to Japan to work for anyone, but we weren't looking that far ahead at the time. Between the wrestlers and the fans, we also might not have gotten out of the Dome alive!

With fire department officials hopping up on the ring apron, Cactus finally gave up and went on with the match.

When we got back to the dressing room, Asano was screaming, "No fire! No fire! You ruin me! You ruin me!"

Then he grabbed the referee and bitchslapped him! He was slapping the referee, I guess, because there was no way he had the balls to try to slap Cactus or me. He didn't mind paintbrushing that poor referee about 20 times, though. I guess it was supposed to impress Cactus and me. That poor referee's head was bobbing back and forth.

All told, though, we busted our asses on that match. After the referee-slapping concluded, Masa Fuchi came up to me and said Baba wanted to talk to me.

I went over to Baba, and we smiled at each other.

He looked at me for a second and said, "Very good. Very good."

That was about the highest praise Baba ever gave someone.

It was the last time Baba and I ever spoke.

But being over there with Cactus was always fun, even if we did tend to come back with some new scars or burns.

Cactus was all about business. Like me, he was in Japan to make as much money as he could. Unlike me, this meant he was willing to sell any goddamned thing he could get his hands on.

One time, we were in Japan, and I was selling T-shirts before the show started. This 45-year-old fan came running up, saying, "Please sign! Please sign this!"

I looked down, and there was this huge pair of underpants, with "Cactus Jack" written on one side, and a faint brown stripe running down the back.

Cactus Jack had sold this son of a bitch his dirty underwear, from right off of his ass!

I asked him about it, and he just looked at me with those innocent eyes and said, "Well, I got 2,000 yen for them, Terry."

CHAPTER 24

Home on the Ranch

My family wasn't thrilled about my hardcore wrestling endeavors in Japan. My wife and both my daughters were worried about me doing more dangerous things, as I got older. But it was my choice, as it has always been. They were not happy with me doing those things, but a man's gotta do what a man's gotta do, and what I've got to do is provide. The way I provided was to be home as much as I could and perform as few times as I could while making us a good living. The pain and sacrifice of a couple of violent matches was not as bad, to me, as the pain and sacrifice of being on a wrestling tour and away from home for weeks, for the same amount of money.

Worrying about me in the ring was nothing new for my daughters. Just as my brother and I had, Brandee and Stacy grew up thinking their dad was really fighting for his life every night. Mike DiBiase told me once, when I was still a rookie in 1965, "You don't ever insult the intelligence of your family. When they reach a certain age, and you'll know when the time is right, you owe it to them to smarten them up to the business. You tell them."

Vicki had known about the business since right after we got married. I knew she'd be worried enough about me without having to worry that my opponent might be really trying to kill me. And to this day she still worries about me.

As if being the love of my life wasn't enough, Vicki was also a great asset to me professionally. She would protect the business as hard as I would, if not harder. She knew that a lot of the people in the audience knew she was my wife, and she was as good a worker in the audience as a lot of guys were in the ring.

I told Stacy first, when she was 13. The business was firmly entrenched in its "wrestling is real" mode, and I truly think waiting until they matured a little made their dialogue at school easier, when the subject of what Dad did came up, because when they defended it as sport, they truly believed. And so they handled it, and the other kids learned quickly not to bother them with it. I was the same way. I'd had a few fights, growing up, but boys are different.

I also think growing up with that mindset gave the kids a healthier respect for the business, just as I'd had, growing up. It was something special, something worth protecting, as opposed to telling a five-year-old, "It's fake. It's phony."

What respect is that kid going to have for it?

These days, it's entertainment, and yes, there's a difference between "fake" and "entertainment." The difference is in the connotation. "Fake" doesn't have a very pleasant definition, but "entertainment" does.

My daughters both always thought the world of the boys, but I was always happy that neither of them ever expressed much of an interest in getting into wrestling. There are easier ways of making a buck, and better ways of making sure you'll have money to retire on—like being a greeter at Wal-Mart. Wrestling is tough on a family, and if anyone knew that, my daughters did.

Not long after they were smartened up to the business, I had a whole new problem to deal with concerning Stacy and Brandee. I've handled a lot of tough situations in my life, stood up to a lot of tough guys and stared down some of the most powerful men in the wrestling business, but I don't know that I was ready for this.

My daughters were starting to date and bring home their boyfriends. And dating had the strangest effects on their personalities. If one of my daughters was dating a smart guy, she would study. If she was going with a triathlete, she would be out running every morning. If one of them was going with an idiot, she would become an idiot. Unfortunately, they were dating idiots most of the time.

Now, in all seriousness, my kids were always pretty good kids, and I'm very proud of them. But they did give me some heartburn with some of their dating choices.

I was never an intimidator as a father, but I got my point across when I needed to. Stacy was dating a guy once who just irritated the hell out of me. I wish I could remember his name.

On second thought, no I don't.

Anyway, I would tell her to get home by 10 p.m. Well, 10 o'clock would come, and this guy wouldn't have her home. He'd bring her home at 10:15 or 10:30. And then, he'd come in with her and sit on my couch and watch the evening news! He'd just sit there with a big smile on his face, just looking around the room like he knew something that I didn't.

Well, this went on for a period of time, and I couldn't knock him, because that wouldn't get rid of him. Nothing else would, and he was getting the best of me. I had to figure something out.

Well, he was a cowboy and very proud of his pickup truck. It was a hell of a nice truck, so when he came over, he'd be sitting there, watching the news, and I'd yawn a little bit, stretch and announce that I was going outside for a little fresh air. I'd go out front, open up his gas tank and piss in it, about a cup's worth.

I got great satisfaction from that. I didn't like the guy—he was driving me nuts, and I couldn't get rid of him. But every time he went to leave, his engine would sputter and cough before starting up. Piss isn't like sugar, which will totally destroy a gas tank, but it can cause some problems. So there's a tip for all the fathers in the world. Got a problem with a daughter's boyfriend? Piss in his gas tank!

This kid eventually stopped coming around, and I don't think he ever had engine trouble again.

But my daughters didn't need boyfriends to get into trouble. One time, while Stacy was in high school, she got a wild hair and ran across the grass at McDonald's and tore the grass up in her pickup truck. The truck was kind of messed up, with a hole in the muffler from her going up on the curb. Of course, someone at the place got her license plate number and called the police, who called us.

I got off the phone and asked, "Stacy, did you do that?"

"No, I didn't do it."

"Well," I said, "are you sure you didn't do it?"

"No! I didn't do it!"

"Well, I guess we'll find out, because I'm gonna have to take you to the sheriff's department."

She insisted, "But I didn't do it!"

"Well, I'm taking you to the sheriff's department. You're gonna have to tell them that."

We pulled up at the sheriff's department, and I turned to look at her before we got out of the truck.

"Well, Stacy, we're going in."

She broke down and started crying.

"I did it, Dad," she said. "I'm sorry!"

And she was, because she was a good kid. She ended up working it out and paying back McDonald's. I just thought it was amazing what you could get out of people, once you put the pressure on them a little.

Brandee just about wore us out, too, and the two of them together were a handful. Once, when Stacy was about eight and Brandee was four, Vicki had bought a jar of pitted olives for a dish she was going to make in about four or five days. She put them in the refrigerator and told the girls that those were a no-no, and not to mess with those olives. Sure enough, the first chance they got, they went right into the olives and were walking around with pitted olive slices on their little fingers, like rings. Then they ate the olives right off of their fingers. Well, of course Vicki noticed that a good portion of her olives were missing. She came to me first and asked, "Did you eat those damn black olives?"

I didn't even know what she was talking about. "No," I said. "What black olives?"

Then she knew it was the kids. She confronted them separately, and all they could tell her was how, no, they never touched those olives! Finally, they kept talking and ended up ratting each other out.

One time, when Brandee was about four, she went out into the pasture with me, because I had a lot of work around the ranch to do. She stayed in the pickup truck, while I did my work. At the end of the day, I got back in the truck to go home. I looked down and thought some Arab terrorist had gotten ahold of my truck, because there was this incomprehensible writing on the edge of the window. I couldn't figure out what that was, and a couple of days later, I walked up to the truck and realized that she had scratched "BRANDEE" into the paint. I had been looking at it upside-down and backwards!

About eight years later, I went to California to make *Wildside,* and one day she just decided she wanted to go for a drive, so my 12-year-old daughter stole my truck! Vicki had come out to visit me, and we decided that since Stacy was 16, she was old enough to keep Brandee herself. Well, we had a snowstorm, and Brandee just took the pickup truck to some friend's house!

From the time they could, I made both the girls work. They worked here at the ranch and had outside jobs, too. I wanted to teach them the value of a buck. It was a lesson that took with Stacy, but not so much with Brandee! Bless her heart—Brandee can spend a few bucks.

Yes sir, I sure did enjoy spending time at home. And one of the reasons I stayed here through the years was that was it such a great environment to bring those girls up in. Financially, I passed up some good opportunities in order to stay, but I never regretted keeping the family in Canyon, and I never regretted staying home as much as I could.

Cactus Jack and I were the only independent wrestlers in the mid-1990s who could make a very good living by picking our shots and being independent wrestlers, up to the time Cactus joined the WWF in 1996. These days I would guess Raven, the former ECW champion, and I are the only ones who make a really good living working on the independent scene.

CHAPTER 25

ECW

Around the same time I was spending the occasional weekend blowing myself up for Atsushi Onita, I ran into Tod Gordon. Gordon was working in Joel Goodhart's independent promotion in Philadelphia, but told me, "Terry, I want to start a promotion of my own."

Goodhart's cards were loaded. Besides me, he brought in The Sheik, Abdullah and a bunch of others. This particular show drew about a $30,000 house, but he spent a lot to bring in that talent, so it wasn't a profitable situation for him.

So Tod wanted to open a new company, and he wanted me. I said, "Tod, it's not gonna work. You're gonna lose your ass, and I don't want to see you lose your money."

But he was determined, and he wanted to know if I'd come on board, so I agreed.

When it first started, it was Eastern Championship Wrestling. I didn't want to put the time into booking it, so he called Eddie Gilbert to come to work and book.

Eddie ran our first show, held in a gymnasium. That show was the biggest fiasco that I have ever witnessed in my life. The dressing rooms were full of wrestlers, non-wrestlers, hunchbacks, fat girls, skinny girls, a very few pretty girls—just the damndest menagerie of humanity you could imagine. One guy I remember was the Sandman. He was there. And he was godawful! He was one of many who became good workers, but who was just the shits that night.

The weather was bad, too, so they didn't have that many people there. We just had a few hundred for the first ECW show. That show was so rotten, you just wouldn't believe it unless you were there.

After my match I grabbed the microphone and said, "You know, I know this show wasn't the greatest, but you people bear with us, and I promise we'll put you on a better product."

And they did—the fans stuck with ECW.

The morning after the show, we were trying to get out, but we were snowed in and ended up stuck at the hotel for two more days. And Eddie Gilbert and I spent those two days creating stuff for ECW. Some stuff in wrestling today is a byproduct of an idea from Eddie Gilbert. People have no idea how influential his ideas really were.

Something else that became popular at ECW shows was something I had popularized—going through tables. Randy Savage was the first (to my knowledge) to send someone through a ringside table when he piledrove Ricky Morton through one in 1984, but I truly think me doing it to Flair in 1989 was what put tables on the map. And when I did it I wasn't even aware that Savage and Morton had done it in Memphis five years earlier.

But a kid named Terry Brunk was the one who really made the tables into a staple of his arsenal. Terry was the nephew of my old friend Ed Farhat, The Sheik. He wrestled as Sabu. The stuff Sabu did from the top rope and his moves through tables were practically unheard of in wrestling in the early 1990s when I first encountered Sabu at an independent show. No one had ever seen moves like the backdive off the second rope into the bodypress. He was a real creator and a real innovator in that ring. Every time you see someone do a high-flying move using the ropes as a springboard, you are watching someone imitating a Sabu invention.

He would also sell that stuff. He wouldn't do some crazy move and then pop right back up. He made sure the fans understood the physical price he was paying by selling every move he made. The generation of guys who borrowed things from Sabu overdid it and killed a lot of those moves by doing too much, too fast, but Sabu's in-ring performance was great. I'm not going to say his work was faultless, but it was damn good.

The first time I saw him, I immediately realized what a huge influence he would be. How could he not? Hell, 80 percent of his matches were things that have never been seen before.

Anytime I went to an ECW show, I tried to do more than was necessary. Sabu did the same, and so did Shane Douglas. We all had a common desire to make the company. We were going to extremes, so it was appropriate when they renamed it Extreme Championship Wrestling.

That "extreme" approach was very influenced by what Onita had done in Japan. Onita himself had started out with a lot of influences (of which I was one, all modesty aside), but he had become a very innovative figure himself, and he had a lot of influence on the business. ECW would never have gone the route it did, if not for the success of FMW, and WCW and the WWF ended up copying aspects of ECW to change up their product, so Onita had a pretty profound effect on wrestling.

The "E" in ECW became "Extreme" in 1994, after a tournament for the NWA world title that occurred while I was working in WCW (more on that in a minute).

The NWA title, supposedly the same title my brother and I had defended in the 1970s, was up for grabs in a tournament in the ECW Arena in Philadelphia. ECW champ Shane Douglas won the title, but then threw down the NWA belt and declared his Extreme Championship Wrestling title to be the only real world's title.

By that time, the NWA was some group of independent promoters who had bought the belt. Maybe it was the NWA belt, in strictly legal terms. That wasn't the NWA world heavyweight championship I remembered, though.

The whole thing did somewhat belittle NWA promoter Dennis Coraluzzo, who I liked, but I just chalked that up to the kind of things that happen in the wrestling business that I had no control over. Dennis and Paul E. had their little fight going on, and that was kind of the culmination of it.

Shane Douglas almost became the face of ECW after that, though, along with Sabu and, later, Tommy Dreamer, Taz and Rob Van Dam. It was just the most amazing bunch of workers, many of whom came out of nowhere to become big stars. That happened because Paul E. allowed them to develop their own characters.

Shane was very good at the time, and I always thought he did an excellent interview. He spent a great deal of time with his promos. You know, some people can do those very easily, very naturally, and without a lot of preparation. For others, it doesn't come as easily, and they have to work a little bit on them. I wouldn't say promos ever came very easily to me—I was always one of the guys who put a lot of work into them.

Over the years, Sabu's contributions to wrestling have been forgotten by a lot of people, it seems, and his historical importance is undervalued by many so-called wrestling "experts." Sabu has also gotten something of a reputation for causing problems in the locker room, but I can tell you I never saw a problem with him. And in the 1990s, there was no one else protecting the business anymore, except Sabu, sometimes to his detriment. He wasn't about to appear in *Beyond the Mat,* because he felt it would be exposing his character in ways he didn't think were right. He truly believed in retaining an air of mystery, something that's all but gone in this era.

Sabu's another guy who's doing pretty well on the independent circuit, but he's busting his ass for his money.

So I ended up in the ring with this great, underrated innovator for a barbed wire match that was the main event of an ECW show on August 9, 1997, called *Born to Be Wired.* That show was one of the worst deals I ever got myself into.

Very shortly into the *Born to Be Wired* match, Sabu took a bump into the corner and got himself hung up into the barbed wire. When he pulled free, the barbed wire tore his bicep at least six inches. His actual bicep muscle was showing, and blood was pouring out.

Sabu asked his ringside manager, Bill "Fonzie" Alphonso, for some tape, wrapped up the arm and went back to the match. At that moment, I had no doubt—I was in there with a rare breed of cat. Later in the match, I went through the ropes and got my neck tangled in the wire. I was seriously choking out, until someone grabbed a pair of wire cutters and cut me loose. I've been in some tough barbed wire matches with Cactus, but this was probably the roughest one I'd ever been in.

Things happen in barbed wire matches. You can't call what's going to happen, either. You have control over yourself, but you can't control where that barbed wire is going to snag you. Anytime barbed wire is strung up around the ring, those wrestlers are in a dangerous situation, and when you take a bump into barbed wire, you're endangering yourself.

Every time I've been in one of those matches, I haven't spent my time in the dressing room bullshitting with the other guys. I sit and I think about it. I'm totally concentrating on it.

But as much as that barbed wire hurt, an ECW match I had with Cactus Jack a couple of years earlier was even worse. During the match, Cactus brought back the flaming steel chair, like the one we had used in Japan. Unlike the one in Japan, however, the seat mat on this one flew off in mid-swing, flaming. It flew out of the chair, as Cactus swung and hit the top rope while I rolled out of the ring. When the burning seat came loose, it landed on me, outside the ring.

Now, every time Cactus tells this story, he says he hit me with the chair, and then I said, "Hit me again."

My ass! I sure as hell didn't want to get hit again with that damn thing! Why the hell would I have been rolling out of the ring, if I'd wanted to get hit again? Once was enough!

Anyway, the seat landed on the back of my arm and just roasted it. And I must say—that was a pretty good roasting.

After it happened, I went into a nonstop rampage, cussing and screaming at anyone within earshot. Friends, wrestlers, doctors, promoters and nurses had to listen to my diatribes, and I bet I could be heard a block away. I called Cactus a "dumb son of a bitch" and many other, colorful things. Of course, I called him later, at his home, and left a message for him on his answering machine, to patch things up.

The bottom line was, and is, Mick is Mick. We've been up and down the pike together and have conceived of so much wild crap together, that stuff like that wasn't going to make us turn against each other. Shit happens, especially with extreme gimmicks like ECW used, and those matches could be very dangerous.

Mick also elevated a lot of guys. One of them was Tommy Dreamer. Tommy didn't have an easy row to hoe in this business. He wanted to be in the business more than anything in the world and was willing to do anything to get into it, and to stay in it. He turned into a good piece of talent, and his feud with Mick helped the ECW fans see that fully. Tommy was a good soldier to Paul E., and always put the business first.

Yes sir, Tommy was a good soldier, taking orders from a so-so general. Paul E. had good, creative ideas about the business, but some of his ideas about financial success for the boys didn't exactly work out the way they should have. But he couldn't help that—there was no way he could make all the guys a living and still balance the books. The money just wasn't there.

Hell, they had a lot of good soldiers there in ECW. And the reason for that was that they were motivated, and not just by Paul E. Yes, Paul was a great motivator, but they were also motivated by the question, "What else is there?"

The guys knew the answer to that question, and they knew they had to hang on from week to week. There was no alternative. But guys who could make something of themselves in ECW generally went on to greater successes in one of the bigger companies. Even today, there are a lot of guys making big money in WWE who should be thanking their lucky stars that they got to be a part of that little organization, because that was how they got their feet in the doorways of this business.

Take Perry Saturn. He and John Kronus had a lot of success in ECW as a tag-team called The Eliminators. Saturn later went on to WCW and the WWF. They were one hell of a team, and really gelled as a team. Some guys just complement each other and make good teams, becoming more together than either one could separately. The Eliminators produced their asses off as a team for ECW. But when they went their separate ways, neither one was as successful as they'd been together. It was like watching The Kangaroos when I was a child—you put Al Costello and Roy Heffernan together, and you had a great team. Split them up, and what did you have? When Don Kent replaced Heffernan on that team, The Kangaroos were never the same. That's not a knock against Don, but they just weren't The Kangaroos.

Another great tag team in ECW really hit it big as a team in the WWF—the Dudleys, Buh Buh Ray and D-Von. Those two guys worked their asses off in ECW, and kept it up when they joined the WWF in 1999. Their hard work paid off, but if there were no ECW, they would have had no place to show off their talents.

But ECW was also a place where a lot of innovations took place. One of those was the triangle match (which WWE calls the "triple threat" match today). The first one was between me, Shane Douglas and Sabu. The trick of that kind of match is timing, because you must pace yourself in such a way that it doesn't come out looking like a clusterfuck. But you can't plan it all out beforehand. You have to just get out there and dance, and that's what we did. I don't think the three of us sat down beforehand and discussed even one spot.

We ended up working to an hour draw between the three of us, and it was dancing at its best. We did three-way sleeperholds and a lot of other inventive spots. All three of us were really on that night.

The idea of the triangle match came about in a conversation between Paul E. and me, and we started working out how to start the match (with two guys and one waiting to tag in, or three in the ring at once). There have been a lot of those kinds of matches since then. In most of the ECW ones, they had elimination rules, where the last guy not to be pinned was the winner. When the WWF started doing the matches a couple of years later, the winner was the first man to score a pinfall on one of his two opponents. I actually think WWF's way might have been better, because in the elimination version of the match, you have to have two guys get beaten, when you really only need one fall to get across the excitement of the match. The WWF way also created exciting scenarios, such as when one guy has to make a save for another guy he also doesn't want to win, just to keep him from getting pinned and the match from ending.

ECW might have started with Tod Gordon, but it had become Paul E.'s baby. He lived and breathed it 24 hours a day. I still don't know what happened with the change in ownership to Paul from Tod, but the last I knew, they were still talking to each other. I don't know if there was a dispute between the two, or if Tod just decided he wasn't going to sink another dime into it and let Paul E. buy him out.

Paul E. is the kind of guy you can be extremely mad at, the kind of guy who'll do something that will make you want to punch him right in the nose. You walk into the arena looking for him, and there he is. Before you can even get to him, to punch him out, you can't do it, because you're laughing before you reach him, and he's telling you something new and absolutely silly. He just has that way about him. That's just Paul E.—a very charismatic person. Not charismatic in the sense of being a TV character, but in walking around dealing with him personally, he has a tremendous personal magnetism.

I liken it to the presence Lou Thesz had as champion in the 1950s. It's obviously not the same kind of thing being projected, but if Thesz was in a room with 50 people in it and you knew only one was a champion, you would immediately know it was Lou. With Paul E., he could walk into a room and instantly command your attention in a different way. He just had a feeling about him that would attract people, an enthusiasm that was contagious.

And he loved to give his Hitler speeches before the ECW shows. He would get everyone, including me, revved up to go out and kick some ass! He would tell the guys how no one thought the company could make it, how they all had something to prove, every single show! When he was finished, all the boys were in a frenzy, and he was their commander in chief. Some of them would have taken a bullet for him.

"Heil, Paul E.!"

He really loved that part of it. Those were his very best promos. He would climb halfway up a flight of stairs, and that was his stage, while the wrestlers were the audience. He did a hell of a job, too. We all knew he was performing, but we all fell into his grasp every time he gave one of his orations.

Paul E. and the boys, including me, had a feel for those fans. The thing was, once we had them, we had them hooked. We had some real fanatics, and they loved that ECW product. And the boys in ECW loved being a part of all that. It was one of the few times in my career when I felt that everything had the right mix. It sure didn't get that way overnight, but those ECW guys created a sense of camaraderie between all of us—between all the boys, and between the wrestlers and the fans.

The ECW fans were different from any other group of fans I'd ever encountered. They were loyal and came every week, but these people were radicals. It wasn't like there were one or two—I'm talking about an arena full of radicals, and they thrived on being known as a radical group. They thrived on being very knowledgeable fans, too, but they also kind of liked the title of "those ECW fools."

They created a few new chants, some of which were quite controversial. A lot of the guys didn't like it when the ECW crowds would chant, "You fucked up! You fucked up!" at them. Well, the thing is, they were right! Whenever a guy got that chant, it was because he fucked up! And we all knew—you'd better not fuck up in front of those people, because they'll let you know about it.

But when you had a good one, they loved it, and they let you know that they appreciated it, more than any other fans in the world (although some of the Japanese crowds were at about the same level). They really loved that product, and believe me, they really miss that product. I sure don't remember wrestling anywhere else where the fans chanted the promotion's name.

I still remember main-eventing ECW's first pay per view, *Barely Legal* in April 1997, against Raven. On this show, I beat Raven for the ECW title, which I would lose to Sabu at the *Born to Be Wired* show I discussed earlier. The president of West Texas State, Dr. Russell Long, and his wife, Natrelle, went to the show with my wife and I and my two daughters. He was utterly dumbfounded by what he saw there. The crowd's reaction to me was amazing; it was something that really moved not just me, but my entire family and friends there. A lot of guys say they're all business and can't be moved by the fans. Well, I was.

I had really become attached to them, and still keep in touch with some, like John Owen. John was a paraplegic with a lot of health problems, and wrestling was a great release for him. He loved it, and the other fans loved him. And another fan, old Mo, took me everywhere, including to the hospital. Her car was no limo, but the price was right.

The ECW wrestlers would give 100 percent every night. They wanted that thing to work so badly. There was a sense that we were underdogs, fighting the giants. At least, we thought we were, and it really helps breed unity when you have a common foe. It gave all the guys a bond, and we were all really tight together.

I broke those bonds a couple of times, though. Once was in late 1997, when I went back to the WWF (a period I'll discuss in the next chapter). The other was a brief return to WCW in 1994.

I'd had a lawsuit over some money I was owed in WCW, and in 1992, Bill Watts (the old Florida booker from my 195-pound days, who was also a successful promoter in the south in the 1970s and 1980s) had become vice president of the company. He said he'd settle with me and get me some of the thousands the company owed me. But I also had to buy $150 of Swipe, this cleaner he was selling on the side, as part of the deal.

These days, he's saying in interviews that we worked out a deal where I'd come in and wrestle on his 1992 *Halloween Havoc* show. Bullshit! I never told him I would wrestle for him on any *Halloween Havoc* show!

However, a year and a half later, I did agree to come in for one shot that turned into a regular stint.

I started on WCW's *Slamboree 1994* pay per view, and worked a match with Tully Blanchard, who had been almost completely inactive for five years. I wasn't really doing much with ECW at that time and I needed a stage. ECW was always a good stage that provided a lot of opportunities to a lot of guys, many of whom are still working today.

I decided to stay on and teamed some with Jimmy Golden, who was wrestling as Bunkhouse Buck. I found myself again working with Dustin Rhodes, who had become a really sharp talent in the ring. He had truly become an excellent worker, and a guy who loved the business—I mean, a true love for the business. Every night with Dustin was a night off. It was just fun, and we tried to do sillier stuff every night than we had done the night before.

I looked around WCW and didn't especially like what I saw. In this business, you have to know when to hold and when to fold, when to blow and when to go, and this was a case where it was time to go almost as soon as I got there. There was no real direction for me there, and I never got the feeling I fit into anyone's plans.

By now, Jim Herd had been gone for more than two years, and the company was being run by Eric Bischoff, who had replaced Bill Watts in 1993. Bischoff had been brought in a couple of years earlier as an announcer.

Shortly after he took over, in 1993, TBS brought me in to talk about taking over as booker. Bill Shaw, one of the executives who ran WCW, asked what I wanted to be paid, and I told him I wanted $350,000 a year.

"That's no problem," he said. "Would you be willing to work for Eric Bischoff?"

Hell, I figured I was on a roll, after the salary thing.

I said, "No."

He thanked me for coming, and I went on home.

I'm not sure I made the right call, because I never would have predicted Eric would have achieved the kind of success he would have by 1996. I also wouldn't have done what he did, in terms of raiding talent from the WWF, because it would never have occurred to me that it would work. And it did!

Of course, he eventually lost control of it all, and he's a big part of the reason WCW no longer exists. He signed guys like Hall and Nash to big contracts in 1996, which paid off at first, but then they got into the mindset of, "Why should I do anything for the company? I'll get paid no matter what, so I'm just doing what I want to do."

There were too many guys with power only looking to protect themselves, even at the expense of the company. And that is what started the ball rolling on the demise of WCW. Kevin Sullivan was officially the booker for much of that time, but it was hard for him to book cards half the time, because only half the guys were there who were supposed to be there. Guys didn't want to travel. They didn't want to work with certain guys. And they got their checks every two weeks, no matter what.

I don't blame the guys who were able to get away with it. Some of them are still doing OK financially, because of those deals during that time, and their idea was to do the least amount of work and make as much money as possible. I blame the guy who was supposed to be in charge. By the time Eric left (the first time) in 1999, no one was sure who the boss was.

Earlier I talked about being a "good soldier," which described a lot of guys in the business. But good leaders, good "generals," were few and far between. For the last 20 years, we wrestlers have been led by assholes, because their egos and the mighty dollar have been more important to them than honesty, pride and dignity.

Where are they in the administrative end of this business? Well, nice guys finish last. The meek might inherit the earth, but they damn sure won't inherit the wrestling business. The good generals, the Paul Boeschs, Don Owens and Sam Muchnicks, are dead and in the ground. They're not coming back.

What the wrestlers need is someone who will say, "Hey, these guys who are busting their asses for me need some medical coverage and some retirement, and I'm going to see they get it. I'm going to see they get a fair shake, because they're making me rich."

That "who's the boss?" feeling was also in WCW when I went there in 1994. Bischoff had turned WCW into a situation where there were "haves" and "have-nots." Bischoff was pretty much doing what he wanted to, and the top wrestlers were doing not what they were told or booked to do, but what they wanted.

And maybe I would have been the same way if I'd had that much power and guaranteed money. I think a lot more people would than would admit to it. But I don't think I would have, and that's more about when and how I was brought up into the wrestling business than anything else. A lot of the guys who became the problems in WCW had come into the business in a different way than I did and didn't grow up with that love for the business and the boys. We are all products of our eras and our environments. How could I expect Kevin Nash to see things like I did when he didn't see the same things and learn the same lessons I did?

The whole place was just totally political. Hulk Hogan had come in and brought in a bunch of his friends, and so began an era of "cliques," which happens periodically in this business.

The inmates were running the asylum, and it had gotten to the point that no one cared about the company, or anything, except how they were doing. In that sense, it was almost like the diametric opposite of ECW. WCW had an unproductive atmosphere at that point. Guys were looking at those big, guaranteed contracts, and it became the era of the contagious concussions.

I finally left WCW in the summer of 1994 because I was going nowhere. I was on a weekly deal, so I just told Bischoff I was going. He nodded but didn't seem to register it much.

I ended up back in ECW, after getting a call from Paul E. Paul E. was glad to have me back, but he never got hot about my going to WCW in the first place.

Most of the times I went into ECW, it was usually on a day's notice. I swear, they were late on everything. I'd be sitting at home, and I'd get a phone call from Paul E., saying he needed me on such-and-such a date. Sometimes, that would be the last I'd hear from him for weeks.

That was just the way it was. Sometimes, they'd just forget to send the plane tickets. And when I say, "they," I mean Paul E.

Like Cornette in Smoky Mountain, Paul was a one-man show in ECW. He was doing everything, from booking talent, to storylines, to TV production, to arranging travel. When one guy is doing so much, crap like that happens. I just wish it never happened to me!

I'm sorry, Paul E.—you were a great booker and still are a good friend, but you were a lousy businessman.

When I came back to ECW, they had a deal where I busted out of a box and attacked Cactus Jack. We had a lot of fun. Hell, I've always enjoyed working with Mick Foley. To me, coming out of the box was really a classic angle. I don't think one person in that entire arena knew it was going to happen.

When I had seen Foley previously in WCW, he had always been a heel, but he had become the ultimate babyface to the ECW fans. And I had always thought Mick's ultimate role in wrestling would be as a babyface. Whenever you have a guy who understands the people and understands what working is really all about, there's no doubt that he can be an excellent babyface or an excellent heel. And Mick had a great feel for his audience and for what they wanted to see. The greatest evidence of that was a year later, in 1995, when he turned heel! Who would have thought that Cactus Jack, who embodied what ECW was all about, could become an effective heel to those fans? He knew exactly what they wanted to see and made himself a heel by actively refusing to give it to them!

Everyone talks about his dangerous bumps, but Foley doesn't get nearly enough credit for his psychology. He's a really smart guy. Foley knew how to read those fans as well as anyone.

And I would specifically like to respond to Ric Flair, who wrote in his biography that Foley was nothing but a glorified stuntman who didn't know how to work, and that he only got over because Vince McMahon and the WWF found a way to get him over.

Bullshit. That is utterly ridiculous. If you look back at the guy's career (and I'm sure Flair has no idea what it's like to bust his ass on the independent scene), Mick Foley came up from a small Dallas promotion. He certainly grabbed me when I happened to tune into it.

I promise you this—Mick made more money in his last five years than Ric did in his 10 best years. And here's the bottom line—if Vince McMahon had a choice of one of those guys, either Flair or Foley, to work on a daily basis to draw TV ratings or people to order pay per views, I bet you he would pick Mick Foley. And that's not because Mick Foley is a freak; it's because of what Mick Foley has become to the fans. He has become a legend; he produces revenue because he gives the people what they will pay to see. And that takes a sharp mind, because what they'll pay to see changes constantly. I've seen Mick Foley have great match-es with guys on the independent scene who weren't going to have good matches with almost anyone else.

I'm not saying Mick Foley is the single greatest worker ever, but he is a great worker, and when you weigh everything about the guy, he didn't get where he got by people saying, "Hey, this guy is going to do some freakish things." He got where he got in the business by making people care about what he was doing, through his interviews and his matches. Mick Foley has been successful because he has a great mind for the psychology of the business, and he's capable of a lot more in that ring than just falling off a cage or a balcony.

And Ric Flair is a great talker, but Foley's promos are unreal. He just has a feel for the audience, even today. If I were a promoter and needed a guy who I could tell, "OK, I need an idea, and we'll go with it, but we need you to come up with the program and the way to build it up over the course of six months," Mick Foley is the guy I'd want, because he knows his faults as well as his attrib-utes. The reason is, he's going to have an idea, and it'll be a good one. There aren't many other guys in the business who I think could do that.

And I'm not here to kiss Mick Foley's ass, because he's got one ugly ass! I'm not just saying this because the guy's a friend of mine. If I didn't think this was true, I just wouldn't even bring it up.

Foley also helped make Tommy Dreamer into a top ECW star, but as I said, Tommy himself also deserves a lot of the credit for that. He turned into a really good performer and was willing to do anything. I don't mean this in a derogato-ry way at all—this is a compliment. After the matches were over and the fans were going home, Tommy Dreamer was out there with a broom, cleaning off the mat and making sure there weren't any problems with anything, so we could have an arena to come back to. He went beyond the call of duty.

The Dudleys were the same way. They would sell tickets at the door, help set things up, whatever needed doing. They knew they needed ECW to stay up and running. They knew—you can't be a performer unless you have a place to perform.

Tommy and I teamed up against Cactus Jack and Raven in a series of matches after Cactus turned heel in 1995. Those were some unusual matches. Raven is a guy with a lot of ideas, and once he had one, by God, he's going to use it! And if Raven can avoid a bump, he's going to avoid it. I can assure you, when Cactus and Raven were partners, it wasn't Raven taking most of the punishment during their matches. Raven figured Cactus should be taking the punishment, but that was because he was under the assumption that he was the captain of that team. But it was only an assumption, and we allowed him to hold onto that assumption.

Raven really is creative, though, and he's three-quarters nuts! But you must understand, it's all about Raven. If I were to have a match with him where Raven's hands and feet were tied, you can be sure we would be in the dressing room beforehand, discussing what spots to do to make sure it was all about Raven. Raven also saw himself as one of the great workers in the business, and when he wanted to be, I'll be damned if he wasn't!

All those guys—Public Enemy, the Rottens, Balls Mahoney (possessor of one of my all-time favorite names in wrestling) and the rest—were great characters in their own rights.

And over the course of his years in ECW, the previously godawful Sandman graduated into being an amazing character. The Sandman was the first authority-flaunting, beer-drinking, ass-kicking babyface. His beer drinking and chain smoking on his way to the ring was like nothing fans had seen before. Vince McMahon and Steve Austin (and Steve was in ECW for a while and saw how over Sandman was) pretty well ripped that idea off from ECW and used it to create the "Stone Cold" character.

I really think Austin is a very talented guy. I don't think he would ever have become a superstar on that level if he had kept the blonde hair on his head. Shaving his head and becoming "Stone Cold" made a world of difference for him. It didn't change his working ability, because he always had that, but being "Stone Cold" was a natural for him, because it was very similar to what he was really like. It sounds silly to think so minor a thing as a haircut would make a difference, but think—can you picture "Stone Cold" with hair?

Some of the ECW characters were just nuts. I remember a show where Bill Alfonso, the manager of Sabu and Rob Van Dam, broke his arm. He went to a grocery store across the street, pulled a bunch of cans down on himself, fell on the floor and said he'd broken his arm there. On second thought, I might not be remembering that right. If that were true (and I'm not saying it is), he could possibly get into some trouble. If it were true.

But there weren't many options for the guys. ECW didn't exactly have a hospitalization plan.

All through this period, whether I was working in ECW and FMW, or doing shows for WCW, or taking acting jobs, I never subjected myself to the kind of travel schedule I'd had in much of the 1980s. I stayed busy, but I always made sure I was striking more of a balance, allowing myself to be with the family more.

My last stretch for ECW was in late 1998, after I left the WWF for a second time (relax, we'll get to it). They put me in a short program with Tommy Dreamer. For the first time in a long time, I was a heel there.

Paul E. had just wanted me to come in for a short pop. We worked a deal where I went nuts and attacked Tommy over and over, but he didn't want to fight back because I was his hardcore wrestling hero. Of course, he ultimately kicked my ass as he became ECW's big babyface.

It was a shame ECW couldn't make it, because Paul E. had a little school going, run by one of the best guys you could have training wrestlers—Peter Serneca, a.k.a. Taz. He taught those young guys a tremendous amount of respect for the business and for the guys who came before. Taz understood that you have to appreciate the heritage of our business, and that the past was important. His methods of taking things very seriously, instilling a sense of history and respect for the toughness of the other guys working a physical style were very similar to the way the Japanese trained their young wrestlers. And it wasn't just him playing some character; that was how he really felt. He was also an excellent evaluator of talent. He knew what made a good wrestler, and he believed in wrestling hard. He would have it no other way.

When I was around the young guys in ECW, I used to get tired of them calling me "Sir," but Taz would make them do it. It really kind of pissed me off! And he had them calling me "Mr. Funk." Well, I don't like being called "mister," and especially not after I reached the age of 50. But that was the respect Taz demanded of his students.

Between the original generation of ECW stars and the Taz students, Paul E. had groomed some new names and faces to be the top stars of ECW. One of them was Rob Van Dam, who worked a lot as a heel in 1996 and 1997 but became too popular with the people to keep him that way. Rob was, and still is, an incredibly talented individual. He really is one of the most creative wrestlers I've seen. He also shared with Sabu an understanding that you have to sell the high-impact stuff in the ring for it to mean anything. Watch him on *Smackdown!* even today. When he hits that frog splash off the top rope, he rolls around for a second, to show you that spectacular move hurts him, too! Who else does that?

Sabu and Van Dam were both trained by The Sheik, and you can tell they learned together, because they both have a lot of the same wonderful characteristics in that ring. The only problem I see is, some of the younger guys watch Sabu and Van Dam, but they just watch the maneuvers. They don't watch their selling capabilities.

That last time I worked for ECW, in late 1998 against Tommy, I saw ECW was trying to branch out into new areas, and within a year, they'd be on the cable network TNN (now called Spike TV).

For them, it was a "do or die" situation. They had to take the chance. I think if ECW could have moved to an area like San Antonio and the surrounding towns in Texas, it might have made it. The company's base wouldn't have been in the East Coast, an area saturated with wrestling. There was a good base of fans in Philadelphia, but I think they would have been better off running in the old Southwest territory.

Truthfully, I'm surprised no one ever made a serious run based out of Texas. The isolation of the area is perfect for growth of a wrestling company. There are some tremendous population bases, close enough that travel expenses would be less, especially with Southwest Airlines and the $50 hops they offer from place to place. One of the most extreme things about ECW's latter days was the amount of money they were paying to go from Philadelphia to a show in Florida. Expanding into Florida and New Orleans sounded great, but the travel expenses made it not very cost efficient.

There's enough population here in Texas to build a base, and there are plenty of towns that can handle having a wrestling TV show. It's untapped potential in my mind. And Texans would make great fans for a regional promotion like that, with the right market penetration, because all Texans are just naturally proud of our state.

Can't you just see it? "This is Texas RASSLIN', by God!"

I know a lot of guys want to be tied to the big population center up there, but that big center is pretty saturated with independents, and it's in the big boys' back yard. There's also more expense flying in talent from all over, all to the Northeast than there would be in a more central location.

But Tod Gordon and Paul E., they were tied to that area, because that was where they were from. They were attached to it, the same way Jim Cornette was attached to the Smoky Mountain area, the same way I'm tied to Amarillo.

And so ECW ceased to be in January of 2001. But it left a huge impression in the wrestling business, in terms of its style that the big two companies borrowed, and in terms of its talent. Vince McMahon has gotten a lot of use out of ECW wrestlers. It was, in a way, the Ohio Valley Wrestling of its time, but for most of its existence, ECW continued to manufacture talent. ECW turned out to be the greatest proving ground for talent the WWF ever had.

Beyond
Beyond the Mat

I was at an independent show in Las Vegas in 1997, working for a guy named T.C. Martin, when I met Barry Blaustein.

Martin's little independent group was actually doing pretty well and getting an ever-improving following among the Las Vegas locals. Unfortunately, T.C. decided he should be the star of the show despite the fact that he wasn't a trained wrestler. Pretty soon he became the play-by-play announcer. Then he became the ring announcer. Then he became the guy walking to and from the ring and managing the guys. Pretty soon he was all over the place, and it didn't take long for people to get sick of him and stop going to his shows.

Realists are few and far between in this business, and T.C. was not one of those rare ones. Of course, if everyone in the business was a realist, there would be no business.

Barry and I had actually originally met in 1978, when we were both guests on *The Merv Griffin Show.* I was on the show with Sly Stallone, plugging the movie. Richard Simmons was on the show, too, as filler, almost, coming in for the last two minutes of the show. This was before Richard made it big, and I remember looking at him and thinking, "Who is this little jerk? He'll never amount to anything!"

And now, he's the richest little jerk in the country!

Anyway, Merv asked me to demonstrate the sleeper hold on one of his writers.

Merv looked offstage and said, "OK, come on out here."

And here came Barry Blaustein.

I said, so everyone could hear me, "All right, just pinch my leg when you start to feel yourself going under."

So of course I put him all the way out. And he pinched the hell out of my leg, too! Several times!

Barry never forgot that initial meeting and reminded me of it when he ran into me at the show in Las Vegas. He was with a mutual friend of ours, another Barry—Hollywood agent Barry Bloom. Barry Bloom had been a friend of Arthur Chobanion's, and was around when I was first talking about going on the *Wildside* show in 1984. Barry Bloom just kind of stepped in and handled all the contract stuff for me, without an agent's fee or anything. He just did it to help me because he liked me.

Blaustein told me he was working on a documentary about wrestling, and he asked me if I'd appear in it. I told him I would. I knew it was a documentary and never expected a penny out of it. I just agreed to help.

Blaustein ended up filming the events leading up to my latest retirement match, at a show called *50 Years of Funk,* celebrating the anniversary of my father's 1947 debut in the city. It was set for September 11, 1997, and was to be my last match in Amarillo. In my mind, I needed another reason besides the "50 years" to make the show a special one, one worth promoting, so I announced it would be my last match in Amarillo. I never intended to retire altogether, even then. I just wanted one last reason to do big business in Amarillo.

That show had some incredible talent, from Japan, ECW and even the WWF. They were guys I knew or had worked with, like the Hart family in Calgary. I asked Bret Hart to come in, and he OKed it with Vince. Vince also OKed my good friend Mick Foley working the show as Mankind, his WWF persona.

One of the more memorable scenes in the movie is one where I'm talking with Dennis Stamp, a former wrestler in the area who I've known since the mid-1960s. Dennis was telling me he had wanted a match on the show, and was refusing my request for him to referee my main event against Bret Hart, although he finally agreed to do it. I've had questions about it from people who think Dennis was working for the camera's benefit, so let me set things straight. That whole conversation was 100 percent real.

Once I realized his feelings had been hurt, I really did regret not having him on the show, because he was exactly the kind of guy I was doing that show for. I was doing it for my friends, for the guys who had wrestled around there, the guys I liked. I really did want Dennis to be a part of it, and I was glad when he finally said, "OK."

Dennis was actually one of my first tag-team partners, when I wrestled for Verne Gagne's AWA in Minnesota. He came down to Amarillo in the mid-1970s and has been here ever since. These days he has a pretty successful bug-spraying business. Dennis was actually a good wrestler, with some amateur wrestling background. He was a solid worker and did not rely on gimmicks, or anything. He believed that straight wrestling was the way to go. To this day, he's very involved with amateur wrestling in the youth leagues. He referees matches and just loves working with kids. He's a very good legitimate, amateur wrestling referee. He takes a great deal of pride in it, and he should.

Dennis was also an excellent referee for my match with Bret. He was in perfect position for everything.

I worked hard promoting this show. I went to one of the TV stations in town and got ECW on the air, for about six weeks before our show. That wasn't a lot of lead time, but it helped to establish who those guys were, so people would know them a little when they came here.

I had well over $35,000 invested in the show, and we ended up grossing about $45,000 on it. As you can see, even under the best of circumstances, an independent promotion is not an easy row to hoe. I think a lot of people who try to become independent promoters have no idea about the expenses involved. As time goes by it gets more expensive. The expenses are unbelievable, especially when you're running spot shows, as opposed to a regular territory, because of the costs of transportation for the talent.

Thirty years ago or more, a promoter would never want to drive a nice car up to a newspaper building. He wanted to drive an old, beat-up car and go in and beg for what he could get for free.

You have to think about your venue. Nowadays, you look at these independent guys running spot shows. It seems like they all want to run Philadelphia. How are you going to buy advertising in the newspaper for your show? It'll cost an arm and a leg!

On the other hand, there are plenty of good-sized markets that aren't the biggest cities in the country, but they're places where WWE hasn't run too much and where you can go and beg to the newspaper, because you can afford their ads. You can afford the radio spots. Amarillo was a pretty good-sized market that fit that description at that time.

And I was very pleased with the *50 Years of Funk* show. One of the things I was most pleased with was that I got to work with Bret Hart.

Bret Hart was my first choice for an opponent at the show, because of his in-ring talent and because of his status in the business. I also wanted him as an opponent to make him a part of it because I loved that family.

When I asked Bret to do the show, he said, "OK. Just send me an airplane ticket."

It was just that simple. Bret was another second-generation wrestler, and he was a very good businessman and a very sharp wrestler. Sometimes younger guys forget that having knowledge of the business and working smart means more than all the tanned muscles in the world. In order to be someone who consistently puts people in seats, you have to be sharp.

And I should stop again here and respond to something from Ric Flair's book, where he called Bret a mediocre wrestling talent.

I think Bret Hart was an excellent worker. He had a great feel for the crowds and had as much athletic ability as anyone, and he had a good mind for the business. Bret was a creator of moves and a real innovator. I think his and Jim Neidhart's matches against Dynamite Kid and Davey Boy Smith were some of the best tag-team matches I've ever seen in the States. Again, I'm totally at odds with Ric in his assessment of Bret Hart.

For *50 Years of Funk*, Bret, the WWF champion, was open to anything—including me beating him! That right there should tell you what kind of a guy Bret Hart is. However, I thought it would be ridiculous for an old fart like me to beat the champion.

I said, "Let's do something no one is expecting."

And I think the match was accepted better with Bret beating me in the middle of the ring than it would have been if I'd beaten him, because it was "50 Years of Funk." It was known that I was promoting it. It was known that this would be my last match in Amarillo. So what are you going to think as a fan?

You'll think, "Oh, it's his show, so you know he's going to win the thing."

Our match was actually the first time I had ever worked with Bret. His dad, Stu Hart, and much of the Hart family came down for the match, too, and I really enjoyed seeing them again.

We had a moment of silence on the show for Fritz Von Erich, who had passed away the day before. Fritz had brain cancer, and so we all knew it was coming. It was a still a sad moment on the show, though, especially for me, remembering that Fritz was the guy who put himself in the hot seat by picking me to be world's champion, after it was a tie among all the other members.

Just about two months after the show, Bret's tenure with the WWF came to an ugly end in Montreal. Vince had told Bret he couldn't afford his contract and freed Bret up to go to WCW. The only problem was, Bret was still Vince's champion. Bret was willing to lose the belt before he left, but the two of them couldn't agree on a scenario, so Vince finally came up with a deal where Bret would go on TV and just give up the belt, say his farewells and go to WCW.

Of course that's not what happened. Vince had Bret and Shawn Michaels (his real-life enemy, not just a foe in the ring) in a match in Montreal, as part of the WWF's 1997 pay per view "Survivor Series." At about what was supposed to be the halfway point of the match, Shawn clamped Bret's own sharpshooter hold on him, and before Bret could react, referee Earl Hebner called for the bell, as if he'd given up. Shawn got the belt and ran off, and Bret was furious.

I thought it was a lousy deal, the way it came down, but it was nothing that I didn't expect. Vince was looking at WCW getting one of his top guys, regardless of how that came about, and Vince wanted to protect his company.

It just goes to show, you'd better be leery in this business. Anyone in as strong a situation as that one was has got to be ready for the worst, and not put himself in harm's way. Bret trusted the wrong people, and he probably should have known better. He gave them his trust, and he expected them to keep it, because he had always kept their trust. But they didn't keep his, and that was wrong.

But you have to understand, Vince and his crew were also going to do everything they could to protect their livelihood. When all that comes together, trust is sometimes lost, but it's lost out of a perceived business necessity. Trust, honor and integrity all go down the tubes when you're talking about the lifeblood of your organization.

As close as Vince and Bret had been, I think something should have been worked out ahead of time. Maybe it just couldn't have been.

But you have to look at it through two sets of eyes—the wrestler's and the promoter's. From Vince's point of view, there was a fear that if he didn't do something drastic he could end up in worse trouble than he already was in. I guess he figured that protecting his company was worth breaking his word to Bret.

In the end, business-wise, it might not have been a bad decision on Vince's part, but I think Vince was totally wrong in what he did to Bret. Shawn Michaels was also wrong for his part in it. Bret might not have been 100 percent in the right, but I have to go with Bret on that one, and not just because he is my friend. Bret got done wrong because he tried to do right. He could have just walked out on the company as soon as he signed with WCW, but he wanted to work through his notice, because he felt like that was his obligation.

That's the thing about giving notice. You're leaving yourself wide open for someone to take a shot or do something to damage your credibility.

But if I was in Shawn Michaels's shoes, it would have been a tough decision to make. Hopefully I would have made a different decision, and I think I would have, but I can see where Shawn made the decision he did, because not going along with the plan might have meant the end of his career, at least in the WWF. At least 10 other guys on the card that night probably would have done the same thing Michaels did. I guess I'm just from a different era.

Ironically, a documentary crew following Bret around caught all of this on tape, just as Barry Blaustein was filming the rest of the wrestler segments for his documentary, *Beyond the Mat*. The documentary about Bret was released about a year later and was called, *Wrestling With Shadows*.

It was a hard time for Bret. A month earlier, he had lost a friend, as I had, when Brian Pillman passed away. Brian was found dead in his hotel room, the day of a WWF pay per view, October 10, 1997.

I was shocked at the news of Brian's death. I still feel sad when I think of Brian, because it was such a surprise. Maybe I should have, but I didn't see it coming. He had crushed his ankle in a car wreck, but it never occurred to him that he wouldn't come back. He always had in mind that he was still in the business and that he'd be getting back in the ring.

In addition to the *50 Years of Funk* show, Barry Blaustein's cameras caught me at a banquet, at my daughter's wedding, at the doctor's office, even getting out of bed one morning!

The strange thing was, the camera started out intrusive, but they followed me around for such a long period of time that, eventually, it just became part of the scenery. At first, I was doing things that weren't my normal things, acting in a way that wasn't natural. In other words, I was performing. But after a period of months, I got used to Barry and his camera being there, and there was no performance.

You might think they'd have been reluctant about having the whole thing shot for a movie, but the wedding party for my daughter Stacy's ceremony was actually pretty excited about the cameras being there.

But my kids have always been like that. They never had to perform for the cameras. They were never shy about cheering me on at my matches, even if they were being filmed in the crowd. In fact, if you go back and watch the tape of my retirement in 1983, my younger daughter Brandee is in the crowd, crying. I guess I did something right, because those girls love their dad, and my matches would often get emotional for them.

Anyway, the wedding ceremony made it into the movie, and when I saw the finished product, I thought Barry did an excellent job with it. I understand Jake Roberts was pretty upset with it.

Jake "The Snake" Roberts had been a big star in the WWF, among other places, in the 1980s. By the time Barry caught up to him, though, Jake wasn't doing that well. He was appearing at small independent shows and, judging from the movie, smoking a fair amount of crack cocaine.

I can't really understand why Jake was upset with the movie. Hell, he smoked crack right there on camera! It wasn't Barry's fault. Barry just filmed Jake doing what Jake did.

My segment came out as me. What you see in that movie is pretty much how I am.

Every now and then, someone will come up to me and say, "You did a great job in that *Beyond the Mat!*"

I always say, "Well, thank you, but I didn't really do anything. I just kind of walked around and was just myself."

CHAPTER 27

Cactus and Chainsaw

One time in the late 1970s, I wrestled once (and only once) in San Antonio under a mask, as "Dr. Knows It All." I honestly thought it was a clever idea to go on one week as the mysterious "Dr. Knows It All."

It didn't last long. As soon as my match was over, I pulled the mask off. I knew it wasn't working.

Another one that didn't work was Chainsaw Charlie.

The WWF was in trouble in late 1997. Eric Bischoff and WCW had recruited away a lot of Vince's stars. Vince damn near lost it all. If WCW had been smart and hadn't gotten complacent in the late 1990s, they could have finished him off. They thought they were smart, but he was the one left standing.

And he was left standing because he was forced to push some new names, and a lot of them clicked with people. One of the ones who clicked was my Japan and ECW running buddy—Mick Foley, a.k.a. Mankind, Dude Love and Cactus Jack. And Mick was about to get a tag-team partner. He hadn't yet reached his peak as a superstar, but he was definitely getting there.

Jim Ross, the great announcer who had come to the WWF and had become Vince's right-hand man, was the one who gave me the call. I'm pretty sure Cactus had promoted to him and Vince the idea of us working together, but hell, if they didn't want me at all, they wouldn't have called.

I agreed to come in because I wanted to help that company. There's just a challenge to going to a company that's an underdog and trying to make whatever changes you can, to be a part of its improvement. And I think I was part of it. I wouldn't say I was the swaying factor, nor did I ever expect I would be, but I pitched in my two cents.

I also wanted to go for Cactus. I wanted to do anything I thought would help Cactus. And I still would. Now, why I would want to do something for the big goof, I'll never know. I guess I just like the guy.

I was actually supposed to work in the WWF in late 1993. They had called me about becoming head booker. They were doing their big Survivor Series show in Boston, and they wanted me to wear some silly outfit with a blue mask, to be one of Jerry Lawler's knights, taking on Bret Hart and three of his brothers in a big tag match. Their plan was, Bret was going to beat me, then take my mask off and put his finishing hold, the sharpshooter, on me and beat me again. After that, "they" said, I would become the creative head of the company, replacing Pat Patterson, my old friend. Patterson had gone from being Ray Stevens' tag partner to being the WWF's booker, but Pat was looking to step down and take it a little easier.

I went to meet with them about it, and going from my ranch, with all the open space, to New York City, with the cabs and people, the hustle and bustle, was culture shock. It was an hour to get here, an hour to get there. There was no place to go that I was going to get to very quickly.

I met with them and then had dinner with Pat. It was great—we laughed a lot and told old stories. Then, I went up to my hotel room and went to bed. As I lay there, I got to thinking, "I'm not sure if I want to follow through with this deal."

I got up the next morning and left a note for Vince. It read, "My horse is sick. I think he's dying. I'll see you later."

A couple of hours later, I was at the airport, when I heard them call my name for a call on the airport paging system. I was running by that time!

And I came home. I escaped again.

As it turned out, that was when Lawler was having his legal troubles, so they replaced him with Shawn Michaels. I would have been one of Shawn Michaels's knights!

When I came to work for him in late 1997, one of the first things Vince said to me was, "So how's your horse?"

The first time I walked in, in 1997, the atmosphere there wasn't really very positive. I don't know if the deal with Bret Hart and Montreal was the cause of it, or if it was just that WCW was kicking the WWF's ass (which it was). There was a definite feeling from McMahon and from the guys in the locker room that WCW had become the real power in the profession.

Coincidentally, this was also around the time Vince was starting to make his stuff counterprogramming, by incorporating some of the hard-edged style that allowed a niche group like ECW to make a national impression.

I got ready for my big debut on *Raw* that Monday night in December, and the plan was for me to come out of a box. Bruce Prichard, one of the backstage guys, was describing to me what they wanted me to do.

I said, "That's it? You just want me to come out of the box?"

"Well, yeah," he said. "Just come out of the box. Do you want to come out as anything?"

Before my brain could fully process the question, my lips blurted out, "Chainsaw Charlie! Get me a chainsaw, so I can go out there!"

I can't explain it. It just popped into my mind.

They asked me what I wanted to wear and then got me some Levi jeans and a pair of suspenders. I already had a red shirt, so I kept that. Then, they got me a woman's pantyhose stocking and some baby powder to put on my head, all at my request (what an idiot). I guess I could have just gone out there without anything over my head, but I wouldn't have been Chainsaw Charlie with Terry Funk's head, would I? I'd have been Chainsaw Terry!

I came out of that box with my chainsaw and my stocking over my head, and the crowd, expecting some great surprise, let out a sound that seemed strangely reminiscent of escaping gas. I had visions of coming out to a tremendous roar, but that wasn't exactly the reaction I got.

I started out teaming with Mick right away, but they had us in a situation where we also liked to fight each other. This culminated in a falls-count-anywhere match on *Raw* where we brawled all over the place.

The match ended with us both in a dumpster that was going to be pushed offstage by The Road Dogg and Billy Gunn, the New Age Outlaws. Road Dogg was Brian James, son of Robert James, whom I had wrestled no telling how many times under his ring name of Bob Armstrong.

We set up for it by Cactus tossing me into a dumpster set up on the stage at the top of the ringside ramp. Then Cactus climbed up the railings alongside the monitor and delivered a big elbow onto me, in the dumpster. It was supposed to be a thrilling, dangerous spot.

But when Cactus did his big dive onto me, the thousands and thousands of little Styrofoam puffs, put in there for our protection, poofed up into the air. That was not our idea of hardcore. I guess we would have rather had just the metal floor on the bottom and killed our damn selves.

We ended up at Wrestlemania XV, the WWF's biggest show of the year, against the New Age Outlaws in a dumpster match, where the only way to win was to put both of your opponents into a dumpster at ringside.

We did a spot during the match where Road Dogg powerbombed me into the dumpster, from the ring. This meant that he would pick me up over his head and fling me forward, sending me back-first over the top rope and into the dumpster below. It was a dangerous spot, because there wasn't much room for error with a metal dumpster, but we thought it was worth it, because we wanted to do some memorable things for the major event. It was especially dangerous, because I was flying blind, so to speak, since I was going backwards. I was pretty much relying completely on Brian's guidance to make sure I landed inside the thing OK.

His guidance was perfectly good, but what we didn't know was that there was a big, two-by-12 plank in the dumpster. We hadn't checked the dumpster beforehand. Hell, who would think that there would be a huge plank in the dumpster we were going to use for our match?

I hit the board right on the right cheek of my ass. Immediately, a hematoma swelled up on me. It looked later like I had a blue watermelon sticking out of the side of my ass. I damn sure didn't feel like moving, but I knew I had a match to finish, so I got on out of there and kept going. Still, it was awfully painful, but that's the kind of thing that happens.

The match ended with us putting them in a dumpster backstage to win the match. Immediately after, I wasn't looking to celebrate the victory. I went to the doctor backstage.

To this day, I have no muscle tone to the right cheek of my ass. The whole cheek just hangs there, drooping. I have an indentation where I once had an ass cheek.

Ever since then, I've been a half-assed wrestler.

Mick and I also made a lot of personal appearances while we were in the WWF. Mick always tried to treat people right, but on one occasion, he got a little preoccupied, and it came back to bite him right in his big butt!

Cactus and I were at an autograph signing, and the people were just coming one right after the other.

I'd ask the guy how he was and what his name was. He'd tell me, I'd write it on the picture with my autograph and then pass it to Cactus, or vice versa. We did this hundreds of times that day, always with the same conversation.

"How are you?"

"I'm fine. How are you?"

"Great. That's great."

Finally, this gal came up and Cactus said, "Well, what's your name?"

She told him, and he wrote it down on the picture.

He said, while signing, "Well, how are you?"

She said, "Well, not too good. My husband just passed away."

He didn't even look up.

"Well, that's great," he said, and passed me the picture.

I stopped.

"Cactus! Did you hear what she said?"

He looked up.

"Whoa, no! What did she say?"

"She said her husband just passed away!"

He felt really bad, but he had just been in that mode, you know? Sign, make small talk, repeat.

Cactus was a really good guy to travel with, though. Just like in Japan, we both wanted to make as much money as we could, which meant spending as little as we could. When we were on the road, we would rent a Pinto, or whatever the cheapest piece of shit was we could get.

Sometimes we'd have another guy with us, so we were splitting the car three ways, splitting a motel room three ways and arguing over who was sleeping on the floor. Hell, we were making good money! We were working for Vince McMahon, and the WWF was making a big comeback! I guess we just didn't want to take any chances, so we'd be ready for the bad times.

Those damn Pintos had that high engine whine, and those little-bitty air-conditioners, and we'd be tooling down the road in our $18-a-day car, while the other guys would cruise by in their limousines and sports cars.

And any time we saw another Pinto coming up the road at us, we knew who it was. He'd pull alongside us, and we'd wave at "Stone Cold" Steve Austin! Yes, the biggest star in all of wrestling was driving the cheapest son of a bitch he could find, too. The young guys could ride in the limos, but the guys who had been down the road before and knew what it was like to have hard times, by God, we weren't sure things were going to continue to be all right!

For a couple of years, Austin was as big a star as I've ever seen in this business. He was not only in the right place at the right time, but he had the ability to produce that "Stone Cold" character and to get it over with the people.

Another star on the rise there was Dwayne Johnson, The Rock. It would be a little more than another year before he really hit the top. I knew from looking that he was a very capable individual and a talking son of a gun. He understood the business very well, from being a third-generation guy (his dad was Rocky Johnson, and his granddad was Peter Maivia, for you remaining 12 simple-minded people who might not have known that). His family was one of the few times I've ever been in the ring with three generations.

Rock's dad, Rocky Johnson, had a lot of charisma. And I had wrestled High Chief Maivia in Houston, in an NWA title defense. He was a great guy to work with and knew how to work his gimmick. Peter was a good draw for Paul Boesch in Houston, as well as all over the West Coast. He was a big Samoan, and tough as hell, but was so easy to work with. You had to be tough to get covered in tattoos from the waist down, which he had to do as part of his becoming a true Samoan high chief. And hell, between Rock and Randy Orton, the third-generation guys are batting a thousand! Maybe Vince ought to find out what Greg Gagne's kids are up to!

Cactus, even in 1998, making as much money as he ever had, would even save on hotels by finding some goofy-ass fan to stay with! He didn't know them from Adam! It would just be some fan he met at the show!

"Hey, Terry, I'm skipping the motel. I'm going to save some money."

"Well, what are you going to do, Cactus?"

"Oh, I'm going to stay with this guy over here."

Well, how did he know it wasn't some goddamned Hannibal Lecter who was going to cut him up and make Cactus Jack stew? Actually, the real question is, how did that fan know that Cactus Jack wasn't Hannibal Lecter? Who would be nuts enough to take a guy who looks like Cactus Jack home with them?

We went through a ton of shit, but I am proud to consider Mick Foley a good friend of mine to this day. My good friend Mick also got me to read his goddamned novel, *Tietam Brown,* by telling me they were going to make a movie out of it, and he thought I'd be perfect for the part of the father. And that's how he got me to read his book, because he knew that was the only way I'd read the fucking thing! That son of a bitch.

I'm just kidding, Mick! Actually, it's a really good story.

But he *did* tell me that it was going to be a movie.

All joking aside, Mick Foley is proof that anyone can achieve something if they bust their ass for it. Here was a guy who certainly didn't appear to have the physical endowments to be a wrestler. He just had the brains and the "want-to." But he really, really wanted to, and he did. Of course, he also tried to kill himself in the ring a couple of times.

Actually, one of the times he probably came closest, he wasn't trying at all.

At the June 1998 pay per view, *King of the Ring,* Cactus was wrestling as Mankind and had a Hell in the Cell match with Undertaker. Now, these are cage matches with one key difference—there is a roof on the cage.

This was the final battle in the two-year feud between Mick and Undertaker, who had possessed one of the better gimmicks to come down the pike. One of the reasons it was so great was that Mark Calaway, the man called the Undertaker, did his gimmick so well and protected it so well. He took a gimmick that should have lasted a couple of years before burning out, and he got a career's worth out of it. And he accomplished this by truly becoming the Undertaker. Hell, undertakers should be looking at him to see how they should be. Seriously, though, who would have thought he would have had that much staying power?

Believe it or not, I gave Mark his previous name, when he came into WCW to team with my friend Dan Spivey, as the Skyscrapers. I came up with "'Mean' Mark Callous," so blame me for that one if you want to.

Mick and I drove up to Pittsburgh where the match was being held, and he was talking about how he wanted to do something spectacular and memorable. We somehow came up with the idea of Cactus taking a big fall off the top. Then, after he came back, to everyone's amazement, Undertaker would still be on the top of the cage and would choke slam him onto the cage roof. The same prop guy was supposed to make sure the two sides of the cage were secure, so the impact from Mick's body would cause the top of the cage to sag and gradually come open, so Mick would tumble into the ring. It would be a hell of a spectacular bump, but Mick figured he'd have the cage breaking his fall.

Well, if you saw the match, you know the fall from the top was awesome. Mick just couldn't have timed it or mapped out his landing any better. You also know that when he went back up, the top of the cage didn't hold at all. The props guy didn't rig it properly, so when Undertaker gave him the choke slam, Cactus went right through the roof, like a warm knife through butter and hit the mat like a piece of lead.

Watching from the back, I thought he was dead. I ran out there and looked down at him, still lying in the ring where he'd landed. His eyes weren't rolled back in his head, but they looked totally glazed over, like a dead fish's eyes.

I got up and went over to the Undertaker, who was standing next to the people checking on Mick, and I told him, "He's not going to be here. That's it. Cactus isn't going to make it."

But we saw him coming around a little and decided to buy some time, so Undertaker gave me a couple of punches and choke slammed me. We just wanted to do anything to give them some time, because we thought Mick was going out of there in an ambulance. I guess I figured I would finish up the deal in the ring with Undertaker while they took care of Cactus.

He gave me the choke slam, and I looked over, and here came Cactus! He was getting up. I was amazed! I could not believe he was even conscious, but he made it to his feet and finished the match, even doing their planned finish with Cactus falling into a pile of thumbtacks before getting pinned. And then, rather than go to the hospital, like a person with any sense would do, he stayed backstage so he could do his planned run-in on the main event with Steve Austin and Kane!

That's just the kind of guy Mick Foley is. He's a tough son of a bitch, and you won't find anyone in the wrestling business with a bigger heart for the guys, or more love for the fans and the business. He also did what he did for the security of his family.

And I know Cactus will get upset with me for saying this, but as I've told him before, I think the only reason he lived through that fall through the cage was because of God's gift to him of a fat ass. That fat ass was the first thing that hit, and it cushioned the fall a little for the rest of his body. The fact that his ass was the heaviest part of Mick's body kept gravity from bringing his head down first, because if he'd landed on his head, we wouldn't have the wonderful "Mick Foley—Millionaire" story to tell. We wouldn't have been reading his books (actually, that might have been a blessing—just kidding, Mick!).

When poor Owen Hart fell from the harness on a May 23, 1999, pay per view and died, he fell a lot farther, but he also landed on his head. Owen was doing a silly superhero gimmick, and they were going to lower him into the ring from the ceiling. But something went wrong, Owen came loose, and he didn't make it.

Whatever problems the Hart family had after Bret got screwed over in Montreal paled in comparison to what happened after Owen Hart died. Martha,

Owen's widow, sued McMahon and the company that made the harness that was to lower him into the ring, but some of the family backed McMahon. I don't know if they truly thought he wasn't to blame for Owen's death, or if they thought there would be something in it for them, but it tore that family apart.

The whole thing was unbelievable. Bruce Hart, Bret and Owen's older brother, called me up the night it happened and told me. I just couldn't believe it. I mean, I really didn't believe it. My first thought was, "Is this some kind of work?"

The whole thing was just heartbreaking. Owen was just 34, and I'd known him since he was 10 years old, hiding in the back of that dadgummed Cadillac, as we paraded through the streets of Calgary.

He had grown up to be a great guy. He was a great ribber, too.

Once it sank in, and especially the more I learned about what happened the night Owen died, the more I got to thinking about some equipment failures I had experienced during my last stint in the WWF.

There was that night, 11 months earlier, when Mick fell through the cage during that Hell in a Cell match with the Undertaker. And that wasn't even the first time I noticed a problem.

Several weeks before the Hell in a Cell match, they had a prop man who was supposed to take care of my chainsaw, so I could go out and be Chainsaw Charlie. It had a chain on it, but the chain was frozen, so I wouldn't hack anyone up swinging the thing around. It also had a grinder on it, which produced sparks. In fact, it produced a great deal of sparks.

Now, bear in mind it was this guy's responsibility to make sure this thing was working, because Vince didn't want me going out there with a chainsaw that didn't work. Hell, I looked silly enough with a chainsaw that did work!

So on this night I was getting ready to go, and the props guy got the chainsaw running and handed it to me. They called for me to go to the ring, and I started heading down the aisle. As I walked to the ring, I raised the chainsaw over my head and clicked the switch to create sparks, without any luck.

After a few seconds of this, I noticed an odd odor and looked at the chainsaw. What I saw alarmed me, somewhat.

From the moment I lifted the thing over my head, gas had been pouring out of it, down my arm and onto my body. The son of a bitch had forgotten to tighten up the lid.

But here's the damndest thing about it. I knew that gas was on me, but I kept trying to get the sparks to go, because, by God, I was Chainsaw Charlie! It was only through a stroke of luck or an act of God that I didn't explode.

I was pretty upset with the guy, and you'd better believe I let him hear about it when I got backstage again, smelling like gasoline and half covered with it.

Now, this was a time when competition was really heavy. WCW was still ahead of Vince, but not for long, and they were neck and neck. *Raw* and *Nitro* were live, head-to-head shows, and both sides were pushing hard. They had timeframes in which they had to do stuff, and you had better be where they needed you, when they needed you there, because they wanted those shows to move. If they didn't move enough, the thought was, people might change the channel and watch the other wrestling show. They were pushing hard to make everything happen during the breaks. And when you're in that frame of mind, mistakes happen. But to me, after Mick took the plunge in that Hell in the Cell match, that was two mistakes too many.

And I don't know if this same guy was involved in what happened to Owen Hart. I tend to doubt he was, but I do feel that Owen died because of the same "pressed for time" mentality that led to my chainsaw leak, that damn beam in that dumpster and Mick's fall through the cage.

Sometimes I think, maybe if we'd made a bigger deal out of the incidents with Cactus and me, maybe they would have looked more carefully at everything else they did after that, including Owen Hart's drop into the ring.

I didn't work exclusively with Cactus the whole time I was there, though. I faced a lot of other WWF guys, and my terrible luck with catchers also continued. Just like a few years earlier, when I tried the same move at that show in Japan, I was doing a match in 1998 with Mark Henry, whom the WWF called "The World's Strongest Man." I went for a moonsault outside the ring with him right below me. To this day, I don't understand how he missed me, coming down like a 250-pound sack of shit dropping from the top rope, when he could lift minivans and shit.

Good thing they didn't call him "The World's Fastest Man!"

During this time, Vince actually presented me with one of the few things I refused to do, and it wasn't an in-ring gimmick. He wanted me to run for one of the Texas seats in the U.S. Senate. He called me up late one night, very excited about his idea, and I said no. It was pretty stupid on my part, really. A decade earlier, I had given Ted DiBiase great advice about jumping at the chance to do something that McMahon was ready to push that hard, and here I was, not taking my own advice.

Through the years, I had contemplated running for the state legislature or senate a few times. In late 2003, I actually gave some serious thought to running in the 31st District and came very close to running. In the end, the guy who had initially asked me to run called the house and asked me not to. There were some other people in the Amarillo political community who were pressuring me not to run, too.

Still, I think I had a very good chance against the incumbent. The area represented was the area I had known all my life, and an area where people knew me. I was really concerned about the water issue here. Boone Pickens has water rights to the Ogelalla, and he wants to supply other major cities of Texas with water from the reservoir. Well, the water is drawn from saturated sand, and it takes years to fill up again. The whole thing is tied up in litigation. I don't want water to get scarce here because he's providing it to someone else. I just don't want my grandkids having to pay every time they flush the toilet. I felt it was an important issue and felt like I could have an impact on it.

I called the guy who had asked me to run and then changed his mind, and told him he had convinced me not to run. But that wasn't really the case.

What really killed it was being in the kitchen one day with my wife and my daughter Brandee. We sat and talked about it, and we all knew it would be very time consuming, with a lot of time spent in Austin. Well, they wanted me home, not arguing about policy hundreds of miles away. My daughter Stacy, who was out of town, had also voiced her opinion on me having a political career, which was similar to Vicki's and Brandee's. They were already tired of me being gone all the time while I was wrestling full time. We talked it over from every angle.

Finally, I said, "All right, let's do this the right way; let's vote. Should I run? Yes or no."

Each of us took a piece of paper, to write down our answers. I looked at my little scrap of paper and thought about how much they hated me gone and how much me doing this would change all of our lives.

We wrote down our votes, and when I opened up the papers, they read, "No," "No," and "No."

And so I didn't run for office. And I don't think I ever will. If there was a right time, that was it, and that time is over.

My last run in the WWF was as a partner of John Layfield, who wrestled as Justin Bradshaw. I liked him, but you'd better watch out for that goofball's clothesline. It was like taking one from Hansen! They're both idiots! Listen—the crowd does not feel your clothesline. They just see it. It's not necessary to take someone's goddamned head off to make the fans appreciate the move!

Bradshaw was also a big Dick Murdoch fan and was half-goofy, just like his hero. What can I say about a guy who idolized Dick Murdoch? Dick Murdoch was a nut! What does that make Bradshaw? It makes him a pretty unique guy. I mean, here was a guy emulating Dick Murdoch, and yet he was a guy writing a book on the stock market and how to invest! Would you trust a guy who wants to be just like Dick Murdoch telling you what stock to buy? Hell, it's a wonder he wasn't pushing Coors! CNBC was probably right to fire his ass!

He got to meet Murdoch early in his career, and even when I worked with him in the WWF, all he would talk about was Dick Murdoch! He thought Murdoch was the greatest guy in the world! Hell, I bet he was one of those guys who got in the pickup with Murdoch early on, with Murdoch telling him, "You and me, we're the only ones around here with any damned sense!"

And Bradshaw believed him! He must have been the only one who didn't know Dick was full of bullshit.

OK now, I want to back up for a second, because I made a joke of Bradshaw getting fired by CNBC, and I think it's worth stopping with the bullshit for a second, going back and talking seriously about the situation that led to that happening.

Bradshaw decided to try to get a rise out of the German fans while touring over there in 2004 by goose-stepping and giving the Nazi salute. When CNBC got wind of it, they fired him as a financial analyst.

I think the ones who should be chastised are the ones who fired Bradshaw, because I think they're the ones who are prejudiced. They don't want someone coming from a "lowly sport" like professional wrestling into their world, while still able to do the things wrestlers sometimes do to get heat.

When Bradshaw did his goose-stepping, he ended up getting the crap beat out of him in the ring, so it was a case of a heel getting what was coming to him. When he sold for Eddy Guerrero and the Undertaker later in that match, he took the idea of what he'd been representing, and he destroyed it. Eddy and Undertaker destroyed the whole Nazi regime in that match! Bradshaw's CNBC firing was utterly ridiculous.

One of my last opponents in the WWF was Vader, a huge man with great mobility. There's one thing I'll say for Vader. In professional wrestling, you have to believe in yourself and in the character you are portraying. And Leon "Vader" White certainly did.

After the little run with Bradshaw, I went to Vince and told him I had done the job I came to do, and that I felt like I'd helped as much as I could. Vince was very professional about it, and thanked me for my work.

Mick was kind of sorry to see me go, but he knew I hadn't been wanting to go in for any long-term deal.

I'll tell you this, though. Vince is a controversial figure, but he has his generous side. Steve Nelson, a tough kid who was the son of lady wrestler Marie Laverne (who had some great matches with Kay Noble) and Gordon "Mr. Wrestling" Nelson and a good wrestler in his own right, was trying to go to a sambo tournament in Russia where he wanted to compete, but he couldn't afford it. Gordon Nelson never wrestled for Vince, but someone informed Vince that the kid needed some money to go over there and compete.

Vince sent him the money without even knowing the kid!

CHAPTER 28

The Twilight of WCW

Like most of my incursions from 1993 onward, this one started with a phone call. The call came from Kevin Sullivan, who was now the booker for WCW. It was January 2000, and WCW had just had a major power shift, with Eric Bischoff finally getting the boot in September 1999. WWF writers Vince Russo and Ed Ferrara came in, but they were also gone before long. Turner Broadcasting executives then made Sullivan the booker, which led to some problems with some of the talent.

Specifically, Chris Benoit had a lot of problems with Kevin Sullivan, both professional and personal. He led a group of WCW stars consisting of himself, Perry Saturn, Dean Malenko and Eddy Guerrero, right over to the WWF. When I got there, they were just about out of there. Shane Douglas had been part of their group, but they ended up going without him, and I don't know why.

I still remember seeing Benoit and Malenko in Japan, and later in ECW. I knew both those guys would do well. Their biggest problem was having a window open for them to show what they could do for the decision-makers in the wrestling business, and to have an opportunity to perform in front of their people.

I think the world of Chris Benoit, but I also considered Sullivan a friend, so I stayed out of that whole mess. As far as I was concerned, I was just there to work my way through it and make a buck. And once I got down there, it became pretty clear that making a buck was going to be the extent of what I could do there.

Sullivan was still a great idea man, but he had forces working against him that were tough to overcome, and he still needed someone to keep him in check.

If there was someone around Kevin to keep him within the boundaries of good sense, he'd be worth his weight in gold to any company, because he has no shortage of really great ideas. If I were going to start a promotion right now, I'd get Kevin Sullivan to be my booker, because by God, he'd have a gazillion ideas for whatever wrestlers I could get working for me, and he has endless energy, something you need in a position like that.

There was so much chaos there that no one could accomplish much of anything. It was constant change, and you never knew who was running what. One day, J.J. Dillon was the guy I needed to talk to about my program. The next week, he wasn't. People were suddenly there, and suddenly gone and sometimes back again.

Kevin Sullivan called and presented me a scenario where I would start as the WCW commissioner. I would be working a program against Kevin Nash, with kind of a power struggle between us.

So I went in and cut some promos and got the thing with Nash set up.

We had a hardcore match, which proved to be another example of a guy stiffing me in the match and giving me nothing. Maybe he thought since he was a foot taller than me, he shouldn't have to make an old man look like he could do him any harm. Who knows?

With me, if I was in a match with someone who gave and gave in the match, I was going to return the favor. Nash apparently didn't have that attitude, but it ultimately fell on the company. When someone brings you in, it's only natural to think that they see some value and want to use you, not abuse you. I probably should have asked where we were going with it. Nash certainly knew where he was going with it—absolutely nowhere.

All of a sudden, he was gone. The guy just disappeared from WCW not long after our match. We never even got into what we were doing. Maybe because of the turmoil regarding who was running the company, a lot of the big guys just vanished from TV. Of course, they were still getting their big paychecks.

Sullivan needed some names he could count on, and I happened to know a guy who worked hard and was something of a name performer. So I got on the phone to Sabu.

ECW, where Sabu had made his biggest name, was really just a stage for the talent to get exposure and to perform. In the 1990s, there were only two real places to make money in wrestling—the WWF and WCW. By 2000, ECW was having some pretty serious problems, and Sabu was looking for a place to make a better living. I told Kevin Sullivan that he wanted to come in, and Kevin said, "Great!"

Kevin knew that Sabu was a real piece of talent and got him a deal worth $250,000 a year, which was pretty damn good money, even with the inflated salaries some of those other guys were making.

Paul Heyman put a stop to it, citing a contract he had with Sabu, even though Paul was barely upholding his end of the deal and owed Sabu money at the time! To this day, I still consider Paul a friend, but this was one of the few times I was really upset with him. I just couldn't stomach the idea that Paul would keep this guy from earning a living. I don't pretend to know everything that went down between Sabu and Paul E. in ECW, but why do that to him?

Seriously, WCW was thrilled about the idea of getting Sabu, and Heyman threatening the possibility of legal action put the kibosh on the whole deal. It just chilled the whole deal.

With all of this going on, Mick Foley's autobiography came out. It was called *Have a Nice Day: A Tale of Blood and Sweatsocks,* and it jumped to the top of the *New York Times* bestsellers list. It contained a less-than-flattering portrayal of Ric Flair, who was something of the elder statesman of WCW. Flair was booker when Cactus worked in WCW, starting in late 1989, and Cactus wrote that Flair was too concerned with other things (such as his hair) to book him in a way that he would get over. We did a short program with me against Flair, and we made the comments in the book part of the angle, but Flair never said one word about the book to me privately. If it truly bugged him, he never let me know about it.

That deal with Flair also exposed me a little to his son, David. Talk about a tough act to follow! I like David, and I think that he would have had a much easier time in the business if he wasn't the son of one of the all-time greats. It was kind of like Dusty and Dustin, except Dustin finally found his niche. David never did, and it was just impossible for him to walk out to the ring without having people making a comparison to one of the greatest professional wrestlers there has ever been. Him having to suffer that comparison was a travesty in its own right.

Being out there with Ric didn't enhance his career; it limited his career. It was different for David than it was for my brother and me starting out. A lot of that had to do with the image my father portrayed, as opposed to the image Ric portrays, and I'm not knocking Ric when I say that. My father had a different image to the Amarillo people—they knew the Funks. We had been around that place for a lifetime. Dory Funk, our dad, was just a regular guy, which was true— he *was* just a regular guy. The character Flair portrayed was larger than life. Dusty Rhodes was another larger-than-life image, and I think that made the difference between David and Dustin, and Junior and me. Greg Gagne ran into the same problems in the AWA, when Verne tried to push him. Verne had pushed himself as the larger-than-life man in that area that he had become the one and only. And he was to those fans. Today you see the same thing with Vince McMahon's children, and you might notice they pull back from having his kids on TV all the time.

Unfortunately, my issue with Flair kind of fizzled out, just as my issue with Kevin Nash had done. It was almost as if it were written in stone that in WCW, there would be no continuity, no building on anything. It was as if, every week, they just threw a bunch of stuff out there, and none of it had time to get over with the audience, which was rapidly shrinking. In 2000, WCW had the unmistakable stink of death on it. There was a feeling in the locker room like everyone felt it wasn't going to last much longer. I don't think anyone doubted it. I knew it was doomed from the moment I walked in the door.

And I wish I could tell you what Sting was like in 1999 and 2000, compared to the Sting I knew a decade earlier, but I was never around him. Sting, like so many other top guys in WCW, appeared and disappeared into his own quarters. I've been in thousands of locker rooms in my life, and I think separating the top stars like that is completely absurd, and completely demeaning to the guys those top stars are wrestling. I wish I'd thought to ask one of them, "You mean that this guy is going to go out there and make you look great, so you can continue to be a star, and yet you can't bring yourself to change in the same room with this guy?"

If I'd been in my prime and someone showed me that kind of disrespect, they might have found themselves doing real battle with me, in the ring. It was insulting and showed no dignity or respect for the people who were making the stars. Maybe I was just never a star the caliber of Sting, Hulk Hogan, or Kevin Nash, but when I was world's champion in 1976, I never dressed separately from the other boys, nor did I find myself bothered by the other boys. I can't think of anyone who was or is so big a star in wrestling that he's just too good to dress with the other boys. Take The Undertaker, for example. He never did that when I was around him, and I'd bet you $100 he doesn't do it now. "Stone Cold" Steve Austin was a bigger star at his peak than *anyone* in WCW was at his peak, and I'd bet you $100 that Austin never did that bullshit.

To get away, to get out of the dressing room for a minute to discuss a finish is one thing. But to alienate yourself from your peers is beyond my comprehension, especially since those peers are doing you a favor by putting their shoulders to the mat.

What that company needed was someone to take the reins a lot sooner. Kevin Sullivan tried it in 2000, but he had a lot of enemies in the company, and in truth, by then it was too late. It had gotten down to a level where a resurgence would have been impossible, especially since most of the guys who had been WCW's top stars were just gone. Kevin was left with a group of guys who, except for Hulk Hogan and Ric Flair, were not the superstars WCW had been focusing on for years. It was also a group that changed constantly, which made long-term planning impossible.

Sullivan was still a great idea man, but it wouldn't be long before he was also shown the door. I think Vince Russo played a part in that, and he was the guy who ended up back in charge, along with Bischoff. The entire company was falling apart, and Kevin Sullivan was there, trying to hold the pieces together. He ended up being WCW's fall guy, the guy blamed for all of that company's problems, even though those problems were there before they put Kevin in charge.

I talked to him right before he left. He said, "Damn, Terry, I'm having to come up with shows, and no one's here."

Kevin Sullivan was one of those rare realists in wrestling, and I think he knew from the day he started that he was there to put together a TV show with whatever he could gather. I think he also knew he was only in for the short term, and that he'd be gone when it all started going to hell. But at least Kevin was trying to create. The ones who would replace him ended up doing nothing but destroying.

In April 2000, Sullivan was out and Bischoff and Russo both came back. Hell, *I* could have told them that wasn't going to work! The last year of that company was a period of total idiocy.

Here you had Vince Russo, who was supposed to be a writer, and all of the sudden, he's Vince Russo, the executive in charge. And then, he's suddenly Vince Russo, the performer! Having a writer as a performer was the wrong move for the company, especially since WCW had the money to hire as many performers as it needed. What WCW ended up with was a "The Emperor Has No Clothes" scenario.

I'll use Sylvester Stallone as an example. We were filming *Paradise Alley* in 1977. Sly was the director, and he was also the lead actor. Sly would finish a scene, and no matter how he did, people on the set would say, "Academy award!"

You get the same thing with someone in Russo's position. No one was willing to be honest with him. You gain more by dishonesty. Remember the story about Dick Murdoch and Jim Herd? Dick told him the truth, but Dick would have been better off by lying to the man.

And if all you hear is how good you're doing, it's easy to start believing you actually *are* good, especially when you're in main issues and you're the one writing all this stuff.

As a creative person, he needed an overseer, as any creative person does. I think the guy could create good stuff, but he could create godawful stuff, too. And somebody needed to be there over him, to tell him which was which. And it needed to be someone who actually knew the wrestling business, someone who knew the kinds of things that worked and the kinds of things that were too off the wall to get over with anyone.

Even Vince McMahon has that problem sometimes. Sometimes McMahon's WWE (as McMahon's company is now known) does something completely off the wall, and it doesn't work. But Vince has people around him, people who can be that conservative voice and help sort out some of those ideas. And even then, the "Stallone syndrome" still exists in that organization, as advanced as WWE is.

You just need a conservative voice, and that's not hard to find in wrestling. Creativity is what's hard to find, and Russo did some creative things. But if you just let a creative person go unchecked ... well, that person might think it's a good idea to go in front of an audience wearing a nylon stocking and baby powder over his head, and carrying a chainsaw.

And even if they did do well onscreen, pushing themselves is not what they should have been doing. Of all the talent WCW had, the best they can come up with to push is ... Eric Bischoff and Vince Russo? What kind of ego would you have to have to think that was a good idea? Bischoff and Russo became the stars of the show, and to make things worse, the show went from being wrestling to being a sitcom of absurdities.

Russo did try to find things to do with guys who had been underused. Hugh Morrus was one of them. He was a guy who could work. I always thought he would find a niche somewhere, but he never really did, and I can't understand why, because he had plenty of talent. He might just have been born too late. He was almost, to me, a Bob Sweetan type. Sweetan was a guy who a regional promoter would take one look at and think, "I won't make a dollar with this guy," but you could! Hell, Sweetan drew a lot of money for Bill Watts in Oklahoma, and he did well for Joe Blanchard in San Antonio. If Hugh had been back in that era, he would have found a niche and his opportunity to show he could draw a buck. But in this business and time, it's very difficult to get a guy like that over. He's not six foot six. He's not the most handsome guy on the show, but if he had gotten a chance, he could have proven himself. But he never got a chance because so much of the business is based on the outward physical appearance of a guy.

Another guy Russo had an idea for was former ECW champion Mike Awesome. Unfortunately, his idea was to turn Mike Awesome from a sadistic monster of a wrestler into a guy who loved fat women, and then into "That '70s Guy."

I've seen some bumbling bullshit in my life, but that is the most absurd thing I've ever seen. That was nothing short of being the destruction of an individual. The way they handled him was a travesty. I mean, here's a guy who is a monster, a big boy, who could do anything. He could backflip off the top rope. He was a good-looking guy, too, with a great physique. He was pretty much everything you could want out of a pro wrestler in this day and age. He had it all!

So what did they do with this incredible piece of talent? They had him lusting after fat women and wearing leisure suits!

I saw him on TV once, wearing some stupid Hawaiian shirt. Well, hell, he was *That '70s Guy!* Think about it—how could you more effectively destroy an individual any more than that? In the year 2000, with wrestling changing quicker than it ever had, with the top minds in the business striving to keep up with the changes, WCW tagged Mike Awesome "That '70s Guy!"

They totally destroyed the guy. It was right up there with the Ding Dongs and Dr. Knows it All. The sad thing was, he'd worked his ass off to get his shot in WCW. He worked for Onita in Japan and was over as a top singles guy, but what you might not realize is that "That '70s Guy" hurt him all the way around the world. He was no longer Mike Awesome, the incredible Gladiator. He was now "That '70s Guy!"

Another thing about Russo, and his sidekick, Ed Ferrara—when they were in the WWF and I got there in late 1997, they never took a minute to say one word to me. I have no idea why. Later, when I got to WCW, I think they were too ashamed to talk to me very much. Maybe they were too busy thinking up their brilliant plan to screw over Hulk Hogan on a live pay per view and cost the company a few million dollars. How innovative!

They booked me into the hardcore division. WCW had just started a hardcore title after the WWF had some success with the idea in 1998. The hardcore title matches were different from other title matches in that you could score a pinfall anywhere. You could fight out of the ring—hell, you could fight outside of the building!

On one episode of WCW's "Thunder" show in May, Chris Candido and I had a hardcore match where we ended up fighting in a horse stable. We were going at it when the damn horse just rared back and kicked the living hell out of me. I was actually very lucky not to be very seriously injured, because he kicked me right in the head. I went loopy and without thinking, jumped up and knocked the shit out of that horse.

I have never had any desire to sue anyone, but that was an instance where I probably could have. We were out at the stable earlier in the day, and I asked the guy running the stable, "Well, how's the horse?"

He said, "Oh, he's just fine."

I said, "Don't you think you ought to ace (meaning give the horse a tranquilizer to keep him from getting riled up) him?"

And they aced him. If they hadn't, I might not be here today, because that horse probably would have torn Candido and me to pieces. As it was, even on ace, the horse got surprised by us fighting in there and momentarily regained all his strength and bearings, just long enough to scramble my brains.

And none of this was the horse's fault. I ended up OK, but it sure could have turned into a bad situation. I've had a horse kick his way out of a metal horse trailer and completely destroy it, just by kicking, so a horse's kick is a pretty powerful thing.

Another time, I was wrestling Jerry "The Wall" Tuite, when I went for a moonsault outside the ring. You guessed it—he completely missed me! I loved The Wall—he was a great guy and a lousy cribbage player. He was also a lousy, lousy catcher!

I yelled at him a little after the match.

"Goddamn, how can you miss me?"

He said, "Sorry, Terry."

Another of my hardcore opponents was Norman Smiley. Smiley was a great guy who got the gimmick of being a coward named "Screamin'" Norman from Russo. What a lot of guys didn't realize was that Norman was whole lot tougher than they thought he was. He had worked for Japan's UWFI, which was a group working in a shoot style, a brutal, punishing way to work. I knew Smiley could go, although he never felt like he had to prove how tough he was. I was also glad I was never someone he decided to prove it to.

And he really had fun with the "Screamin'" Norman thing. He must have loved it, or he wouldn't have done it so well. The only problem I saw was, that was going to be a hard gimmick to overcome later. It was a fun character, but it was a character that was going to stay near the bottom of the card. There was no way "Screamin'" Norman was ever going to be a main-event deal.

They even had a deal where Bischoff beat me for the hardcore title. It was kind of a goofy deal, but hell, I didn't care, it was their title. That was their business, and their business was amok.

I should take a moment here and talk about Eric Bischoff. He was brilliant in some of his first endeavors. He brought in Hulk Hogan when a lot of people in the business thought Hogan was washed up, and made millions with him. He launched *Nitro*, the first time anyone dared take on Vince McMahon on a weekly basis. He brought in a lot of other WWF talent and gave them new leases on life. I probably wouldn't have done any of that if I'd been in his place.

Having said that, Eric didn't have a real understanding of the business overall, and I think he knows that now. His biggest mistake might have been becoming so involved with it himself as a performer, or allowing himself to be manipulated by others while he was supposed to be the boss. I don't think he would allow that to happen now.

And it wasn't even so much the guaranteed contracts themselves—it was who they gave the guaranteed money to. You have to use good judgment when you're giving a guy that much power.

But hell, what do I know? Maybe Kevin Nash understands the business better than I do, after all. I was always someone who had compassion for the other guys in the locker room. Nash made himself a lot of money with his philosophy of the business. That philosophy was to make Kevin Nash as much money as possible, at the expense of all others. And he was certainly not the only one who thought that way, either. Worst of all, those guys had no concern for their profession. They didn't give a shit about wrestling itself, or else they'd have been working every week. Not one of them was concerned with the product they were putting out.

Actually, one of the guys who got a reputation for being a difficult guy was someone I thought a lot of—Scott Steiner. He was a good kid and I always enjoyed being around him. When I was around him in 2000 in WCW, he hadn't changed and still hasn't, at least to me. He was still a great guy, and I still talk to him to this day. Scott and his brother Rick were two great guys, and they were smart. Both of them saved their money from wrestling, and I'm sure they're doing OK now.

In the end, Bischoff had a good plan for short-term success, but that was all he had. If you're running a wrestling company, you have to surround yourself with people who love the business, in order to succeed long term. You have to pick the guys who are going to be good soldiers, and eliminate the other ones. The beauty of the wrestling business is you can do that. A company can handle one or two people of that mentality, if they're big enough draws to justify it, but WCW had a locker room half-full of people like that. And that was no one's fault but the guy running the company—Bischoff.

Making movie actor David Arquette the world champion would have to rank up there with the stupidest ideas ever, too. How much does he weigh? 180? Hell, that shows that *everyone* has a chance! *Anyone* can be a professional wrestler! That was nothing short of an insult to the fans and to the other wrestlers.

So Eric was a guy capable of both a great idea and total idiocy. I don't think he was a wrestling genius by any means, and I think he ought to count himself lucky that he's able to draw a weekly paycheck from this business, working as an on-air character for Vince McMahon. He should be damned thankful for that check.

I think if he had it to do all over again, he'd do a lot differently. I think he would have built some stars of his own early, so he could have people who weren't such massive problems. He should have started creating talent instead of relying on guys who were known problems like Kevin Nash and Scott Hall.

That was one thing Paul E. was always great at in ECW, until the end. No matter who the WWF or WCW took from him, he always had somebody waiting in the wings. He was always making someone who could step into a position at the top level.

Eric also had found some success with smaller wrestlers who did more high-flying, the cruiserweights. The origin of the term "cruiserweight" in wrestling came from a car ride that I shared with Chris Benoit and Diamond Dallas Page, in 1993. We were heading to an independent show, which, as it turned out, would be the only time I worked with Chris. I really loved working that match with him and wish I could have worked with him more, because he was (and is) a great, great worker.

Anyway, we were in the car, and Page was asking me a million questions about what I'd do if I ran WCW. I told him that what I thought would be great would be go with a cruiserweight division and have it be totally separate. At the time, wrestling in the United States was all heavyweights (WCW had done a light-heavyweight division but never did much with it), and I thought the smaller guys could put on different styles of matches.

What I didn't know was that apparently Bill Watts was on his way out as head of WCW, and Page's buddy Bischoff was talking to the TBS people about replacing him.

About a year after Bischoff got in, he got the cruiserweight division going. But I have to tell you, I don't think Bischoff thought up that name all by himself. I think his buddy Diamond Dallas Page might have suggested that one.

My idea, though, was to do "Cruiserweight TV," with no mixing against heavyweights and all matches best of three falls. I also thought of experimenting with the idea of using a one-count as a pinfall for the cruiserweights.

I still think if WWE were to split their guys by weight, with one show nothing but cruiserweights, it would be interesting to see who got the better rating. It would certainly make for a clear distinction between the two shows they have, since *Raw* and *Smackdown!* are supposed to be different divisions. I'm not sure the heavyweight could produce the action like the cruiserweights, to sustain a better rating. Cruiserweights, in this day and age, are not just a unique attraction—they are a necessity, because of their speed and the unique action they can create. They can perform moves that you're just not going to see a 300-pound guy do, especially off the top rope. Maybe if they raised the ropes another three feet, they might be able to do them, but that's about the only way I can see.

It was obvious the end was near when the top guys just started vanishing, one by one. Hell, even Eric Bischoff secluded in his office in the back, somehow came down with a case of the contagious concussion!

Bischoff ended up leaving the company when Vince Russo pulled what might have been the single stupidest stunt of his career on a major pay per view in July 2000. They did a deal where Hogan went to the ring, and Jeff Jarrett laid down to let Hogan pin him for the title. This was all some pre-arranged deal, but what wasn't pre-arranged (at least with Hogan) was that Russo did a profanity-laced tirade on Hogan after the match and declared Hogan was champion of nothing. Hogan ended up suing the company, so they at least lost money on attorney's fees, and I bet you that thing didn't draw one new viewer or fan to WCW.

You just don't deal with a piece of talent that way, especially a piece of talent that has produced the box office Hogan has.

Actually, that might not be the most absurd thing those two were part of. The more I think about it, the more I think the most absurd thing they ever did was to think that they were proficient promoters and bookers in the wrestling business.

In a strange way, working for a company I knew was doomed helped me to have a good time there. I did my little part, just had a good time with the boys, and didn't worry about the rest. Still, I will never understand why someone, before it was too late, didn't look at the figures and say, "Hey, this thing's going in the wrong direction."

And what does it say about that company, or about me, that even I got that attitude, toward the end? Here I was, a guy who was supposed to act out of a love for the business, and I was reduced to just thinking of it as "just a job." By 2000, they had taken the heart out of just about everybody.

Wrestling's a joint venture—the promoters and boys have to work together, or it will fail. The top guys all had their own agendas, and none of them were to help the company.

In contrast to the stagnation that started WCW's fall, Vince looked long and hard at his company in 1997, and changed a lot of things, going for more of an ECW style and doing some other things, and it was successful for him. But that was because he owned it and he had the concern for it.

Who had that kind of love and concern for WCW? No one, and somebody should have, because it was a wonderful place for guys. Looking through a wrestler's eyes, and not an owner or promoter's eyes, it is not healthy for one company to be the only one in the business, and that's what we have now.

Even the WCW announcers were out of control! One night I was watching a show, and Mark Madden was calling the match. Whatever wrestler it was dug under the ring and came up with a table. Madden laughed and said, very sarcastically, "Would you believe there's a table under the ring?"

Well, that did a hell of a job getting over how clever Mark Madden was, but it didn't do a damn thing to make anyone want to order a pay per view, or even watch the next match. He wanted to get himself over, at the expense of the talent.

Of course, maybe I was spoiled, because I came up in the business around greats like Steve Stack, Gordon Solie and Lance Russell, but I thought WCW's announcing sucked. Now, I don't think Tony Schiavone or Mike Tenay suck, but I think they had gotten away from describing wrestling with simplicity, which is the cornerstone of great wrestling announcing. They had gotten into a pattern of describing moves almost in code, using all these fancy, contrived names that don't really tell the people what the move is. You're gaining new fans all the time, so it's important to explain things to people in a basic way. I shouldn't have to get out my slide rule to figure out a 360, a 450, a 720, or a 1080, or whatever. By the time I've finished adding and subtracting, and figured out the degree of the flip, the goddamned match is over!

Gordon Solie, probably one of the greatest announcers ever, probably used no more than 35 to 40 wrestling terms, and even those, he used over and over, to make people understand what he was talking about. He didn't bombard people's senses with new terms for things that really shouldn't be that hard to comprehend.

It's bullshit like Madden's commentary and world champion David Arquette that make me think, "Thank God Vince bought off what was left of WCW. Thank God he bought out that godawful pile of dogshit!"

Of course, I slid around in the shit for a while, took my money and went on back home to the ranch. I'd probably even roll in shit, if the money was right. I can always take a shower and get rid of the stink.

But WCW wasn't the worst place I ever worked. Several independent promotions are tied for that honor. A lot of my independent experiences over the years have ended with me chasing the sorry, son-of-a-bitch promoter down the road to get my money! Now *that* is a bad workplace! In WCW I never had to worry. My paychecks came just like clockwork.

Those independent promoters were some strange individuals, and sometimes I questioned their priorities. I won't mention names here, but I worked for an independent promotion run by two guys who were supposedly the best of friends.

Well one night we were in the dressing room, and one of them came in and announced, "It's over! We are dissolving the partnership!"

I asked, "Why are you doing that?"

"Because that bastard stole my arena rat!"

Now, an arena rat was a wrestling groupie, like a girl who hangs out at the matches, hoping to "get together" with a wrestler. Now, can you imagine that shit? And she was fat and ugly, too, just a horrible-looking broad!

CHAPTER 29

The End of the Wrestling War

In 2000, there were still one or two places I hadn't worked yet, so I thought I'd get to them. XPW was an ECW-like group operating on the West Coast. The owner was Rob Black, who produced porn movies and is a very controversial figure, even in that industry. But I have no complaints about him, or about that group. He paid me my money, and he treated me very well while I was there. Vicki came with me, and they treated her like a million dollars, too.

The show was on June 22, eight days before my birthday, so they even brought in a cake for me. And there was no porno girl jumping out of the cake or anything like that.

It was great working with Sabu again, and great getting out to California and getting to see some old friends out there. I did think their show was a little crazy, but one thing that really impressed me was the camera work. The camera guy doing the promos was a better shooter than anyone I'd ever worked with before. I mean, this guy could shoot some incredible promos. He was in and out, had a different look to each one, and they were all fantastic.

I said to him, "My God, you do a great job of that. Where did you learn how to do that so well?"

He said, "Well, uh, I really don't want to tell you, but I've been shooting pornos for eight years."

But the guy was a great cameraman! Vince should look this guy up and hire him! He knew when to go in for a close-up and when to pull back. The guy's timing was amazing, and those XPW promos looked unique and fantastic. I think he also wrestled that night.

In January 2001, I worked a show for All Japan, teaming with Atsushi Onita against Abdullah the Butcher and Giant Kimala II. They had called me and asked me to come in for the show.

I was expecting a sad scene since Baba had passed away two years earlier, in January 1999. But it really wasn't. His wife, Motoko, was there. The company was still afloat and together. However, there was the definite feeling there that it was never again going to be what it once was that All Japan was on the descent, not the ascent. You didn't have to be the sharpest knife in the drawer to see that in terms of ratings, attendance and even company discipline, All Japan was sliding. That show was kind of a last hurrah.

All Japan took a big hit when top stars Mitsuharu Misawa, Kenta Kobashi, Jun Akiyama, Akira Taue and others left in 2000 to form Pro Wrestling NOAH. Of the top stars from the 1990s, only Toshiaki Kawada stayed in All Japan. For American fans who don't follow Japanese wrestling, that would be like if Triple H, Kurt Angle, Chris Benoit and Eddy Guerrero left WWE to form a new company, leaving only The Undertaker among the top main-eventers.

Even though Misawa had been Baba's boy, he was perfectly within his rights to leave and strike out on his own. After all, Baba himself had split off of the Japanese Wrestling Association to start All Japan nearly 30 years earlier.

I had always tried to avoid that match, the return to All Japan after all those years, especially since that match ended up involving Abdullah. The reason for that was it had been 20 years since the angle with Abdullah stabbing my arm with a fork. Even though a lot of time had passed, that image was still impressed and enlarged in a lot of those fans' minds, like a photographic negative. There was no way, even if Abby and I were still in our primes, that we could live up to the fans' memories of that angle. No matter what we did, it would be secondary to the image in people's minds of what that match was, because people still talk about it to this day. So why rattle it? Why risk destroying that memory?

I went because they asked, because it was to be my first chance to see and talk to Mrs. Baba in years, and because I wanted to give them my own "last hurrah," of sorts. I saw it as one last chance to participate in a show for All Japan where I could help them at the box office.

We went out to eat after the matches. Gene Kiniski and Nick Bockwinkel were there, and when you have them both at the same table, your end of the conversation is going to be very limited, because they are going to do much of the talking.

Aside from that, it was very, very cordial and a lot of fun talking about all those old times.

Keiji Muto, my old partner in 1989 when he was The Great Muta, ended up buying the company, and he's now in a very difficult situation. Wrestling in Japan has changed so much and so has the audience. There are certain things you just can't follow, and following Baba's footsteps has been all but impossible for them. Misawa might have actually been a genius, because he's now running a completely different company. Muto is running All Japan, and that name will always mean "Baba's company" to the people of Japan.

Just a few days after that All Japan match, I found out ECW was out of business. I wish I could say the news of ECW's death was a surprise, but I had been half-expecting that phone call ever since they started going national. I understand they had been under financial strain for a while. They were paying a lot of money to a lot of their TV stations, and they just weren't taking in enough to match the costs. You don't have to be a financial genius or a wrestling genius to know that a company that's not going in the right direction, moneywise, is going to be gone sooner or later.

WCW going under in March of that same year wasn't really much of a surprise, either. I was actually surprised that it lasted as long as it did. I hate to say it, but it was the boys who killed WCW. They killed the goose that laid the golden eggs. It had started with they guys making a gazillion dollars, guaranteed, not wanting to do this and griping about doing that, and after that, it was monkey-see, monkey-do. That was also the case with the contagious concussions. If you see a top star get away with a prolonged absence, the next guy's going to try it, and the next guy.

I also wasn't too surprised that McMahon was the one who bought the assets. It was a pretty smart move on his part, especially since part of the deal was that there would be no new wrestling show on the Turner networks for the next few years. Think about it—was he buying the assets (the tapes, some of the contracts, the "WCW" initials), or was he buying the no competition?

The end of the wrestling war was chronicled over the Internet. Starting in the early 1990s, people on the Internet had begun to discuss wrestling online, and sites had been popping up all over. The Internet and the fans who communicate on it certainly have a great influence on the business, sometimes positively and sometimes negatively. It has an effect on the decisions being made by the people in power. If I watched a match right now and then pulled up a discussion of it on the Internet, I bet a lot of the people there would have the same views on what was good and what was bad that I would have. But the thing is, I'm not always right, either. I think it can be a great tool for those in the business to see what some of the fans think, but I don't think wrestling should live and die by the Internet.

It can also be a sort of crutch, because one thing's for sure—if I'm in the WWE and Triple H, as a top guy who's married to the boss's daughter, has a stinkeroo of a match, it's a heck of a lot easier for me to say, "Hey, the Internet is saying you had a stinkeroo," than it is for me to tell him I think he had a stinkeroo.

And later in 2001, I did something I had once thought I would never do—on October 8, 2001, I wrestled a match for New Japan. You might think there would be a strange feeling for me, being in a New Japan dressing room, but I had fully made the separation from Baba a decade earlier, and Junior had ended up leaving there, too.

It was a special match to commemorate 50 years of wrestling in Japan, with Junior and me against Tatsumi Fujinami and Bob Backlund. It was also going to be one of Fujinami's last matches. He was one of the original great junior heavyweights in that company, and was one of its best workers for years. He had always wanted to wrestle me, and it was really an honor for me to get into the ring with him and to work with Backlund. Actually, Fujinami's wife played a big role in that, I think, because she had been a great Terry Funk fan growing up in Japan.

The whole time I was there for that show, I never talked to Inoki. However, a couple of years later, Inoki and I did an appearance together on a talk show that was going to air in Japan. I sat down and listened to him. Of course we never could have met like that years ago, because the promotional rivalry was so intense.

If you think about it, Inoki has been very much a visionary of wrestling, and someone who has been able to change with the times. Our discussion was very cordial, if a bit strained at first. We had been adversaries for so long, and to get to hear the history of the wrestling war in Japan from his perspective was a great experience for me.

CHAPTER 30

These Days

I was a special guest at the WWE show in Amarillo on April 30, 2004, just a couple of months before I started working on this book.

I had fun, and it really made West Texas State, or West Texas A&M, as it's now known, a good amount of money, which was the thing most important to me. Still, it was good to see a lot of the boys again, and good to be in front of the hometown crowd one more time.

For the record, I thought the university's name change was a successful deal. At the time they changed the name, I wanted them to leave it alone, but as time has passed by, even I've started calling it West Texas A&M. It has turned out that the best thing that ever happened to the university, for state funding and for the buildings, was for it to become an affiliate of Texas A&M.

The show was also a good deal for WWE, because they had a nice crowd, and I had gotten them a good rate on the building. WWE made more money than they could have otherwise, and West Texas made more money than they ever could have by trying to run an independent show as a fundraiser.

I saw a lot that night, and I actually took a minute to reflect on more than 50 years that I had been either in or around the wrestling business. The thing that surprised me most was, the matches I was watching were still different from the matches of 30 years ago but were a lot closer than they were to the matches of six months ago.

I saw more selling, and I saw a great deal more storytelling. I also saw a lot more mat wrestling that night than I had a couple of years ago, when it looked like a bunch of half-assed acrobatics. And when I say half-assed, that still makes those guys pretty damned good acrobats. But they got to a point where they were reliant on those moves, which don't give you a whole lot of longevity.

A lot of those acrobatics were the product of the competition between the WWF and WCW. Each wrestler wanted to be better than the guys on the other show, and that put the guys in a position of constantly having to outdo each other. Ultimately, that mentality has shortened careers because of all the neck injuries that have resulted. The return to wrestling is a good thing for the performers, because it should be slowing that down, especially now that there's no serious competition. The office itself has, and should, put a stop to the extreme amounts of punishment the guys are taking.

Of course, sometimes you never know what is going to be a crippling move. In October 2001, Hayabusa, who impressed me so much in Japan, slipped on the ropes while performing a move called a quebrada, landed on his head and ended up in a wheelchair. That move is one Chris Jericho does every week on *Raw*. He calls it the lionsault, and it doesn't immediately look like the kind of thing that could cripple a man. It just goes to show that any move can be a dangerous one.

I understand what drives someone to take those kinds of chances, especially with the way the business was in the late 1990s and even now. It's a wonderful business to be in if you're in the right place and being used properly. It's a business where you can make enough money to retire at a young age, but you also need to make sure you'll physically be able to enjoy those retirement years. It's nice to be able to afford a gold-plated wheelchair I guess, but it's not a place I would want to be.

The only thing that's going to have longevity in this business is wrestling itself. I could go out and do hardcore stuff, and it will leave an impression I can draw from for a while, but it doesn't have longevity, because then you're off to the next thing, acrobatics, or whatever. After a period of time, the acrobatics are gone, the hardcore is gone, and so it goes. But wrestling will never be gone.

I think Hunter, or Triple H, as he's known now, and the rest of the WWE guys saw what was happening, with all the injuries due to that style, and pulled it the other way. Maybe I'm blowing too much smoke up Hunter's ass, but he's got great psychology, and the McMahons added a real asset to their family when he married Stephanie.

A lot of the guys from my era don't see things the way I do, and I don't necessarily mean that as a bad thing against Bill Watts, Ole Anderson, or any of those guys.

Like them, I don't watch it on TV every week, but I stay involved enough and keep my finger on certain things to where I can still feel some of these things that can be difficult for them to understand, because they don't follow it at all.

And any of us "old-timers" can gripe about how "Vince did this," or "Vince did that," but I'll say one thing—Vince's daughter Stephanie married a guy who's got some goddamned brains, and some respect for the way things should be done to keep the business strong. This guy Hunter loves wrestling.

And he catches a lot of heat for his position. People gripe, saying stuff like, "Well, he's always got the belt!"

Well, hell, he's not going to get all pissed and run crying out of the door like Shawn Michaels used to do, is he? He can't! He can't quit and go home, because the business, in the form of his wife, is waiting for him at home!

And get used to seeing him, because Vince is going to rely on him more and more. When he needs a truthful word, a decision from someone who knows the business itself, he's going to go to Hunter.

And Hunter is a guy who strives for excellence inside that ring. He busts his ass to get all he can out of every match.

And Stephanie's out there, too. She watches every match, to see reactions.

My wife used to do that, too. I used to hate to ask Vicki, "How was my match?"

She'd point out every single thing I did wrong, and the reason I hated it was she was always right.

What I saw made me optimistic for the future—the future of WWE, anyway. If you had told me 20 years ago that I'd be talking about that company as the industry leader in this country, I'd have laughed in your face. But they're not just the industry leader in this country—they're the industry itself!

And, you know, I've got no reason to make up good things to say about them. I'm not ever going back up there, especially after my horse went and got sick 10 years ago.

A couple of weeks before my appearance at the WWE Amarillo show, my old friend Mick Foley had come out of retirement for a short series of matches with Randy Orton. Mick really let me down, though, because he had retired and then came back. And that's one thing I feel very strongly that wrestlers shouldn't do!

Seriously, I think Mick did a great job with it, and he was working with a real talent. Randy is a third-generation guy. His father and grandfather, the two Bob Ortons, both had tremendous ability. I worked a lot with Randy's father and just loved being around him. I saw Randy's grandfather wrestle quite a bit, and I had a lot of respect for him. They were both great workers.

I think Vince has been very smart to groom Randy, and in how he's been grooming Randy. Mick Foley was a good choice of opponent, because Mick will always be over with the fans, and they'll always care about what he's involved with.

I hate to keep going on about this, because I don't want this to turn into some big, book-length love affair between Mick and me. I will say, though, that Mick looks at the business very similarly to how I look at it, although I am a lot smarter, of course. Mick has a good eye for what's good and what he can do that will help. He is the total opposite of the self-centered attitude that so many had in WCW. In 2000, Foley made Triple H into a solid main-eventer by putting him over as strongly as he did, and four years later he helped give Randy Orton a good push. I would like to think his selflessness is something other guys in the business choose to emulate, because him putting the younger guys over is just an example of someone with a true love for the wrestling business.

I see the WWE going back to wrestling, reverting back to wrestling holds, maneuvers and psychology, perhaps out of necessity. But it's working, because the guys on top are doing it, and the younger guys underneath are seeing what works. A good leader doesn't lead by telling you what to do. A good leader shows you what you should do, and the leading wrestlers are setting an example of wrestling.

And they're getting back to the idea of doing things by feel instead of choreographing entire matches ahead of time. In April 2004, I watched Triple H and Benoit at their show in Amarillo, and I knew they were doing the dance.

I know that fans don't know if a good match is called in the ring or completely choreographed beforehand, but I think planning it all out before the bell rings takes away from a wrestler's creativity. Is choreographing matches sometimes necessary? Sure, because of TV time constraints or whatever. But when wrestlers choreograph, they are just getting into a routine and losing the natural feel for what's going to work for that particular match in front of that particular crowd. And they get into a mindset that they must get in every, single thing that they have scripted. It's planned to fit perfectly the amount of time they have, so they run through everything. A lot of times, even if you have a plan for how a match is going to unfold, the crowd might not be reacting to it, and there's a more natural course that would be a better way to go. A good worker should always be able to have a feel for the crowd and be able to change a match accordingly.

I bet that's a lesson being taught to the next generation of stars in Ohio Valley Wrestling, a training ground run by Danny Davis and Jim Cornette that uses a lot of WWE developmental talent.

I think we'll also be seeing a couple of other territories pop up, run by McMahon's company, to provide more training grounds. They'll run shows, be modestly successful, and when Vince feels like guys there are ready for the big time, he'll bring them up. I'll guarantee you, those guys like Chris Benoit and Triple H, who are working those great matches, are not scripting them all the way through. I think scripting is going to be a thing of the past, except for maybe when the TV timeslots are tight.

I've been asked about training young wrestlers from time to time, but frankly, the thought scares me. My brother does well with his school in Florida, but I don't think that's the way for me to go. If I had a wrestling school, I'd have carloads of my students drive 250 miles with about eight guys in each Chevy Nova, with all their bags and stuff. Then I'd have them set up the ring, feed them a couple of hot dogs and make them go in there and do an hour broadway. Then they'd have to pile back into those cramped cars after taking the ring down and drive another 250 miles while drinking a couple of cases of beer. That would be the final exam. If you make it back home safely, you graduate.

I think my test to see if they could make it in the wrestling business might not be that relevant, because nowadays they fly everywhere. So my frame of reference is dated.

I do love to help. If a guy asked me to watch his match, I always used to watch his match. I love to critique the matches for the younger guys who ask, but these days I'm so old that I have to start stretching from the time I get to the arena, just to be loosened up in time for my match. Unfortunately, that doesn't leave me a lot of time to watch the other matches, but I offer advice when I can. I love the young guys in the business, but I don't want to be involved with getting someone into the business.

I guess the Number Two promotion right now would be the Total Nonstop Action group, which until recently ran weekly pay per views. I actually worked a show for them in 2003 and thought they had some very good talent.

Their problem is that they have their "X Division" matches, where the guys do insanely risky stuff. And like I said about ECW, there's not health coverage for those guys. Those guys go and do their damnedest to put on a good match. I mean, they do everything they can to put on a good match, and I'm not talking about going through tables, hardcore chair spots or anything else like that. They do maneuver, after maneuver, after maneuver. And I guess that's what they need to do because they want to hold their jobs. If they don't pop the crowd, they're not going to keep their jobs.

Problem is, the next match comes out, and those guys do the same thing—move, after move, after move. And that means the fans will get to see some spectacular stuff, but they see so much that it's hard to make anything stand out. That's going to cause them some problems ultimately, because they're going to burn themselves out.

They've got to go back to selling wrestling. They should be aware that they're following a direct line that Vince and WWE once went down—the dangers of doing riskier and riskier moves.

I also questioned their logic of continuing to put on weekly pay per views, instead of just doing one big one each month, which they finally switched to in November 2004. What they were doing put constant pressure on the company to deliver something for the paying audience, instead of letting them build up to one big thing each month.

On the independent scene, there's Ring of Honor, a company that does sell wrestling. That's a well-run group, but they also get into that mentality of doing a ton of moves without the wrestlers selling any of them. They also put in some strong in-ring performances, but if they keep doing things that way, they're also going to burn out their fanbase.

Their other problem is that their former owner, Rob Feinstein, got caught on a TV news report where they had people posing as underage kids trying to lure adults into meeting them after setting it up online. I was shocked when I heard about the news report, just totally taken aback. I had known him for years and never would have guessed he'd have gotten caught up in something like that.

He's out of Ring of Honor now, but I think they might want to just cut all the ties and change the name. But I think they'll survive that. Hell, Amarillo survived Gorgeous George. In 1961, George was under investigation for allegedly getting involved with an underage girl, and it hit the news about four days before he was supposed to wrestle my father here. Everyone in the office thought it was going to be death for the house.

He sold out! People were packed into the arena that night, just to get the chance to chant, "Baby banger!" at him.

I actually appeared on one of the most successful independent shows in years in August 2004. It was another match with Jerry Lawler in Memphis. We built up to it with some of the best promos made in a long time, as we discussed in Chapter 13.

Lawler approached me about doing the show earlier in 2004, when we both worked a show for the Insane Clown Posse. The Insane Clown Posse is a pair of rappers, Violent Jay and Shaggy 2 Dope, who paint their faces up like clowns.

They're also completely insane and a couple of wrestling fans. They put out a videotape where they were commenting on old matches. One of the matches had me versus Abdullah the Butcher, and they kept knocking us and laughing at us.

"Look at those two big goofs, acting like they're wrestling. Ha ha ha!"

After I heard about that, every time someone told me they were going to see the Insane Clown Posse, I said, "Tell them if I see them, I'm going to go ahead and kick their asses! Goofy bastards, knocking me on a tape and using it without consent!"

Of course, I wouldn't have known the Insane Clown Posse from Adam and Eve, if I'd seen them on the street. I sure wasn't listening to their damn music!

Finally, I got a call at the ranch from Sabu: "Terry, I've got the Insane Clown Posse here. They want to come and see you, but they don't know if you're mad at them or not."

"Well," I said, "bring the sons of bitches out here."

They had just finished a show in Corpus Christi, and their next one was in Houston, so they took their bus all the way from Corpus Christi to Amarillo, and then back down to Houston after they met me! I *told* you they were nuts!

And so the Insane Clown Posse came into the house, and Vicki had some chili cooked up. They sat down and ate a bowl of chili apiece and talked to me. They said they were sorry if I was upset over what they said on that tape, and we buried the hatchet.

Then, Violent Jay said, "Terry, we want to leave you some money for using that tape of you."

I said, "No, no, don't do that!"

"Yes, Terry, we're going to leave it under this jar, on this counter here!"

I kept telling them not to, but I walked into the next room before them. They followed me in, and told me they had to go. We said our goodbyes, and the Insane Clown Posse drove off in their bus.

And I walked back into the other room, to get the money I knew they'd left. I have to tell you, I was excited. I was thinking, "Oh boy, I bet they left me twenty bucks, or maybe even forty," which would have just tickled me pink. I thought I'd have enough to pay for the chili, at least, and so I was really happy at the notion of having twenty bucks.

I went in there, lifted up the jar ... and there was four thousand dollars there!

And so let me tell you people something right now—I love the Insane Clown Posse! The next retirement match I have, they're going to be in the semi-final! They're the greatest band in the world, and I have all their records. Haven't got around to listening to them yet, but I have them here somewhere.

Later, I got a call that they wanted me to work at a show they were putting on, and I went. And I was amazed. Vince McMahon could learn a thing or two from the Insane Clown Posse, and I'm not lying. Those boys run a better show, and a smarter one, than even WWE does.

It was a four-day event, held outdoors, about 40 miles from the middle of nowhere. They drew a total of about 11,000 people, and they were charging 180 bucks a pop, just to get in. And it's two guys! That's all it is! The Insane Clown Posse is a two-man outfit! I think of a posse as 20 idiots running around with rifles. But this was just two guys. It reminded me, in a way, of the show my father did, where his match with "Iron" Mike DiBiase was the only one on the card. They paid the people who worked for them a set amount, and then they split the lion's share of the proceeds, because they're the stars! Those two goofy bastards are two of the smartest people I've ever met!

And it was the greatest place in the world to sell T-shirts. I had my Terry Funk T-shirts and was selling them when I wasn't wrestling. Well, those people were so smoked up on that marijuana, they didn't need much convincing.

Someone would walk by and see me and say, "Hey, Terry, how are you doin'?"

I'd say, "Come on over here and buy a shirt."

"Nah, Terry, I don't wanna buy a shirt."

"Oh, come on and buy a shirt!"

"No, I don't know, man."

"Oh, come on and buy a damn shirt!"

"Well, OK."

I didn't even wear my own shirt to the ring. I left my vest, my chaps and all that crap. I wore my Juggalo T-shirt, with the Insane Clown Posse on the front. I like to think of myself as the honorary third member of the Insane Clown Posse now!

They had the wrestling matches on two different days, and then they had stuff like Vanilla Ice on one stage, and someone else over here. But hell, Vanilla Ice isn't exactly hot these days, so he didn't cost them a lot of money. And the Insane Clown Posse would get up there with their quarter-gallon bottles of grape pop, and they'd shake that stuff up and undo the lids, and those bottles would fly like a rocket in the air, just squirting that sticky, purple shit all over everyone! And those people, 11,000 idiots wearing clown makeup, loved it.

I'm serious! The whole audience was clowns. And they were happy, peaceful, smoked-up clowns. But they were united in purpose. One time, one band on stage tried to get the fans on one side to yell, "Fuck you" to the other side, but these people were all Juggalos. They were all Insane Clown Posse people, and they saw these guys on stage trying to split them up. Well, they weren't going to have any of that crap! They started booing and throwing stuff at the guys onstage. The police had to come and get those guys off the stage! Those people did not want anyone trying to break up their clown nation.

Dusty and Lawler were at the show with me, and we couldn't believe it. This crowd was the damnedest commotion we'd ever seen, but they were all clowns, and they all got along!

There was another guy there, a crazy wrestler named Madman Pondo. He sees himself as a combination of Cactus Jack and Jack the Ripper. He dreams about wrestling me. Every time I see him, he tells me how much he'd like to work with me. It's his dream and ambition!

And I think once I've wrestled Madman Pondo, then I can call it a career. Once we've hit each other over the head with neon light tubes, shot each other with staple guns and all that other crap, then I'll feel like I've done it all, because I've wrestled them all, except for Madman Pondo.

The funny thing was, the Insane Clown Posse were pretty damn good workers. My big match on the first show was me and the Insane Clown Posse against Lawler and two partners.

On the second show, I wrestled Dusty, but it wasn't exactly just like old times. We'd both slowed down a bit. The day before, we walked to lunch together. It took an hour to get from our hotel to the restaurant, and it was only a block and a half away.

After my match with Dusty, I was watching the Insane Clown Posse against Madman Pondo and another psychopath, Necro Butcher. During the match, they did a spot that you might not think would get over, but it sure as hell did with this crowd.

At one point in the match, Shaggy 2 Dope was lying outside the ring, terribly hurt from the beating he'd taken. Pondo and Butcher were in the ring with Violent Jay. I was looking at Shaggy 2 Dope, trying to figure out what he was doing on the side of the ring, there. Well, he took out a lighter and was trying to light up a gigantic joint.

Seriously, the damn thing was about 18 inches long! Shaggy 2 Dope got it lit really good, then threw it over the top rope to Violent Jay. Violent Jay, in a great deal of pain, took a bit hit off that 18-inch-long joint ... and he hulked up! He took another hit, and he hulked up more! He took a third hit, and he was, by God, invincible. He beat those guys all over the place, and the fans were just going out of their minds. I always thought the spinning toehold was a good finisher. Maybe I should have been keeping an 18-inch joint under the ring all that time! Who said marijuana was a depressant?

The smartest thing they did was, they figured out a way to make sure they weren't getting screwed on the concessions. Live event promoters have always gotten screwed on concessions, because it seems a lot of the time the amount the concession people pay percentages on is less than what they actually sold. I'm not saying this goes on at every event, but it happens a lot. Well, the Insane Clown Posse figured out a way that it wouldn't happen to them.

When you went through the gates at the Insane Clown Posse events, you traded in cash for Insane Clown Posse coins, and the only way you could buy your concessions was with those coins. At the end of the show, every concessionaire has to report all their sales, because they have to turn in their Insane Clown Posse coins for cash. The clowns win again!

And it was at that show that Lawler talked to me about doing some promos to build up for a match in Memphis. And that's what we did, leading up to a match in August 2004.

Lawler was technically the heel, but I wanted to make my heel promos, and they still played like babyface promos, because our business has gotten to the point that there are no more babyfaces or heels.

The match itself, me and Corey Macklin versus Lawler and Jimmy Hart, was good, especially considering you had two old wrestlers and two non-wrestlers out there. I enjoyed the hell out of it. The crowd reacted pretty much how I expected. Lawler was a legend there, but he didn't have that hard-edged crowd heat. Lawler's a great entertainer, but he's been there so long that the people have seen him go from heel to babyface and back, over and over. Those people love Lawler, and even when he was a heel there, for our match, the people loved him, even the ones who booed him. They were just acting like they didn't love him, because that was what they were supposed to do. They truly love him—they just like acting as if they hate him.

And there are people making a living in the wrestling business, today. Two of them are the best world champs we ever had—my brother and Harley Race. Junior makes a buck off of running a wrestling school, as well as a promotion. Harley is also running shows and making some appearances with Misawa's group in Japan.

You can be successful in this business without having to set the world on fire. That's the problem with a lot of guys. They come in and want to be the next Vince McMahon overnight. Well, hell, even Vince McMahon didn't become Vince McMahon overnight.

And a lot of the successes are having problems staying strong. As I write this in 2004, I see the Japanese wrestling companies cooperating with each other, sending talent from one promotion to another. That never could have happened when Junior and I booked All Japan, because the rivalries were so business. But I guess it's just another progression in the business, a new and necessary way to find new ways to draw.

To me, one of the strengths of Japanese wrestling was that they had very few "characters." Most of the guys, ninety-five percent or so, were just themselves. There weren't a bunch of name changes. When the Japanese press would talk to the guys, they would answer questions almost as honestly as they could, which is something we never really gave them in the States. What kept us from being strong with the media was the same thing we thought gave us life in the territorial era. We had life through not letting the media in and not leveling with people, keeping an air of mystery about it. Japanese culture allowed the people there to be more tolerant of something that was a work than we felt people here would have been.

We weren't the circus coming to town. The circus comes once a year and does business. It might not have been the greatest show on earth, but when it only comes once a year, they can sell it that way. Wrestling, especially in the territorial days, went on week after week and night after night in the same area. If we told them we were totally entertainment, then that entertainment was going to get old a lot faster than sport. That was the reason we tried to maintain the façade we were a sport. Even though we didn't get into the newspapers much, the people who did come believed what we were doing was real.

It worked for a long time, but we've progressed and gone more and more into entertainment as we went along. We were self-destructing on a weekly basis and didn't even know it. The feeling was, if we wanted to keep doing business, we'd have to do something at least as good as we did last week.

There's room for several angles on every show. One should be a long-term deal, and the others should be quick deals. There's no real formula. It's not like

I would go to book a show and say, "Let's see, according to my calculations, I need three-point-five angles on this show."

You just have to have a feel for it, and a feel for what's working and when you need to add something. It's always good to have underneath angles going, but there should always be one angle that is clearly your main thing.

But anything can be an angle if it's promoted right. Wrestlemania itself is an angle because it's something out there that fans are anticipating, and an angle is anything you talk about to create interest for a show down the road. It's very healthy because WWE always has something to build to, and it's something everyone knows is coming.

And people today think that doing a work is a thing of the past. But works are everywhere. Look at reality TV shows. Those are supposed to be people acting as they really would, but the cameras always magically seem to know when to go in for a closeup of someone. They're all worked!

What is real today? My dad used to tell me, "Don't believe that everything in life is a work."

Well, I'm not so sure. It's scary to think how much of this world is a work. And anything where money is involved, if it's not a work, is at least manipulated. The buck is more important than the purity of the sport.

Hell, high school football is manipulated. Ever notice how a team gets a 20-point lead at halftime and then sends in the second string? That's almost a work! They're influencing the outcome by sending in a squad that does not give the school its best chance of staying ahead. I understand why they do it. They don't want to kill that other school, because the next time they meet, it might not be as big of a draw. But it's still manipulation.

Sometimes it's amazing to me how much the business has changed. But the manipulation has always been there.

The situation has changed for the wrestlers themselves. In the 1950s and 1960s, we had Cadillac Row in Amarillo, because all the wrestlers were making good enough money that they could buy the nicest cars. They were making $300 a week at a time when most people were making $50 to $75 a week. Today there are a few slots where you can become a millionaire, but those very few slots are in WWE, and if you're not there, you're having a hell of a time trying to make a living in the wrestling business.

In terms of the style and the product, the changes have been huge. When I was a rookie in 1965, wrestling was very accepted as a sport, maybe not in every area, but here in West Texas. The most spectacular move anyone saw in those days was a dropkick. And gimmick matches were few and far between. Remember—my dad did the death match with Mike DiBiase, and then they spent a whole year building up the second one.

Gradually though, everything progresses and changes. You have to be able to top what you showed the people last week, or at least have something new for them, to keep bringing them back and to do business. So the matches got wilder and the characters got bolder over time. No one did those things trying to hurt the business. It was all a matter of trying to stay in business.

And 1965 was the year things really started to pick up speed, as blood became more and more commonly used, and there were more and more stipulation matches. By the 1970s, we went heavily into the gimmick matches because we had run through all the 60- and 90-minute matches the people were going to stand.

And when competition became prevalent in the 1980s, it sped up that progression even more, because now you had companies trying to top each other. The stipulations have gotten wilder and more common, and the style of wrestling has sped up.

And it's still progressing today. So what's next? Well, progression can go in more than one direction. Ten years from now I see the progression leading the business to the point that the shoot wrestling will be the dominant thing, or what we really believe is shoot wrestling.

These shoot fight groups—they're all manipulated. I see it every time they put together an apparent mismatch. They are doing that because they are looking to create a star, and they are looking for a specific result in that mismatch. These companies invest a lot of money in the Bob Sapps of the world, and keeping their stars strong is in their financial best interests. It might not start that way, but it turns into that.

What I don't understand is how any of the Japanese fans believe in anything they see, when the atmosphere over there now is that guys go from shoot fights to worked wrestling matches and back again. To me, once a guy participates in a worked scenario and you bring him back in a shoot, you are tainting the purity of the competition.

Sometimes they even intermingle works and shoots on the same cards. How do you tell the fans, "This one might not be real, but the next one will be?"

Once you do that, your business is a work. That might not mean that everything you do is a work, but you are manipulated.

But we follow Japan a lot. We follow them in wrestling and we follow them in business. They had their recession a few years back, and we're having ours now. In wrestling, the Japanese have been very progressive, in large part because of the amount of media coverage the business gets over there. Now they have gone in a shoot direction, because they saw that was the way to progress, dollar-wise, at the box office. Why did things go from no bleeding to bleeding every night? Because it produces more money at the box office, or at least you think it does.

And American wrestling is going to progress in the same direction, whether you, or Vince McMahon, or I like it, or not. That will be the ultimate progression. We'll still have wrestling from Vince, but the biggest dollars will be drawn through the shoot wrestling industry, regardless of whether they are actual shoots, or just proclaimed as shoots.

I actually think Vince would be the perfect guy to promote that. I wonder why he's never tried that. Here he was, pushing bodybuilding leagues and goofy-ass football teams, but over here was another form of something he knew—wrestling. He's got the arenas, the equipment and the production teams already. If McMahon were to promote shoots the way he has promoted his worked matches, he might see the best ratings he's ever had. And what the hell—if they're working in six months on the shoot show, who cares, as long as they're not obvious about it? We want to be entertained, and if we think two guys are really kicking the shit out of each other, that's going to entertain us.

That's the only direction left. Worked wrestling has already gone to its greatest limit. What could be next? Reality is next.

And once we get to that point, the whole thing will start over. They say wrestling is a cyclical business, but the real cycle of its history will start over with shoots, and with the inevitable manipulation of those shoots.

The first time shoot wrestling gets on national TV and has a good show, that's it. They're off and running. They might not run every week, but they'll run a few times a year. And eventually they'll run a little more, so they can make more money. Then they'll decide to manipulate things a little more strongly to protect the guys they've figured out are their superstars.

And wouldn't you know it? When that happens, we're working again!

I wouldn't call it a "vicious cycle." It is only the wonderful world of wrestling!

EPILOGUE

On a shelf in my study is a picture of Brock Glear, a young kid who had brain cancer. I went to see him before he died. He was the sweetest kid in the world, a wrestling fan, which was how I met him. He was nine years old when he died on New Year's Day, 2001. Dennis Stamp, who sprays trees now, was spraying by Brock's house, and got to talking with the kid. Dennis really loved him, too.

It was a shitty deal, but it helps you keep things in perspective. That kid knew what he had, and knew how it would end, but, by God, he was going down the road! That's a pretty tough kid.

I keep his picture up to remind me of that kid, but also to remind me what my friend John Ayers had to battle in the last years of his life. John, who played in two Super Bowls, who did so many wonderful things in his life, died after fighting liver cancer, such a terrible death.

When they had his funeral, we had a reception here at the ranch. It was amazing to see who all had turned out to pay their respects. Half of John's 49er teammates, from Joe Montana on down, came all the way out here, out of respect for him, to say goodbye. He had so much respect from his peers.

And he loved the wrestlers. I had gotten him involved in Crockett's NWA group in the 1980s, and he just loved being around the business. I think he'd have made his mark in wrestling if he hadn't had so much success as a football player. Frankly, I'm glad he didn't get into the business, because he was a guy with a laid-back attitude, and I don't know how he would have fared with the manipulations of some of the people in the business. He might have been too honorable a guy to be in the business.

This was the kind of man John Ayers was. I would take off on a wrestling tour, and he would come every day and take care of my cattle and my horses while I was gone.

He was my best friend and was always willing to help me out in any way he could, even though he endured quite a bit because of me.

In the first round of the 1978 NFL draft, the 49ers picked Ernie Hughes, an All-America offensive guard (John's position) from Notre Dame. John was playing first team, but he was spending all summer drinking beer and playing around.

One of John's favorite tricks was to bring three or four people to the house, people I didn't even know. They'd all be there in the den, where I had a bar and a keg at the time. Vicki and I would go to bed, and John would keep his entourage there until the wee hours! I had strangers drinking all my beer!

He also loved driving his Jeep all over my ranch, leaving tracks in my grass. That was really funny to him!

Anyway, he had been carrying on for a while, and I thought to myself, "John's not getting prepared enough for this Ernie Hughes."

I decided to call a local florist.

A few days later, a bouquet of green (Notre Dame's color) carnations showed up at John's house, along with a note that read, "Good luck, sucker! Notre Dame is number one and always will be. Signed, Ernie."

And I'll be a son of a bitch if he wasn't out every morning at sunup, running around my pasture, dragging around a tractor tire he had tied to himself with a huge rope. He was training from the time he woke up to the time he went to bed. He became a crazy man! He wouldn't slow down, wouldn't have a beer with me, wouldn't do anything. He wanted to kill Ernie Hughes and was getting prepared to do it.

It was like this for about three weeks. John was killing himself getting into shape, but even worse, I had lost my beer-drinking buddy. I finally decided to call him.

"John," I said, "I'm sorry, but I'm the one who sent you those flowers."

He was pretty mad at me, but hell—he was in tremendous shape!

I thought that trick worked pretty well, so a couple of years later, I used it again, when West Texas State played Abilene Christian in the Lone Star Conference championship game.

I had Vicki send to West Texas State's locker room a bouquet with a note that said, "Sorry about the game today. Tough luck. Abilene Christian is number one."

They had a riot! West Texas State won the game, but they were fighting from the time they got out onto the field. Even the coach was damn near ready to fight Abilene Christian's coach.

What a motivator that is! You can really piss somebody off just with flowers and a carefully worded note.

I decided in this case it would be best to wait about five years to keep my mouth shut. When I finally told the West Texas State coach, he just half-smiled and said, "You son of a bitch! You damn near got me killed. I damn near lost my job over that!"

John had let the bouquet motivate him to get in shape, while my alma mater just got whipped into a frenzy.

I have tried to be there for John's kids, the way I know he'd be there for mine if I'd been taken, instead of him. I love his daughter Jolee to death, and his death was very difficult on her and her brother John T., and on their mother. John T. ended up playing at West Texas State, like his dad, and he graduated with a 3.75, which is no small feat. He's working in Houston now, and we always see him when he comes to visit his mother. Jolee is a 4.0 student at Texas Tech, and she'll graduate this year. She's married now, and I don't see her as often as I used to.

They both remind me of John, but Jolee is probably more like him. She's just got that easy way about her.

I think of John a lot, along with my dad and so many other friends. In June 2004, I turned six years older than the age my father was when he passed away. As I said, I've done a lot of living, but I've lost a lot of people in my life. I see them every day in the pictures on my study wall.

Some of them I get mad at. Larry Hennig is a dear friend, and has been for a long time. When he lost his son Curt to a drug overdose, it devastated him. I was torn up, too, but it pissed me off, too, because it was induced by Curt himself. I really think it killed a part of Larry, and I can't help but blame Curt for doing that to his dad and his family.

I get mad at Eddie Gilbert, too. I tried many times to help him, to tell him he needed to be careful, but it's hard. You see someone with a problem, but you also see that person as a friend, and you never can tell which guys you need to be watching out for. It's not like there's a glow around their heads to where you could say, "Wow, I'd better talk to him. He's going to be the next one to go."

Eddie knew he had a problem, and it was something he fought hard against. Eddie was extremely proud of himself in the summer of 1994. He was clean and sober and was actually trying to go into politics in Lexington, Tennessee, where he was from. He saw an escape and a totally different way of living.

About six months later he overdosed on cocaine and died in Puerto Rican hotel room while on a wrestling tour. If he had won that constable's election, I think he'd still be alive today and still be drug-free.

Even though I knew he'd had a problem, the news of his death came as a terrible shock. He was only 34, and had such a great mind for the wrestling business. He was another second-generation guy. I also knew both his father, Tommy, and his brother, Doug, well. Tommy spent a couple of years wrestling for us and was a good man. Eddie had a very strong, tight-knit family, and I can't imagine what they're going through, even to this day. The toughest thing in the world must be, as a parent, to lose one of your own, and Vicki and I hope that God blesses us with death prior to either of our daughters.

Eddie Gilbert was a friend. But I'm at the point where, when I get news about one of them passing away, and drugs are involved, I'm pissed off at them. I'm mad, and I don't know if that's right or not, but it's how I feel.

I don't think it's callousness, but I want to yell at them, "Goddammit, you're cheating me, you're cheating your friends, and and you're cheating your family! By God, learn to count! How many pills have you had? Keep track!"

Hell, I even get mad at Eddie Graham, sometimes, for killing himself and taking himself away from all the people who loved him.

The sad thing is, a lot of times, I just feel numb to the news, when someone calls to tell me about another young guy in the business dying. There have been so many, I've almost just grown numb to it. I know that anger and numbness is a horrible combination of feelings to have in reaction to news like that, but I feel like I've gotten that phone call 100 times.

And I think again, of the Von Erich boys who died young—David, Kerry, Mike and Chris.

There were some horrible stories about the Von Erichs, and I tend to believe a lot of the stories. I guess it was just a case of too much money and fame for kids that young.

I remember being on a plane in the mid-1980s with Kerry, headed for Saint Louis. Kerry and I were talking and he said, "Boy, I really feel good. I've really cleaned up. I don't drink, or do drugs anymore. I'm finally clean and sober, and I finally feel like I've got my life back in line."

Then the stewardess walked by, and Kerry ordered a vodka and 7-Up.

I thought it was quite funny at the time, but looking back, it's really a sad story.

I remember when Kerry went to Japan for the first time, in March 1983. He walked around the room and introduced himself to everyone.

"Hello, Mr. Baba, how are you? Mr. Higuchi, how are you?"

After walking around the room and shaking everyone's hand, he sat down for a few minutes. Then, he got up and walked around the room again, shaking everyone's hands.

"Hello, Mr. Baba, how are you? Mr. Higuchi, how are you?"

I knew it wasn't a good situation, but Kerry was able to work, so what were we going to do?

And there's Kevin, Fritz's oldest son, who had some problems of his own. God bless him—I'm proud of him. He's discovered that money and family are better drugs than anything else. That's the thing about being addicted to money—you have to live pretty clean to make it and keep it.

I remember Vicki and I used to go out with Randy Savage and his wife, Elizabeth, when Randy and I were both working for the WWF in the mid-1980s.

Elizabeth was a wonderful person, but things with Randy and her fell apart in the early 1990s, and she ended up dying a couple of years ago, mixing alcohol and drugs. I wonder how she could have gotten to that point, because when Randy and I would go out with our wives, Elizabeth wouldn't even take a glass of wine.

She was living with Lex Luger at the time of her death. Now I never considered Luger someone I wanted to go have a beer with, but I don't know how he could have let her get to that point.

What I do know is that must have been a horrible deal for her. Maybe this is just chauvinism on my part, but I don't get mad at Elizabeth when I think of it, the way I get mad at Curt Hennig or Eddie Gilbert. I truly think hers was an exceptional case. I don't think Liz would have been surrounding herself with that shit on her own. I can't imagine Liz ever looking at Luger and saying, "Hey, let's go get some drugs and do them." I just don't think it started that way. There's no way it would have. I think she was enticed along the way. I think all that shit was made a part of her life, and it certainly wasn't a part of her life when she was with Randy.

Sometimes, we become our characters in this business. Randy became the wired "Macho Man" on occasion. Luger probably doesn't know who he is, to this day. He probably still thinks he's the "Total Package." I think that persona consumed him, and I hate to say that, but it's true. It happens a lot, in this business.

I remember the last time I talked to my friend Mike Hegstrand, Road Warrior Hawk, just a few hours before he died.

A few days earlier, my wife had gotten a call from someone whose voice, she said, was awfully garbled. The caller said something like, "This is Hawk," and then a bunch of stuff Vicki couldn't even make out.

Now, we used to get a lot of strange calls at the house from wrestling fans, so in our last conversation, I asked Hawk if that had been him who had called the house.

"No," he said. "It wasn't me."

He also told me how worn out he was.

"I tell you, Terry, I've been moving all day, and I'm just dead tired."

We talked a little while longer and then, I told him I had to go. From what I understand, he hung up, laid down to rest and went to sleep. He didn't wake up again.

I also talked to him a couple of months earlier. He called, asking if I knew anywhere he could pick up some work.

"I don't really care where it is," he said. "I just want to pick up some work. Do you know any of those independents that might be able to use me?"

Well, hell, this guy was one of the top names in the entire business in the 1980s, so there should be somebody, right? I checked with Court Bauer, who ran an independent group in Florida, and Court said he'd "think about it." He never did say anything back to me on it.

Some guys didn't get killed, but they sure hurt their careers. Scott Hall was, in my mind, a very talented worker in the 1990s, and he still could be an asset to someone in 2004. But he's squandered so much time, and the real shame is that he's hurt both himself (both healthwise and in terms of money in the bank) and the business (by keeping it from having another marketable star available much of the time). I hope he'll kick himself in the ass at some point and get his head on straight, because I truly believe he's one of the more talented guys in the business when he's working right. I hope it's not too late for him to turn things around, as a guy in his mid-40s. I'm afraid he might be approaching that point, where it's just too late for him to turn it around. If he's going to do it, he'd better do it soon.

I know a lot of people who don't agree with me on this, but I'm telling you, having seen the guy, he can get heat with the best of them, and he also knows how to be a good babyface. I can knock the way the guy lives his life, but there's no knocking his ability to get over with a crowd. Why throw it down the drain?

You can't blame the drug deaths on Vince McMahon or wrestling. It's not the promoters, or the agents who are the enablers. The enabler to all this stuff is the road itself. These were guys rolling around with a lot of cash in hand, and a lot of time on their hands while going from show to show. You had to be in charge of yourself. You had to take control of your life. The drug problem would be minute if the towns could come to the boys, instead of the wrestlers coming to the towns.

You don't watch singers overdose and drop dead, and then say, "Oh, music is killing people."

Yet the entire wrestling profession gets tied to these problems. It shouldn't be the profession. It has to be the individual. It has to get to the point of wrestlers assuming responsibility for themselves.

You can look at Vince McMahon and say he should do more, but he has done a great deal through the years. He's fired a lot of guys for being visibly high. He's put a few who needed it through rehab. And over the past couple of years, it hasn't been WWE that's had the problem—it's been the independent promotions, the guys who used to be with WWF, WCW, or ECW.

I believe the drug problem in wrestling is subsiding and will continue to subside because there are people in the business who are realizing that staying employed in it is a way to become a successful individual and maybe even retire at a young age. Career spans will shorten as time goes by, not only because of injuries caused by guys working such a physical style nightly, but because of the monetary opportunities.

And that might be a good thing, because this business of wrestling can be hard, and it forgets you. I think of Wahoo McDaniel, the only guy I ever saw who would fight for the underneath boys, every single place he went, to get them more money. He always busted his ass in the ring, and then he'd be in the back, fighting for somebody else's payoff, which no one did. You weren't going to find anyone else to do that, but Wahoo would.

My wife and I drove 250 miles to his funeral in Odessa, Texas, a couple of years ago. There were two people connected to the wrestling business there—my wife and I.

Guys don't realize that Wahoo was someone who fought for them all those years. He was always the leader, the "Crusader Rabbit," always the guy who'd go pitch the bitch to the promoter.

What the business really needs is a wrestler's union. In the old days, it would have been impossible because you would have had guys trying to bust one organization at a time when there were 30 organizations. That promoter could call one of the other 30 promoters and say, "Hey, I need a little help," and there'd be new talent in the promotion, while whoever tried to start the union would find themselves alienated from the business.

Today I think it's possible. And I'm not talking about something that would mess up things for Vince McMahon or his company. I'm talking about something that would do nothing but help. Right now would actually be the easiest time in the world to do it. Wrestlers starting a union isn't the same as wrestlers just trying to hang up Vince by his balls. People have to get over that idea that a union is the enemy. It's not to put Vince, or anyone else, out of business. It's just something to make sure something is set aside for guys who need medical care for their in-ring injuries, especially those guys who spend 15 years putting over the Triple Hs and Undertakers of the world, because those top stars didn't get to where they are, making that huge money, without some help. And that help came from scores of guys who put them over, but who never made that huge money. Those are the guys who should be looked after, and it should be those top stars who are fighting for a way to take care of those other guys. Those underneath guys deserve a little something for busting their asses to help make the business the success it is.

A union is not there to ruin Vince. It's to help with health care, to do some good for the guys who have done good for that company for so long. Eventually, I wouldn't be surprised if the one who figures this out is Vince himself. But it needs to be done, and it's not for old Terry Funk, because I'm out of it, but the business needs to look out after guys, the guys who spend their time in it and don't make enough to retire on. The few who are making that five million a year need to look at the other guys with some compassion. I bet you Benoit, Guerrero, Triple H and Undertaker all see it, because each one of them has been in the position where they weren't making money hand over fist.

And it wouldn't be a big bite out of Vince, but it is something that needs to be looked at, because believe me, there's a guy in that company for years who has made a decent living. And maybe he's not the smartest guy in the world, or the most marketable, but he's done a lot of jobs for you. And if it weren't for guys like him putting the stars over, how would the wrestling business make stars? Maybe some will benefit who don't deserve it, but better that than the guys who deserve the help not getting it. There have been and are a lot of guys who lived in this business who either need some help, or will, for the 2,000 backdrops they've taken in their career, or all the power bombs they've taken.

The only thing is, people have to stop looking at it like it's there to hurt the business. Unions want employers to succeed because when they don't, suddenly there are a lot of lost union jobs, so they have a stake in the company doing well. If WWE had been taking $500 a night from every house show for the last 20 years, they'd have something started, for guys who needed it. I'm not talking about giving a guy $100,000 so he can buy caviar, or re-tile his swimming pool. I'm talking about helping the Wahoo McDaniels and Johnny Valentines of future generations, who would otherwise die with nothing, no way to pay their hospital bills, in their last days.

When John Ayers died, his wife was able to send those kids to school because he had some benefits from the NFL players' union. And she doesn't live in the lap of luxury, and she still has to work to earn a buck every day.

The business is getting a little better about acknowledging its history and the legends of the past, but a lot of greats don't get the recognition they deserve.

I can't finish this book without mentioning one guy who should always be remembered—Danny Hodge.

Of all the guys I ever knew in wrestling, the one guy I never, ever would want to shoot with would be Danny Hodge in his prime. Hell, take Danny Hodge now, in his 70s, amputate his arms and legs, and I might have a 50 percent chance with him.

I watch the shootfighting groups like Pride and Ultimate Fighting Championship, and they have some tough guys. But let me tell you—you can have all the Gracies, all the Shamrocks you want. They couldn't hold a candle to Danny Hodge.

Danny Hodge was a three-time NCAA wrestling champion, and one of the strongest men I've ever known. His grip strength was unbelievable—I've seen him crush a pair of steel pliers with one hand.

Danny was world junior heavyweight champion for years and was a perfect fit as a legend in Oklahoma and other parts of the South and the Midwest. The rest of the country had no idea what they were missing.

As a person, Danny was a great guy, just a lot of fun to be around. He was also the greatest shooting wrestler in the world for years, but if you dropped him into New York as the world junior heavyweight champion, the people there would look at him and say, "Oh, come on! Who are you trying to bullshit?"

They would have prejudged him based on his size and appearance, because he didn't have a musclebound physique, and I don't know how his southern talk, peppered with "dadgums," and "gollys," would have gone over.

But he was a great one, and everyone in Oklahoma and everywhere else he wrestled knew there was only one Danny Hodge. And there's never been anything like him since.

In a way, though, he reminds me of Jim Raschke, who wrestled for years in the AWA and Georgia as Baron Von Raschke. The baron was a tall, bald German who goose-stepped and used a clawhold. He reminds me of Hodge because the baron also did not have a very impressive physique. He was another guy you might take a look at and think, "Well, he couldn't whip anybody."

But Raschke was a great amateur wrestler and one of the toughest guys you were likely to meet in the wrestling profession. He could stretch the hell out of damn near anybody if he'd really wanted to.

So as we come to the end, I hope I've given you at least a sense of the great, crazy guys who made pro wrestling such a wild business. I encountered so many great characters, and it's sad to think they'd be forgotten in future generations.

And me? I wouldn't move for anything. There is no opportunity in the wrestling business that could make me move from this place.

And there's not a lot I regret about my career. I got to wrestle almost everyone who was a top guy over the course of the 1960s, 1970s, 1980s and 1990s. I do wish I had gotten to work with Chris Benoit more than that one time, just because he was so talented and such a pleasure in the ring. I worked with Joe and Dean Malenko just a few times in Japan. They were a great tag team, and I would have liked to work more with them. And this might seem funny, but one guy I would have loved to work with was Art Barr. Art teamed with Eddy Guerrero in Mexico as Los Gringos Locos in the early 1990s, and he was so far ahead of his time it's not even funny. Art died of a drug overdose in 1994, just a couple of weeks after his biggest match ever, on a pay per view put on in the States by the Mexican promotion AAA. Art and Eddy just burned the house down whenever I saw them on TV.

I also never got to work with Verne Gagne, who I got to watch when I was just breaking into the business. Verne's AWA ended up dying a slow death in the 1980s, and a lot of people knock Verne for his company going under, but that son of a bitch was a phenomenal worker.

There are others, but I was lucky enough to work with a lot of the true talents of this business.

I do miss being around my brother. Junior moved to Florida a little more than 20 years ago, to book for Eddie Graham, and he never moved back. We still see each other now and then, but not like when we were young.

You might have noticed that I have lived my life somewhat differently than a lot of wrestlers. I haven't been on the road, nonstop, for 20 years. More than 30 years ago, I let myself get sucked into the business to the point that it cost me my marriage. Well I was surely blessed to get her back and get a second chance, and I was sure as hell not going to let it happen again. And I haven't.

And I've been very fortunate, very lucky. I enjoy the hell out of my home, and the wrestling business has been good enough to me to allow me to be centered in the middle of nowhere. And no matter where I've worked, I've been able to come back here as much as I want.

Stacy lives in Amarillo, now, and Brandee's in Phoenix, but she travels quite a bit in her job, and we get to see her a lot. I wish Brandee was here, of course, but I love the fact she's only a couple of hours away on an airplane. She's also a registered nurse, helping to deliver babies and working on her master's degree, to become a nurse practitioner.

They're both flight attendants, and I do worry about them being in the air so much. When 9/11 happened, everyone remembered the policemen. Everyone remembered the firemen. Everyone remembered the people who died in the World Trade Center. Everyone remembered the passengers on those planes.

The travesty of the crashes was that those flight attendants had their throats cut, and hardly anyone has mentioned them. That's a pretty hard way to go. I tell my daughters constantly, "Watch out! Keep your eyes open and be aware!"

But at least I see them regularly enough that I get to tell them that often.

And there's one more member of the family I haven't mentioned—my Jack Russell terrier, Tooter Brown. I've had dogs all my life and loved dogs, and when the girls were growing up, we had three dogs—Masa, Scooby and Boo. They all died the same year, and it was tough. I told Vicki, "I don't want another one."

But she found Tooter in Waco, and brought him home. And we haven't had a quiet moment since. One time, he went down to the creek on our property, and found a beaver hole. He wouldn't come out, and we had to dig a 15-foot tunnel for his little ass.

But I love the people here, I love my family, and I love to be home. If you want to know why I've done all the crazy things I've done, it's very simple—it was to be home, to have a life, other than just wrestling. Believe me, I love the wrestling part, but I love this part of the country and I'm not going to go anyplace else.

Why did I go to New York City 12 years ago, only to turn right around and come back? Hell, I don't want to spend a lot of time in New York City. Why did I go to Japan and do the insane things I've done? I've been able to do something that a lot of wrestlers, even in this day and age, would love to be able to do—to have fun in the profession and be my own boss, and still get to spend time at home, where I want to be.

It's not the most successful thing for me financially, and I realize that, but it hasn't been bad. I can't think of much else that I want. Money has always been a necessity, but it's not my guiding force. My guiding force has been my family.

I've seen a lot of guys get those things reversed, and believe me, I've gotten them reversed in my lifetime, but by God, I got it straightened out. I've had it straight for more than 25 years, and I've done it right. I'm proud of that fact.

In fact, you probably won't see me out on the independent circuit too much, anymore. I know that sounds like bullshit coming from me, but it's the truth. It's getting to where it takes more and more to get me to leave the house.

And there are health concerns. I have had some retinal injury to my right eye, I recently learned. It's not something that bothers me constantly, but it is the kind of thing that can get worse if I take a blow to the head. At times it's worse than other times, and sometimes looks like my right eye is looking through wax paper, because things can be that hazy.

It's not just my eye, (or "My eye! My eye!" for you empty arena match fans). If you saw *Beyond the Mat*, you might remember the scene where the doctor was telling me I needed a right knee replacement, because I'm bone on bone down there from the years of taking a pounding in wrestling. Well, seven years after that doctor visit, my knees are still godawful. My body goes ahead and screams every morning when I get up. What it usually screams is, "Stay down! Stay in bed!"

But I get up every morning anyway. More than 10 years ago, I had knee surgery by Dr. James Andrews, a well known sports physician. He later treated Ernie Ladd's knees and told Ernie, "Geez, Ernie, I've only seen one person with a worse knee than you."

Guess who?

I realize I could get a replacement, and people wonder why I haven't gotten one. Well, they say those things only last for about 15 years, and I don't want to have to get two of them done, so I'm going to wait until I'm 105 to have my knee replacement. That way, it'll last me the rest of my lifetime. But just barely.

I'm still able to get around, which means I've been pretty lucky, but I've also had cracked vertebrae and more concussions than I could count, all because I like to work physical.

Besides the physical aspect of it, I'm getting too damned old.

Every now and then, a wrinkled, old man will shuffle up to me, tap me with his cane and say, "Terry Funk! I used to watch you wrestle when I was a kid!"

I know that one day soon, I really will retire, from the entire business, once and for all. I wouldn't mind going around the country and having a retirement match in every town, but whatever it entails, I'm pretty near the end of my wrestling days, and pretty glad to be there. I can promise you one thing—if I do accept an independent booking, and you go to the show, don't be expecting to see any goddamned moonsaults out of me! I don't have any left in me.

We all have windows of time in this wrestling business. They open and they shut. I've been lucky enough to have a window that's been broken, on the open side. I've seen a lot of talented guys whose windows were just jammed shut, for whatever reason, but mine's been open for a great number of years, and I've been very fortunate. A few times it's slammed shut on me, but I've always figured out a way to get it open again. Nowadays I'm looking at closing it, once and for all.

I have a friend who just passed away from liver cancer in May 2004. He spent more than $100,000 on special treatment he could only get in Philadelphia. He got the treatment, but he still died.

I don't mean this specifically about him, but maybe the way we'll know who wins and who doesn't in this life is by seeing who lives. For all the guys who lived fast and died young, maybe I win when I live one more day than they do. That's how simple it is.

You can have all the money in the world, like Bill Gates, but what would you pay to have that one extra day of living, especially if you're home, where you want to be?

Right here on the Double Cross Ranch is where I want to be.

INDEX